THE WARRIORS

THE PRIDDEN SAGA: BOOK THREE

Cover Art by Deranged Doctor Designs

Editor: Laura LaRocca

ISBN: 978-1-7389742-6-9

Printed in United States of America
Published by JMT Publishing, Canada
www.sjmtpublishing.com
Second Edition, 2023

THE WARRIORS

THE PRIDDEN SAGA: BOOK THREE

J. M. TIBBOTT

DEDICATION

To Rob who always encouraged… and still does.

ACKNOWLEDGMENTS

Special thanks to:

The River Writers for reminding me that my readers cannot read my mind.

To my favorite editor, who catches me when I tend to travel off on a tangent, and definitely helps me to become a better writer

To my writing friends for reminding me I am never alone in my challenges

To Ed Greenwood who is the ultimate fantasy mentor

To my sister, an ocean away physically, but close in my heart.

To my dear friend who helps to soothe those frantic writing days with chocolate.

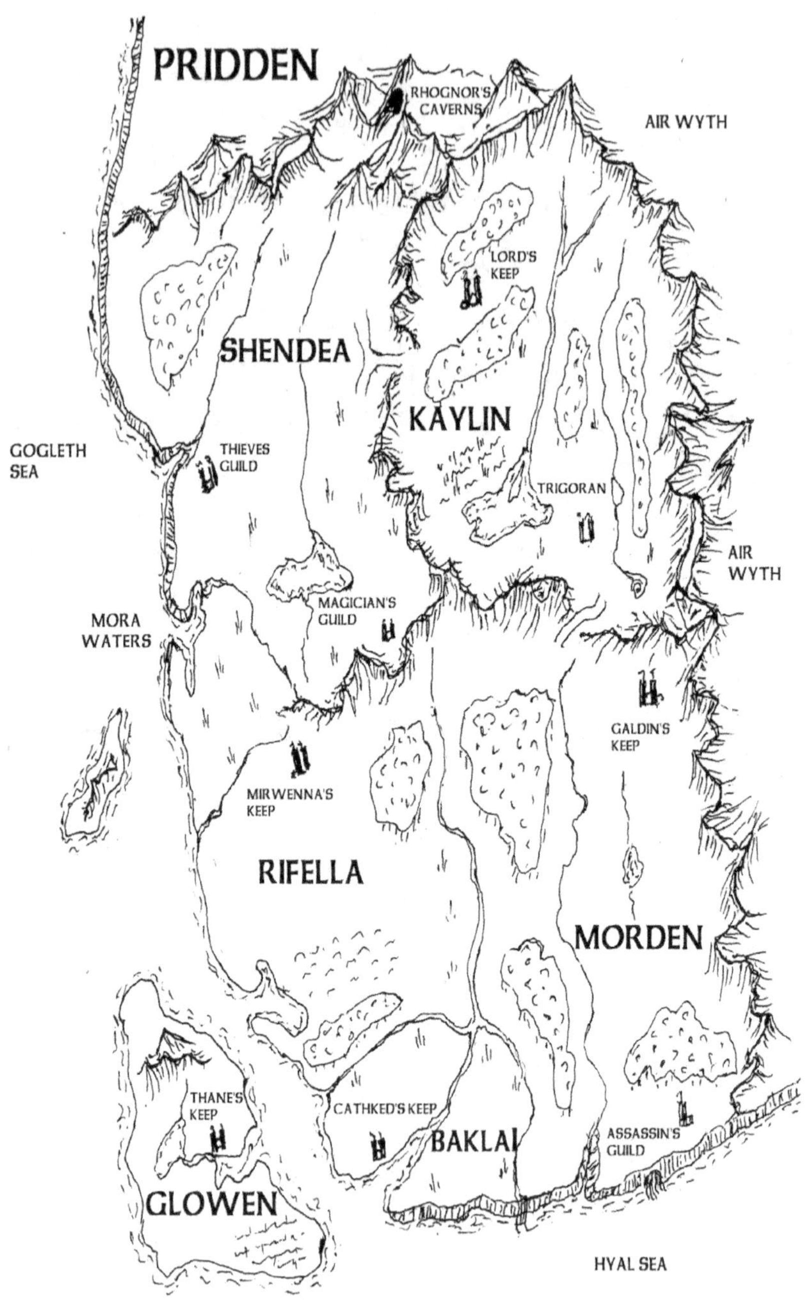
PRIDDEN
RHOGNOR'S CAVERNS
AIR WYTH
LORD'S KEEP
SHENDEA
KAYLIN
GOGLETH SEA
THIEVES GUILD
TRIGORAN
AIR WYTH
MAGICIAN'S GUILD
MORA WATERS
GALDIN'S KEEP
MIRWENNA'S KEEP
RIFELLA
MORDEN
THANE'S KEEP
CATHKED'S KEEP
BAKLAI
ASSASSIN'S GUILD
GLOWEN
HYAL SEA

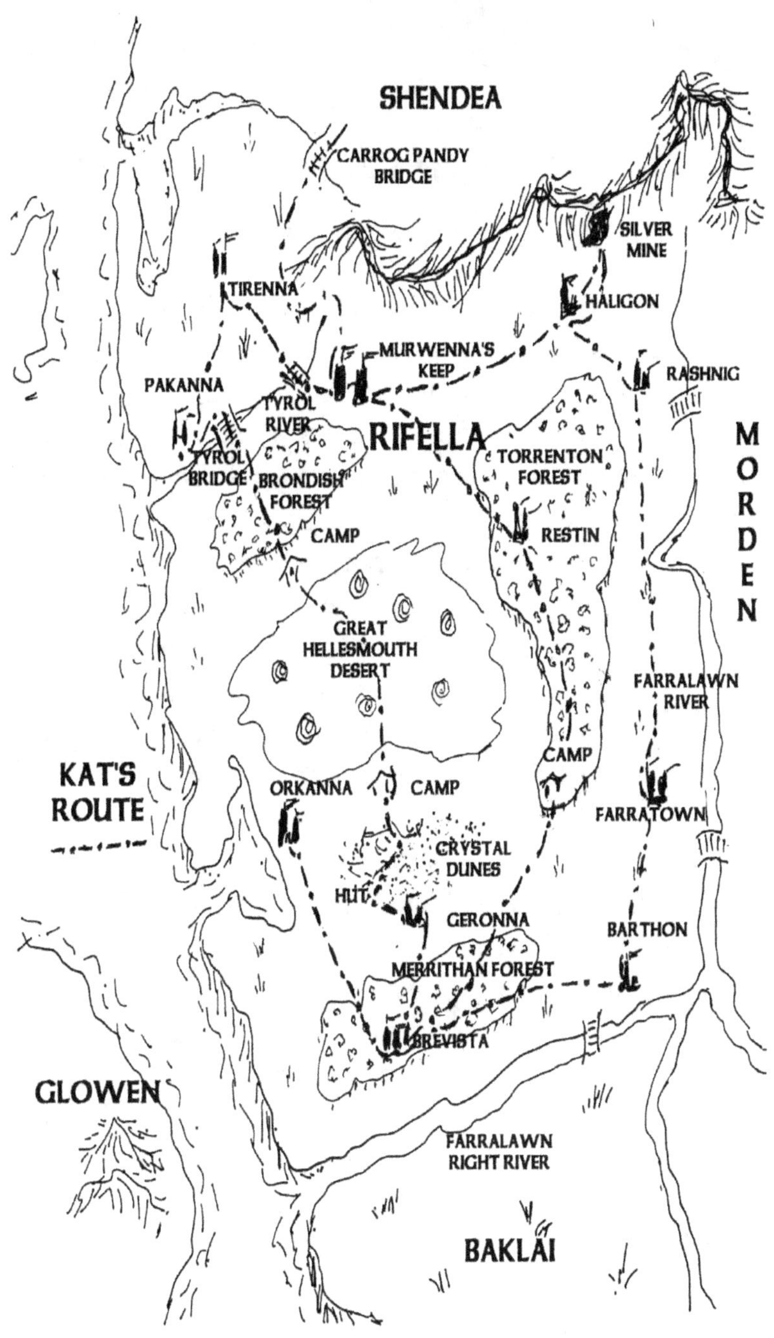
SHENDEA
CARROG PANDY
BRIDGE
SILVER
MINE
TIRENNA
HALIGON
MURWENNA'S
KEEP
RASHNIG
PAKANNA
TYROL
RIVER
RIFELLA
TYROL
BRIDGE
BRONDISH
FOREST
TORRENTON
FOREST
MORDEN
CAMP
RESTIN
GREAT
HELLESMOUTH
DESERT
FARRALAWN
RIVER
CAMP
KAT'S
ROUTE
ORKANNA
CAMP
FARRATOWN
CRYSTAL
DUNES
HUT
GERONNA
BARTHON
MERRITHAN FOREST
BREVISTA
GLOWEN
FARRALAWN
RIGHT RIVER
BAKLAI

WHAT HAS HAPPENED SO FAR

Kat, a brilliant, solitary video game designer, discovers she's in danger of being fired for not working well in team situations. Given the option to consider her future with the new management's style, she takes a leave on the Island of Tortola in the British Virgins. Opening a strange door in some ruins behind the hotel, without warning, she gets caught in a vortex and is transported away from home.

Kat wakes in a strange new land, Pridden, and at first believes she is dreaming and is in one of her own video games. She is befriended by the healer Wynneth, and Eduardo, who is the lord of this land. When Kat asks for help to find her way home, Eduardo offers a trade. She must help him determine who is causing challenges between the peoples of Pridden, which might lead to war and, in doing so, discover those, who when their powers are combined, will be able to return her home.

She decides to record her experiences so she might transfer them to a new video game when she returns to her own world. In the current land of Kaylin, Kat discovers the inhabitants are so straitlaced, they forbid close relationships between men and women before bonding for life. Kat needs to learn the social requirements of life in this land. She is reminded of this when she accidentally exposes her legs to Haydar, the Horse-Master, and thus is denied the use of a horse.

Seeking help, Kat meets with two attractive Rifellans, Praetor Bardu and his wife Irina, whose pheromones, without the calming effect of a tea called Karri-san, affect Kat's passions with great force.

Eduardo assigns his counsellor, Drainin, whom Kat dislikes, to accompany her through the land of Kaylin on her first journey. During her travels, she meets with the enticing Liandock, the Metal-Smith, who designs a unique pendant for her which allows her to discern between friends and enemies. She also encounters Penrow, the bear-like, but joyful Master Builder. In Trigoran, she confronts men from Morden, which angers Drainin enough to chastise her.

Later, Drainin attempts to seduce her using the Kaylin equivalent of roofies, and Kat refuses to travel with him again.

When Eduardo's promise of a horse to travel to the next land lags, Kat, frustrated, attempts to steal one from Haydar. Eduardo saves her from the death penalty for this action by taking on the responsibility for her attempted thievery.

Eduardo now introduces her to Mouse, a timid little man in a grey robe who hails from Morden, to guide her through the rest of Pridden.

In the meantime, Kat is lured to creepy Old Town and is kidnapped by the Assassin's Guild, who contracted to bring her to Galdin, the Thane of Morden. He needs her presence to supply him with power over all Pridden. Drainin is shown to be an ally to Galdin, and helps with the kidnapping.

Many of the people Kat encountered during her journey through Kaylin ride to her rescue to free her, but, in the ensuing battle, a number are killed. Most of the Assassins, and Drainin also die during the violent skirmish.

Kat realizes her prejudices were unfounded, and she asks forgiveness from those she misjudged. She requests Eduardo, who is a Wielder of Power, be the person from Kaylin to help her return home, and he agrees.

Kat, with a pen made from a cathnog tooth and a cute furry messenger pyrock, plus the odd little man called Mouse, sets out for Shendea.

Once in this next land, she and her guide are attacked by a dangerous cathnog, which appears to be killed by a hydodd, its sworn enemy. The two travel to the stronghold of Lord Rhognor, whom she finds fussy and thus doubts his ability to lead. Healer Deleth, who is a twin sister to Wynneth from Kaylin, supplies her with help in Shendea. Kat discovers a creature known as a boradai, whom she names Breen, and with whom she bonds and communicates telepathically. During her journey through Shendea, Kat encounters Hesginn, Rhognor's chief adviser, a most attractive man who spurns Kat's advances. When pressed, he reveals he is in love with someone else. Later, Hesginn's brother Walden, a man with a much better sense of humor, confesses to Kat that Hesginn forced him to become a magician in the Magician's Guild, rather than a Tapestry Assistant, which he preferred.

After an unpleasant attack by a robber in the passageways of the Stronghold, Rhognor and his bonded mate, Halfin, persuade Kat to continue on her journey with Mouse.

Within a short time after they leave the stronghold, Kat is joined by a magnificent black panther-like creature who is invisible to everyone but Kat and other animals, and who acts as her protector and communicates with Breen. Kat names her Shade.

A visit to the Crimson Cauldron for a delightful spa-type mud bath ends in an encounter with two violent assassins, whom Kat and her guide, Mouse, are forced to dispatch. After this unexpected attack, Mouse determines someone targeted them and changes the planned route through Shendea. They visit a number of smaller villages and arrive at the Thieves Guild, where they view a Thieving ceremony. Kat now understands that Thieves in Pridden do not steal but reverse time for deserving candidates.

During a stop at Roothlan, Shendea's own holiday resort town, Kat is attacked once again, but disables her attacker with such force, she breaks his leg. Ballinor, the Rifellan captain of the guards in Roothlan, is fascinated by her abilities and requests she teach his troops the same technique. His intended seduction of her fails, when after dinner, images of Liandock come between them.

On their way back to the Stronghold to report in, Vendi, the innkeeper, offers Mouse the cathnog skin, which he refuses, suggesting instead he gift the pelt to Lord Rhognor, as he and Kat cannot take the fur with them in their travels.

Lord Rhognor expresses satisfaction at what Kat achieved so far and gives them permission to continue their journey to Rifella. Since they will be stopping at the Magicians' Guild, Rhognor says he will join them in Blain and requests they allow his mate, Halfin, to accompany them. They agree.

Kat, ignores Mouse and Deleth's warning not to take Breen with her, as the removal of a boradai from Shendea means death by fire, because Breen insists she must accompany Kat. Our game designer decides they cannot kill her, as they need her to accomplish the task Eduardo handed to her.

When Halfin joins them, she discovers Breen is accompanying Kat and insists upon a trial to determine Kat's fate. However, Halfin understands Breen's communication and absolves Kat of guilt because the boradai insists she must accompany her.

Shortly after this encounter, Halfin, the last member of the Enchanters' Guild, discovers the existence of Shade and speaks with her. Enchanters' Guild members are able to converse with all creatures. Halfin senses hidden secrets, and when she receives the cathnog pelt from Vendi, she touches the fur, and understands that the cathnog was killed by a hydodd, and views Mouse with renewed interest.

Mouse leaves the party less than a turn before they arrive in Blain, where Halfin and Rhognor meet to continue their journey together.

In the meantime, Galdin meets with Ssarff, the head of the Assassins' Guild, and insists Kat must be brought through the little-known tunnel between Shendea and Morden so he can use her for his own purposes. He informs Ssarff his contact in Shendea is Hesginn.

Hesginn and Ssarff meet in the tunnel, and Hesginn insists he will help, provided they kill Rhognor, thus freeing Halfin to become Hesginn's mate.

Their discussion is overheard by Kat, who does her best to reach Rhognor to warn him before Hesginn and Ssarff can kill him. In addition, she sends her pyrock to Mouse to request help.

Rhognor appears as Hesginn and Ssarff are approaching, and Kat calls out a warning. Ssarff hurls the deadly syeth at Rhognor, and when Halfin throws herself in front of her mate, the snake sinks poisonous fangs into her neck. Because the venom is injected so close to the brain and heart, she loses consciousness and dies within minutes.

Rhognor is beside himself, and Hesginn is horrified. He yells at Ssarff to kill Kat, because she is at fault for Halfin's death.

The syeth bites Kat on the wrist as she raises her arm to protect herself, and she falls to the ground, but its venom is less strong on this second attack.

Ssarff, Hesginn, and the grey magicians grab Kat and flee for the tunnel. Rhognor, enraged and out for revenge, follows with his guards. He encounters Mouse, accompanied by Walden, who both realized Hesginn and all the grey magicians were headed for Blain. With few words, Rhognor conveys what happened, and he persuades Mouse and a large number of white magicians to head for the tunnel to rescue Kat.

In the tunnel, Breen bites Kat's wrist and begins to suck the poison from her blood stream. Kat is worried the poison will kill Breen, but the boradai assures her she has plans to save both of them. Hesginn discovers Breen attempting to save Kat and grabs the boradai, who twists around and bites Hesginn and begins to pour the poison into his veins.

At that point, Mouse and Walden catch up with the litter carrying Kat. They kill the bearers, and, Walden plunges a dagger into Hesginn, killing him. But Breen possessed insufficient time to empty all the poison into Hesginn and she too dies, still retaining too much of the poison to survive. Mouse carries Kat, holding Breen's lifeless body, out of the tunnel and returns to clean up the rest of the assassins and grey magicians.

Rhognor prepares Halfin for Caleesh's fire and sets out for the Magicians' Guild. He meets with the white magicians and issues a rule that grey magicians will no longer be tolerated in Shendea, and Walden will assume the title of head of the Magicians' Guild.

Kat, grieving for both Breen and Halfin, apologizes to everyone at a subsequent meeting and tells them all that she now understands why asking for help is so important. She pledges her help to anyone who wishes to ask in the future.

In a private meeting later, Rhognor is given the cathnog pelt, but says the beautiful fur is too laden with sad memories, and, requests Kat gift the skin to Lord Murwenna of Rifella. In return, Kat requests his help to send her home when the time comes, and he agrees.

Mouse insists they must leave for Rifella the following morning. When she retires for bed, Kat, still ill from the after effects of the syeth poison, is surprised to find her stone dull and lifeless.

She remembers what Liandock advised her to do, but she can't summon energy for self gratification. Shade climbs on the bed and lies across her chest, purring, and Kat is comforted by the warmth of Shade's body enveloping her. The cat's eyes are brilliant green and shining. As Kat beholds her, Shade begins to fade from existence until she disappears. Stunned, Kat discovers her stone is once more a brilliant green and glows brightly. Her health regained, Kat speculates that Shade might be a gift from Liandock.

CHAPTER ONE

The trip from the Magicians' Guild in Shendea continued, slow, tedious, and silent. The two travelers clopped on the Carrog Pandy Bridge and began the pass from Shendea to Rifella. Kat stopped her horse midway. At her back, the winds blew cool and gentle, yet dispassionate. She glanced behind her.

Mouse rode his animal up beside her. "Shendea is over."

She nodded. She found her peace with the death of Halfin, but she still missed Breen so much. To lose the ability to speak with a creature with the intelligence of the boradai left her with a sense of emptiness. She relied on Breen for information and guidance about social customs and people's agendas, while she traveled through the land of the healers. Wink, her pyrock, a sweet and cuddly ball of fur, possessed little intelligence and appeared limited to delivering messages, eating, and sleeping.

Shade's departure created a different vacuum within Kat. Her glorious panther protected her from dangers, but when the challenges of Shendea ceased, Shade appeared to be no longer needed. *I think Liandock somehow tied her to my ston*e. Positive the gorgeous Rifellan held responsibility for the huge black animal, belied her initial conclusion that he possessed only limited power. He appeared to control something far more arcane than she encountered with any other.

She breathed the air blowing toward her. The wind from in front of her, warm, fecund, beckoning, filled her with strength. The winds reminded her of Africa.

Mouse, still paused beside her, glanced anxiously at her. "What?"

"Can you sense the land? Rifella?"

Mouse closed his eyes, breathed in and out, turned to her, his eyes now open, and nodded.

As they left the bridge and set hooves on Rifella, the landscape changed. Ahead and to the right, the terrain lay flat before them, covered in knee-high grasses, stunted trees, and bushy undergrowth that stretched for miles. Not far to the left, however, loomed the crags of Clog Arth, on the Rifellan side.

Kat stopped her horse again. "Does Murwenna live in the mountain like Rhognor?"

Mouse paused beside her. "No. She lives within her own keep, which is home to many of Rifellan royalty. Please remember, Kat, when we are in her company, use Lord Murwenna's title."

"You've told me about titles often enough. You don't need to keep reminding me. It's like teaching a pig to sing. First, pigs can't sing, and, second, you annoy the hell out of them."

Mouse blinked rapidly at her. "What are you talking about? Pigs cannot sing?"

"You are correct; pigs can't sing. What I should say is, you're annoying me so much with your constant reminders about protocol, I'm beginning to ignore your words. I suggest you allow me to be myself, and only correct me when I make a mistake."

Mouse hesitated. "Kat, such an action would be appropriate, except when you make errors, they are quite substantial."

"So? Explain to them I am not of this world, and I'm still learning about the customs. I'm confident most will accept your words. I wish you all would accept me as I am, 'cause I'm trying."

Mouse sighed and rolled his eyes.

Kat gasped. *Why is my stone so icy cold all of a sudden?*

Without warning, half a dozen creatures, each the size of a fox, sprang from the undergrowth and headed for them, grunting and growling.

"Move, Kat. Fast." He swatted the pack horse on the flank and, spurring his own animal forward, headed for the less bushy areas at the foothills of Clog Arth.

"What are they?" Kat called to him as they galloped toward the mountains.

Mouse yelled back at her. "Brantors. And they run in packs and can bring down a full grown horse if slow enough. Keep riding."

Kat rode, and the grunting noises became fainter as the three horses galloped for their lives.

Silence reigned. "Did we outrun them?" She slowed her mount.

"Um, I think so." Mouse began. "Oh, oh." He rode over to the pack horse, where, clinging by its teeth to a sack on the luggage frame on the horse's back, hung an animal with tufts of black fur on its head, surrounding two small horns. Each foot sported two massive claws, perfect for disemboweling prey.

Kat gasped at the size of the claws. *No wonder Mouse urged me to move fast.*

Mouse raised his dagger and plunged the point into the neck of the brantor. Blood gushed from the wound, and the gross-looking animal tumbled to the ground. "This one got caught in the sacking, and could not free itself. The teeth tell you they are formidable creatures. It is fortunate their legs are so short, as they experience difficulty keeping up with animals who can run faster. But what they lose in speed, they make up for in stamina. Their quarry almost always collapse from exhaustion, and fall victim to the foul creatures."

Kat gazed closer and shuddered. The animal, covered in a leathery skin similar to an elephant, possessed a repulsive face. Bulbous blood-shot eyes, surrounded by black hair and the horns that Kat glimpsed as the animal hung from the sacking, gave the appearance of a nearsighted miniature Satan. All this sat atop a yellow snout, from which dripped a viscous green fluid. The teeth, which Mouse so kindly pointed out as formidable, shone midnight black, and provided a sharp contrast with the yellow interior of the mouth. "Is this one of the creatures I needed to shoot with my spring bow?"

"Indeed. Please ready your bow, because while we evaded one pack, more may be waiting ahead. We will leave this one in the grass, as any others who follow us, will make a meal of the dead one before pursuing us further."

Kat pulled her bow from the sheath on the saddle, lifted her foot from the stirrup, and set the spring. Her arrows in their quiver hung over her back. She hung the set bow from her saddle, and the three horses trotted toward Clog Arth. *Am I getting used to gross animals? I'm not out of breath. Damn. I gotta return home. Horror and tragedy are becoming too normal.*

They passed out of the area of bushy undergrowth, and the trees grew more stately as they neared the distant keep. *Safe now. My stone is warm.*

Mouse turned in his saddle to glance at Kat. "I want to remind… " He stopped.

Kat hoped her glare at him contained as much venom as possible.

"I did not intend to remind you of protocol. I merely wished to suggest you wear one of your new leathers when we are called to meet with Murwenna. I believe we will be well served if you remind her of your strong resemblance to Rifellan royalty."

Kat gulped. *Oops, I thought he was going to correct me again. My bad.* "Oh. Yes. You're right. Good idea."

As they neared the walled keep, similar to the castle-like structure of Eduardo's towers, Kat admired the neat farms and plots of land on which grew a variety of vegetables, dotted between fruit trees in full flower. Attached to almost every home stood a stable for two to three horses. The paths leading between the houses and up to the prime gates of the keep, laid with cobbled stones, created a soothing rhythm with the sound of their horses' hooves.

At the gates, two guards stepped forward.

Mouse stopped his horse and slid to the ground. "You are Lord Murwenna's guards?"

When they answered in the affirmative, he walked toward them. "I am Mouse, and this is the Lady Kat. Lord Murwenna expects us."

Kat dismounted and held the reins of her horse, waiting for someone to relieve her of them.

Both guards stood a little straighter, and ushered them forward, offering to take their horses to the stable. Mouse thanked them and enquired as to where they would collect their baggage.

The closest guard snapped his fingers, and a page came running. He gave the young man a few orders and returned to his post.

The page addressed them as he led them both to the enormous entrance hall. "Sire, my Lady, as soon as we are aware of which rooms you will occupy, your baggage will be delivered, and you will be escorted to them. I am positive Lord Murwenna will wish for you to dine with her for the evening meal. Another apprentice will come for you to squire you to the dining center. In the meantime, would you please await your apprentice helper in the ante-room."

"Thanks to you." Mouse turned back to Kat. "We will wait in this room." He pointed to what resembled a parlor, off to the side of the monumental hall.

Kat followed him to a small chamber, furnished with sofas and comfortable chairs, where they waited to be shown to their rooms.

Kat turned to Mouse. "I'm beginning to realize, being expected is pleasant."

"In most lands this is true."

Kat peered at him in surprise. *Now what did he mean?*

CHAPTER TWO

A tall, brown-haired, attractive woman, in a light blue robe, peered at them from the doorway. She smiled. "You must be the Lady Kat, correct?"

Kat nodded. She sighed internally. *I wish they'd forget the Lady bit.*

The woman glanced at Mouse. "And you sir, must be my Lord Mouse."

He winced. "I am no lord. I am Mouse."

The woman furrowed her brow, and tensed her shoulders. "My apologies, Sire. I meant no offense. I am Healer Fenneth and am assigned to Lord Murwenna's keep."

Mouse bowed his head. "Well met, Healer Fenneth."

Fenneth relaxed her shoulders and smiled again. "I am here to conduct you both to your rooms. I am sure you wish to refresh yourselves."

Kat sighed. "I do. Unluckily, we encountered brantors on our way here. I swallowed a cloud of dust, and I will welcome a visit to the personal to shake out my clothes."

Fenneth's eyes widened. "Brantors pursued you?" She exhaled with a whoosh. "You are so fortunate you made your way to our keep unscathed."

"I'm aware how lucky we are. He—" she gestured at Mouse "—is an excellent guide."

Fenneth smiled at them both and turned to leave, calling back to them. "Please follow me. Your luggage will be delivered straight to your rooms."

Mouse shot a glance at Kat.

He appears suspicious. I believe he thinks I'm insulting him. She frowned back at him, her left eyebrow raised in query.

The three walked down the corridor, Mouse on Fenneth's left, and Kat on her right.

"Lord Murwenna will meet with both of you on the morrow. I will bring you to the dining hall for your evening meal, unless I am needed by Lord Murwenna. She expects to birth her heir within the next nine to twelve star turns, and is often in need of me because of her current discomfort." Fenneth chuckled. "Lords are no different from all women in the last few turns of their expectancy. They are also uncomfortable, grumpy, and impatient. Despite the fact she is our Lord and leads us most beneficially, Murwenna is still a woman facing the birth of progeny." She glanced at Kat. "Are you familiar with the challenges of bearing progeny, Lady Kat?"

"Not as yet, Fenneth. And from my experience, I believe I'm quite satisfied I'm not."

Fenneth laughed. "You will change your mind when the time comes, Lady Kat. Most woman do."

"You raise children of your own?"

"Interesting."

"Excuse me. What's interesting?"

"You used the word children. I cannot recall any Rifellans, except those of royal birth who use such a term."

"I'm not from Rifella."

"So I am told. However, Lady Kat, you do resemble one of royal birth, and you also use many of our words."

"Please would you call me Kat. I'm uncomfortable being referred to with such formality as Lady Kat."

"As you wish." She smiled. "I heard you preferred less formality. In that you are much like us in Rifella.

The three arrived at a massive and finely decorated door, replete with carvings of horses of different sizes and colors.

"These are your rooms, La… Kat."

Kat smiled at her. "Thank you." She opened her door and entered, as Fenneth led Mouse to his room, two doors away.

Kat pulled off her backpack and unhooked Wink's cage, which she carried to the dresser. She reached into the pack for the pyrock treats. Wink, perhaps sensing food in the offing, raised her head and squeaked in anticipation. Kat fed the little creature and stroked her furry body. Wink butted at her, curled around three times, tucked her nose under a leathery wing, and fell asleep.

Kat located her luggage and set up Wink's permanent cage on a tall side table. She reached into the travel cage, lifted out the round ball of fur and deposited the sleeping animal in the larger quarters, nestling her within warm fabric in the cage. Wink murmured a couple of purring chirps.

After deciding which clothes to wear to the dining hall, Kat headed to the personal. She showered off the dust gathered while escaping the brantors and, when clean and dry, donned her culotte type pants and a pale yellow shirt.

She brushed the dust from her leathers when a knock at the door summoned her. Mouse and Fenneth waited for her.

"Kat, we're here to escort you to the dining chamber."

"Thank you, and thanks for not using the Lady honorific."

"Of course, I understand. We do not practice much formality either. I will become accustomed to referring to you as Kat."

Fenneth and Kat strolled toward the half-open doors of the dining room, with Mouse lagging behind.

"Fenneth, I thought we might be in the presence of Lord Murwenna for our evening meal. I assume she is not available."

"I believe she hoped she might meet with you, but she needs to rest this turn. We will see her on the morrow."

The buzz of conversation reached their ears before they entered, and the vibration of animated chatter reverberated around the hall.

Kat glanced at Fenneth, puzzled. "Everybody is so excited about something."

"They are. Lord Murwenna will be birthing her heir within the next twelve star turns, and many of the men created a game, speculating when the turn and time will occur. The number of chits in the game jar is increasing daily."

"Sounds like fun."

"The most fun will be for the man who wins the game."

"I wish I possessed chits to guess with."

"Our males are those who most often enjoy games of chance, but a few women do play. If you wish to venture an entry, I can supply you with a chit."

"Truly?"

"Of course. You are our guest, and you are more than welcome to join in any of our events. The board with the remaining unselected turns and times is mounted on the wall at the far end of the hall." She stopped, drew a chit from her pocket, and handed it to Kat. "Write your name on this, go to the wall, and write your name again on one of the empty spaces."

Kat regarded Mouse helplessly. "How do I write my name in your writing?"

Mouse grinned at her, and reached for the pen and ink sitting on the table. "Here." He wrote a word on the chit. "Copy this on the space you choose."

"How will I decipher which turn and time I choose?"

He laughed this time. "Here is another bit of parchment. Copy what is on the board, and I will translate the words for you."

Kat thanked him and took her chit, the blank piece of parchment, and a pen poised in the ink container from the table, and walked to the wall. She copied the name from the parchment on a blank space on the chart on the wall and dropped her chit in the jar. After the note dropped in the container she copied the name from the wall to the second piece of parchment. When she faced the room to return to her table, she stopped. Hundreds of eyes stared at her. She gulped and strode back to her table, head held high. *If Fenneth encouraged me, I'm sure I didn't goof.*

She returned the pen and ink to the table, sat, and handed the piece of parchment to Mouse.

"Well Kat. Your estimate is Lord Murwenna will birth her offspring eight turns from now, a short period after star set."

"Thanks." Kat peered around at Fenneth. "Why is everyone here looking at me with such curiosity? You mentioned some women do enter the game."

Fenneth laughed. "You are unknown to them, but your hair coloring indicates Rifellan royalty. They are only curious."

"Oh." Kat shrugged. "Are we able to order food now? I am ravenous after fleeing from the brantors."

Fenneth raise her eyebrows. "Brantors? Ah yes, you mentioned them when we first met. They are fierce and unforgiving creatures. I am fortunate I never encountered any. You must relay your experience for me later. In full detail. And yes, we can order food." As she spoke, she waved at an apprentice server.

The young man recorded their orders and, within minutes, returned with a tray laden with frothy drinks and steaming aromatic bowls of some exotic stew. He deposited bowls and mugs on the glossy wooden table top.

“Thank you. Would you bring me Karri-san tea as soon as possible?”

“Of course, my Lady.”

Kat dipped her spoon in the mixture and rolled the stew around in her mouth. The meat in the bowl, combined and simmered in a mixture of spices unknown to her, tasted divine. The flavor of a slight hint of salt, and overtones of a honey-like texture, tickled her palette, but stumped her with the identity of the other additives. “This is delicious. What is the meat?

Fenneth raised her eyes and peered up at Kat. “Brantor. Though I never saw one, I have eaten many.”

“How are they caught? They travel in packs, and they are nasty in the extreme.”

“All our brantor meat comes from the village of Tirenna. The villagers work together to set snares and arrange a regular drive, where they force extreme numbers of brantors into a trap. Once the trap is full, the brantors are dispatched with speed. The meat is smoked, dried, and sold everywhere in Rifella. We reconstitute the dried meat, and the result is what you are eating.”

Kat laughed aloud. “I find all this so appropriate.” She paused dramatically. “The life of a brantor is to eat or be eaten.”

Fenneth giggled. “I prefer to eat them and not meet them.”

Even Mouse chuckled at her remark.

The three ate in silence for a while, Kat savoring each mouthful. Once she finished her meal, Kat began to drink her

Karri-san. “So we will meet Lord Murwenna on the morrow. Can you tell me a little about how she operates?”

“Rifellans are not complicated people, Kat, so Lord Murwenna’s dealings with her subjects are achieved with clarity and simplicity. Lady Melindar, Lord Murwenna’s sibling is her chief council. Melindar is head of a group of seven advisors who consist of Praetor Arrogol, the head of the warriors in Rifella, and six other leaders in their fields. They cover such things as economy, relationships with other lands, food production, metal and wood production, ship building, and general internal matters in Rifella.”

“I’m delighted to discover Rifellans are efficient.”

“We all do what works.”

Kat rubbed her eyebrow. “Murwenna is the only female Lord in Pridden, am I correct?”

Fenneth nodded. “Lords are the leaders who are able to trace their bloodlines back to Argelwyd, the original Lord of Pridden, who remains the most powerful Wielder in our recorded history. Argelwyd divided our world into six lands, and each of his immediate progeny became responsible for ruling a defined area. When succession first began, Lordship went to the first-born male, but the lines thinned out, and many bondings occurred between those without Wielder power. Rifella long recognized the value of a female ruler, and Murwenna’s parents bore no sons.”

“Is this the reason why only three Lords reside on Pridden?”

“Yes. Because Argelwyd bore only sons, most of the lands behaved in a foolish manner and decided only males should assume the Lordships. Murwenna’s line decided to be less rigid in their approach.”

“So, who is Murwenna’s bond mate?”

"Lady Janella is bonded with her."

"Lady Janella? But Murwenna's expecting."

"Indeed. She chose, with clear and focused foresight, a male who would guarantee the best progeny for her. She picked Praetor Arrogol, and when you meet him, you will understand how fortuitous her choice was. As thanks to Arrogol, she arranged a future bonding for him with Lady Olwyn, a woman of wealth and strength who is from a royal lineage. When Olwyn and Arrogol bear their own progeny, they will be assured of a continuing line who will also possess some power."

Kat blinked at the amount of information and glanced at Mouse. His eyes glazed over at the discussion of the relationships among the Rifellans; he appeared bored. "Sorry Mouse, we've been talking so much, we almost forgot you are here."

He only sighed.

Fenneth blushed. "My apologies, Sire Mouse. Kat is correct. I tend to talk too much." She rose. "I must return to my duties. I arranged a meeting for both of you with Lord Murwenna after your morning meal. I will take you to her." She stretched. "You are both able to locate your rooms without my help now?"

They indicated they were.

As she left the hall, Mouse rose. "Kat, I am weary, and I suspect you are as well. I suggest we retire and meet here on the morrow for our morning meal. I will bring the cathnog hide ready to present to Murwenna when Fenneth comes for us."

Kat rose and headed toward the door of the hall with Mouse. "Perfect. I am tired." *And my head is so full of facts about Rifellans and their liaisons, the poor thing's aching. Fenneth erred. Things are not simple at all.*

CHAPTER THREE

The following morning, clean, dressed and prepared for her day, Kat set off to meet Mouse. Although the primary construction consisted of stone, the halls of the keep through which she strode, boasted wood panels fitted with care and polished to a high sheen. The honey-blond color was the perfect background for the rows of painted scenes of family life in Rifella. By the time Kat arrived at the main dining hall, redolent of the aromas of succulent roasts and the heady scent of fresh baked bread, her stomach grumbled for food. Once seated, with plates and cups in front of her, Kat rolled the journeyklim around her mouth, blending it with a pale white sauce. The mixture reminded her of whipped cream, drizzled with vanilla and maple syrup. What the actual contents consisted of, she would not be able to guess, but she relished them with glee. She savored the flavor, eyes closed, enjoying the moment.

"Are you sleeping or meditating?" Mouse's voice beside her ear, startled her and she jerked in her seat.

Her eyes flew open, and she caught sight of him as he seated himself opposite her. "You caught me by surprise." She laughed self-consciously. "I'm meditating on the wonderful sauce on this journeyklim. I adore the flavor and the texture."

Mouse said nothing but regarded her with a speculative expression on his face.

"What?"

"You amaze me. So often, times exist when you are strong and emotionless in your evaluations. Yet you view many things from an artist's point of view. and your descriptions of foods are quite sensual."

"Is this a problem for you?"

"No, of course not. It is… well…" He hesitated.

"What?"

"You so often appear to be a person of extreme contrasts. I find this unusual."

Kat rolled her eyes. "People always want to analyze me, and it is rare they are correct in their assumptions."

Before Mouse added anything to the discussion, Fenneth approached them. "Good morrow to both of you. Did you rest well?"

"I'm not aware of how Mouse rested, but I crashed on my bed, down for the count." Kat caught Fenneth's surprised raised eyebrows. "I mean I fell asleep the moment my head touched the pillow, and I was so comfortable. I didn't wake until your star rose above the mountains, and the bird songs added their noisy cries."

"Excellent. The beds in the keep are generally considered most comfortable." She smiled at them both. "If you are prepared, Lord Murwenna is ready to meet with you."

"If you lead, Fenneth, we'll follow." Kat glanced at Mouse. "Did you bring the hide with you?"

He pointed at a sizable package beside his chair. "Yes."

They stood and followed Fenneth from the room.

As they strolled to Murwenna's quarters, Fenneth pointed out the sections of the keep that housed the services required to run an entire household in a well-organized way. "Down this passageway is the communal laundry for all those who live at the keep."

The scent of fresh warm linens curled around Kat's nostrils as they passed.

The healer explained further. "Most of the workers and apprentices establish their own homes adjacent to the keep, but for the permanent residents, we possess laundry facilities, dining areas, food preparation sections, and sewing areas. We boast an excellent seamstress, and her assistants are famed in all Rifella. While those who own their homes rely on most of these services within their homes, many do make use of Wealin, who is our official tailor."

Kat stared at each section assigned to the running of Rifella's royal house, catching glimpses of men and women kneading breads, others hanging bolts of brilliant fabrics from rungs, and yet another room crammed with desks overflowing with parchments. "Wow. I discovered how Shendeans and Kaylins run the residences of their Lords, and Murwenna's keep appears to operate in a similar manner. I find this extraordinary how well you and your people organize everything. Murwenna's home operates like a village."

"I suppose when you consider all the needs of our keep which she must consider, the concept of a village appears logical."

"How do the guards operate?"

"Each of the guards live in their own lodgings, located close to the keep. They are outside the walls, however, because they require stables for the horses. Those animals belonging to Murwenna's retinue and to the Lord herself, are all housed in the stable attached to the outer wall of the keep. Horses must always be available without delay."

"Do some of the guards reside in the keep, because I am conscious warriors are always on hand?"

"Yes and no. None of the guards rely on permanent homes within these walls. A platoon of guards is housed within the keep for thirty star turns at a time. During those turns, they are familiarized with all the duties of the keep, and their horses are housed in the attached stable. After their thirty turns are over, they return to guard duties outside the keep, and a new set of guards arrive. Praetor Arrogol, as head of the guards, keeps track of the assignments. His home is attached to the keep, so he is almost always on call. This is a major responsibility, but his position is closest in power to Murwenna's. Being a warrior guard in Rifella is a position of respect and power, and Arrogol as leader of the guards earns much admiration."

Mouse, who lagged behind and peered into the area assigned to the scribes, caught up to Fenneth and Kat. "Are we close to Murwenna's quarters?"

Fenneth turned to face him. "We are almost at her rooms. I will request her guard to announce us." She hurried ahead a few steps and spoke to the tall, muscular, blond guard standing at attention in the hall.

At Fenneth's words, he nodded; knocked; opened the carved, iron-banded door; and announced the three visitors. With assent given, he stood aside and ushered them in the room.

Kat glanced back at him as they entered and did a double-take. Another one. *Rifellans are so gorgeous. The women as well. Whew.*

The three entered a huge room, decorated with tapestries and wall paintings of battles, and of warriors astride their horses. Each exuded the sensation of victory and power. At the far end of the room, in an enormous gold-veneered chair, filled with cushions and comforters, sat Murwenna. Her hair, brushed to a sheen, created a halo of flame about her head, and she glowed. Her skin, a light bronze color, appeared as if dusted with gold. Although extremely pregnant, she sat tall and regal in her chair. Kat did not doubt, Murwenna, with the power that vibrated from her and as the epitome of splendor, always filled any room she occupied. *The woman is a goddess.*

Her voice, a deep husky contralto, broadcast her power and sensuality to all within earshot. “Welcome, Lady Kat and Sire Mouse, to my keep. Thank you, Fenneth, for bringing the visitors to me. And thank you as well for the tea you gave me at the morning meal. My comfort level is much increased.”

She even sounds like a goddess.

Mouse walked forward. “Lord Murwenna. I bear a gift from Lord Rhognor for you. This is the hide of a magnificent cathnog, which innkeeper Vendi presented to his Lady Halfin. As you may be aware, Lady Halfin returned to the bosom of Caleesh, and Lord Rhognor misses her. Since she is unable to appreciate this lovely hide, he wished us to present this to you, so you may enjoy the fur for its beauty. He also deemed this gift as appropriate for the coming of your heir.” Mouse held out the glorious snow-white fur, dotted with tufts of black.

“Please approach, Sire Mouse. I am not as nimble as I am in my normal state.”

Mouse walked up to the throne-like chair, and handed the fur to Murwenna. He bowed his head. “Lord.”

Murwenna stroked the soft fur. “Beautiful. A truly magnificent gift, Sire Mouse. Please convey my thanks to Lord Rhognor, and my condolences for the absence from his life of Lady Halfin. I found her to be the most spiritual of women. I am sure all Shendea will miss her presence."

"I will pass on your kind words and thanks."

"Excellent. Now, Fenneth, if you would, request my guards bring chairs closer to mine, and set a table in front of me. Would you also arrange more of my special tea and locate refreshments for my guests?"

Kat cleared her throat. "Lord Murwenna, if you would be so kind, may I request Karri-san tea?

Murwenna laughed. "Ah, Kat, so you are not as Rifellan as you appear."

"I'm not, Lord Murwenna."

"We are done with the formalities now. I would prefer if you would call me Murwenna, and I shall call you Kat."

Kat breathed a sigh of relief. "My thanks, Murwenna. I'm not one for being formal."

Fenneth returned with an assistant, and the two deposited tea and small cakes upon the table for the group. Murwenna poured and handed each a cup. She thanked Fenneth, who left the room. Murwenna turned to Mouse. "I believe you wish to show me the intended route for your travels in Rifella."

"Indeed." Mouse pulled a map from the bag at his side and, moving the tea cups, spread the parchment on the table.

Murwenna bent her head over the map, following Mouse's finger as he outlined the route, nodding in agreement with his plans. Kat concentrated on her tea and cookies. She and Mouse would go over the plans later, so she didn't need to stick her head in the way. Mouse held this meeting for Murwenna's benefit.

As they completed their analysis of the route, Murwenna requested Mouse tug on the tassel in the corner of the room.

Within minutes, Fenneth appeared at the door. "What do you wish Murwenna?"

"Fenneth, would you summon Janella, as I wish her to meet my visitors." She paused. "Oh yes, also request Arrogol's presence."

Fenneth nodded and left the room.

Murwenna faced Kat. "As one who will be viewing the challenges within Rifella, I do believe meeting both my bond mate, Janella, and Arrogol, who is the male responsible for my coming heir, is important."

"Thank you Murwenna, I'm sure the knowledge will prove important in our travels." Kat, not convinced she told the truth, but decided it politic to say so. *I'm becoming a political animal —and I'm telling fibs.*

"One of the places you should visit, Kat, is the village of Pakanna, which is where our leather armor is made. Our craftsmen in Pakanna are the best in Pridden, and many of Morden's assassins purchase armor in their shops."

"You deal with the assassins?"

Murwenna shrugged. "Why not? Rifellan warriors are the best in Pridden. We need fear nothing from the Assassins' Guild. Many turns ago, they attempted to violate our borders, and we trounced them with sufficient force to deter them in the future."

Kat grimaced. "I've been the target of their treachery, and they are duplicitous and sly in their attacks. They use snakes." She shuddered. "The odd thing is I never feared snakes before. But their syeths manage to instill a total revulsion of reptiles in my psyche."

Murwenna nodded her head. "I do agree. Syeths are not normal snakes. Like the assassins who own them, a deep furtive aspect surrounds them."

A knock at the door, and Janella and Arrogol appeared and walked toward the throne.

"Janella. Can you order more tea for us, and come sit beside me?" Murwenna held out her hand. "Arrogol. For many star turns, I noted your absence from the keep."

Mouth dry, Kat stared. *Blond. Muscles. Bare arms. Absolutely drool-worthy.*

Arrogol took Murwenna's hand. "Olwyn and I are spending much effort setting up our household prior to our official bonding ceremony. Women often do this, I am told. Their concerns appear to be similar to the nesting habits of many birds." He gave Murwenna a wry smile. "However, you are at fault. You chose her for me."

She smiled at him, a fond expression on her face. "Yes, I did. I'm glad the liaison is working for you." She shook her head. "But I am not doing my duty. I want both you and Janella to meet Kat, who comes to tour our land, thanks to Lord Eduardo. He is convinced she is able to discover the subversive element who are at work in Pridden. Both he and Lord Rhognor appear to value her abilities, so I would ask the two of you to give Kat and her guide, Mouse, your full cooperation."

Both Janella and Arrogol turned and stared at Kat. They nodded. "We will do your bidding, Murwenna."

"Excellent." She shifted in obvious discomfort. "Janella, you stay. The rest of you, please depart. I need to sleep."

Mouse appeared taken aback but lowered his head and moved away from the throne area.

As they departed the room, Arrogol chuckled. "Lord Murwenna is unpredictable these days. Olwyn advises me this is normal in the last weeks before a birth."

Kat nodded. "I believe she is correct. Your Lord appears

most uncomfortable." *I remember Nick, my boss telling me about his wife complaining with great bitterness near the end of her second pregnancy*. She hid a grin. *He told me she felt like a beached whale. Guess Murwenna's being a normal woman.*

They walked down the wood paneled hall, and Kat addressed her companions. "Mouse, I'm going to eat a light meal in my room, and I'll meet you at the morning meal on the morrow. I know you want to go over the route with me." She turned and beamed at Arrogol. "And you, sir… a pleasure indeed… er… meeting you. "*What I said is true—he's a major hunk.*

CHAPTER FOUR

Raucous cries and screeches of a bird, unknown to Kat, woke her the following morning. *What the…?* She clutched at her necklace, the stone ice cold. Frantic cheeps from Wink attracted Kat's attention to the pyrock. A black bird, the size of a turkey, appeared to be attempting to remove Wink from her cage. The pyrock pressed back against the rear bars, flapped her little wings; and, as Kat stared, astonished, Wink opened her mouth and spat a thin pencil of flame at the attacker.

"Wink? What?"

Aware of the danger to Wink from the huge bird, Kat leaped from the bed and grabbing her leather pants from a chair, she flew at the predator and landed a few blows on the substantial black body, driving the creature toward the open window. Anxious to escape, the monstrous bird flew out the window, with loud harsh cries. Kat dropped the pants of her leathers on the floor and slammed the window shutters closed. Her heart hammering, she turned to the pyrock, wings no longer flapping, but still sitting wide-eyed in her cage. Kat ran to the cage and scooped up the tiny creature. She stroked the furry little body, experiencing the anxious beating of Wink's heart beneath her fingers. "Wink, what are you? Did you spit out fire? Are you a teeny, tiny dragon?"

Wink chirruped and nuzzled Kat's hand with her downy head. Still carrying the little animal, Kat peered at the bars of the cage and discovered singe marks. "You did spit fire."

Kat grinned at the small creature. “I always wanted a dragon but never dreamed I might be the owner of a real one.” Wink gazed up at Kat and squeaked plaintively.

“Ah, you want food.” Kat rummaged among the containers on her dresser, and found three pieces of pyrock treats. Wink appeared to possess an enormous appetite this morning, demanded more, and only settled down after six of them disappeared down her gullet.

The danger over, and with Wink now deposited and asleep in her cage, Kat showered and dressed in her comfortable split skirt and a cool top. With her stone, once again warm against her skin, she headed for the communal dining lounge.

At the entrance to the public room, Kat paused and sniffed the air, laden with the spicy aromas of fine food. A hum of conversation filled the hall, and among a majority of Rifellans, she caught sight of a few Shendeans, clad in elegant robes, and a number of small, dark-skinned Baklai. Halfway down the rows of tables, a hand raised, and Kat recognized Mouse, sitting with Fenneth. She joined them, grinning, and greeted both of them.

Fenneth asked Kat what she preferred for her morning meal.

“Do you supply journeyklim regularly in Rifella? I find it’s my favorite meal in the morning.”

“Of course, Kat.” Fenneth raised her hand and beckoned to a young apprentice. “Would you please bring Lady Kat an order of journeyklim, with the usual topping?” She turned to Kat again. “What would you like to drink?”

“Would I be able to obtain some Karri-san tea, please?”

Fenneth smiled. “Of course.” She placed the order with the apprentice.

“Why are you smiling?”

“Because, Kat, to think of you as Rifellan is so easy because of your appearance, but your request for Karri-san reminds me you are not, in reality, one of us.”

“Oh.” Kat swallowed and blinked. She leaned forward, grinning “I must tell you both something. I experienced the strangest thing when I woke. An enormous bird came into my room and attacked my pyrock.”

Fenneth put her hand to her mouth. “Kat forgive me. I forgot to give you safety instructions about the windows. The bird is called a haggapoe, and they are noisy and inveterate robbers. They will take any bright shiny objects in your possession. They only appear at the keep in the harvest season. So keep the shutters closed at all times. You will still be able to allow fresh air in the room because they cannot insert themselves between the wooden slats. They are carrion birds, and are most vicious toward smaller creatures. However, they are normally unable to catch pyrocks, who can most often escape by jumping to another place.”

“I don’t believe poor little Wink, trapped in her cage would be able to jump anywhere. Luckily, the cage is wrapped in cloth. So when we begin our travels again, she should be safe. And I’ll be sure not to flash any bright shiny objects at them.” Kat paused and leaned further forward. “But I must tell you more.” Kat told the other two about the thin flame emitted by Wink. “Is she a dragon?”

Fenneth opened her mouth and stared at Kat. “No one ever told me of a such a thing. What is a dragon? I also am unfamiliar with a pyrock spitting flame. This is most astonishing.”

“A dragon is a mythical creature in my world who is gargantuan, covered in scales, can fly, and is able to emit huge gouts of flame. They are considered fearsome.”

Mouse rubbed his chin. "I too, never heard the word dragon before, nor do we on Pridden possess myths about such creatures." He stared at Kat, curiosity written over his face. "But I am aware of rare occasions when a pyrock spat out a flame. I believe this is most unusual."

Mouse and Fenneth continued to speak about the haggapoes, and pyrocks spitting flame.

Kat ate mechanically, wrapped in her own thoughts. *I don't care if they never learned of dragons. Wink is my tiny dragon.* She smirked to herself, warm and happy.

"Kat?" Mouse's voice penetrated her thoughts.

"Sorry, what did you say?"

"I need to prepare everything for our first journey through Rifella and locate items we will use during our travels, so you can enjoy this turn for yourself. Plus, the Rifellan guards invited me to join them for the evening meal. They plan to supply me with maps of Rifella. Are you able to keep yourself occupied?"

Fenneth jumped into the conversation. "Kat would you enjoy a tour of our marketplace? We can experience the offerings from most of the lands of Pridden. I would also appreciate a conversation about how Wynneth and Deleth are faring. I have not been in their company for more than two paths. I miss their wisdom." She smiled with a wistful expression. "We can partake of a midturn meal as well. What say you?"

"A fine idea, Fenneth. I appreciate your suggestions. I need to change to my leathers back in my room, and I'll join you at the exit to the keep."

Fenneth nodded, and both set off for their rooms.

❦ ❦ ❦

Kat met Fenneth inside the entrance to the keep.

"Kat, welcome. As you can tell, the paths leading away from the entrance are designed for specific functions. To our left is the route to the stables, and, to the right, if we follow the inside wall of the keep, we will come to the market place. The keep always housed the markets within its walls—in the beginning for protection during the wars Pridden suffered hundreds of paths ago. The walls surrounding the keep are extensive, because during the time of the conflicts, all our citizens, their families, their trades, and their homes needed the protection the keep offered. Now, after all these paths, we live in more peaceful times, and many of the smaller villages are no longer walled." Fenneth grimaced. "Except those along the Morden border."

"I gather the Mordens cause some problems."

"Those in the north do. Southern Mordens are quite different. They are more easy going, and most of them possess a sense of humor. They are pleasant people."

Kat stopped in awe at the entrance to a mass of shops. Music and laughter and singing surrounded them, with flags and banners adorning the entrance. "This is some market. I believe this will be fun."

"Let us enter. If you admire anything you would like to own, advise me. The keep will cover the cost, as you are our valued guest."

"Thank you for the offer, but since I still need to do so much traveling, I'm trying to keep my belongings to a minimum."

"As you wish, but you may need other types of clothing. So, what would you like to experience first?"

"I need some more arrows for my spring bow. May we visit a stall with those types of weapons?"

"Follow me."

Kat followed Fenneth among the various merchants, stopping every once in a while to admire beautiful jewelry. Nestled among handcrafted silver wires lay lustrous yellow citrine, tigers eye of pale brown and buttery gold, deep blue amethysts, fiery red rubies, and brilliant green emeralds, which reminded Kat of her own necklace. She fingered her stone through the folds of her blouse. Everything expressed glorious glamor, but Kat considered her stone more beautiful than any displayed there.

At a booth a little farther away, Kay spied scarves, dyed in myriads of colors. One caught her eye. The silky fabric reminded her of a glorious sunset, beginning with a deep red, mixed with brilliant orange, which faded to pale yellow, the pinks of early dawn, and, ended in blue and mauve, similar to the sky when Pridden's star fell below the horizon.

"Oh." Kat breathed in awe. "How gorgeous."

"If this strikes you with such force, you must own the shawl." Fenneth approached the shop-keeper and handed him a chit for the scarf. She passed the diaphanous fabric to Kat. "You can wear this like a scarf or spread the entire material over your shoulders for light protection from the cool of evening. You can wind the fabric around your waist as a belt, if you desire. But, you are right, the color is magnificent."

"Fenneth, this is too much." Kat wound the fabric around her waist, leaving part of the scarf showing, similar to a short overskirt. *I don't usually indulge in such delicate fabric, but this gives me the sensation of being royal and glamorous.* "Thank you." She glanced in a mirror the stall keeper displayed for his customers. *Yup. Royalty.* "Fenneth we better move to the weaponry—everything here is so amazing, I might want to purchase every piece, simply to gaze at them."

Fenneth laughed. “No matter how warrior-like, all women appreciate beautiful things.” She strode on, Kat lagging behind, admiring the scarf in every mirror she passed.

Soon the two approached the weaponry shop. Kat stared at all the different fighting implements on display. She approached the shopkeeper and requested a dozen arrows for her spring bow. He brought some out to show her, and she discovered the tips on these arrows were sharper and stronger than the ones she purchased in Kaylin. He scrunched up his face and regarded her with puzzlement. “Do you do much riding?

“Yes, why do you ask?”

“Spring bows are fine weapons when on foot, but Rifellan guards discovered many turns ago that the long bow is much better when riding on horseback. Setting a spring bow while perched on a horse is slow and can put the person at a disadvantage.”

Kat frowned. “You make sense. What would you suggest?”

The stall keeper motioned as he wandered over toward a collection of long bows. He brought out three different lengths and held them up against her. “This one suits your height best. Now let us test the strength of the weapon.” He brought out four different bows of the same length and asked her to pull on each one, first handing her a glove with which to hold the bow in a firm grip, and a tab to protect her fingers from the string. She pulled the first, second, and third bows with relative ease, but the fourth one became more difficult. The owner of the stall raised his eyebrows almost to his hairline. “You are strong, my Lady. If you planned to use the long bow as much as the guards do, I would recommend the fourth one. However, I would suggest you purchase the third, as the draw weight best suits your current abilities."

Kat beamed at him. "Thank you, I find this one similar to my own bow back in my homeland."

"You will need an extended quiver, because this bow uses arrows which are much longer."

Kat chose a quiver of pale brown, and arrows with fletching of red and black. She figured she would be able to locate loosed arrows with greater ease if fitted with a red cock feather.

Before she departed the stall, Kat caught sight of a number of excellent daggers.

She remembered how Mouse saved their lives with his and thought she would be wise to possess one of her own. She enrolled the shopkeeper into helping her choose an appropriate weapon. He presented a number of shiny metallic blades of various sizes, and she caught sight of one of the perfect length. The bright blade resembled a sgian dubh she'd spied on a Scottish friend, a regular member of a Highland pipe band. This small dagger, inserted in the socks of Highlanders when on parade, became part of their magnificent costumes. Kat's dagger, with a carved bone hilt, sheathed in a plain leather scabbard, and attached to a thin leather belt, fitted snuggly around her waist under the silken scarf. *Perfect. No unsightly bulges or anything showing. Plus I can reach the dagger quickly and without effort.*

Kat turned to Fenneth to request a chit for her purchases and caught a smile of amusement on the healer's face. "What?"

Fenneth chuckled. "You appear to be preparing for war."

Kat laughed.

They stared at each other for a few moments.

"Is your shopping complete, Kat?"

She nodded.

"I will request the owner deliver your goods to your quarters. Except what you are wearing, of course. We should head further into the market for a midturn meal."

"Excellent. Now, I think about food, I'm starving."

Kat followed Fenneth toward savory aromas. *Preparing for war? In many ways, I suppose I am.*

CHAPTER FIVE

The food court area of the market rang with laughter and happy conversation. Friends called to each other, and a trio of musicians played rollicking tunes off to the side. The middle area, surrounded by merchants offering a number of local dishes, and filled with tables and chairs, welcomed visitors of different lands. The scent of spices and roasting meats and vegetables hung in the air, tempting the shoppers to try a variety of foods. Kat, positive she detected the aroma of gornog among the offerings, headed to a stall with a lengthy lineup, followed closely by Fenneth.

"We are fortunate indeed, Kat. Tannis only comes to the market two turns each season, but he brings with him heavenly gornog meat. Quick, stand in the line."

"The line is long. Will gornog still be left when we reach the front?"

"He glanced my way, and Tannis always saves a portion for me and any guest I might bring to his stall."

"I'm delighted you have pull."

Fenneth peered at Kat. "Pull?"

Oh bother. I must stop using expressions they don't understand. "What I mean, Fenneth is… um—you possess influence."

"Pull. A strange expression, but it does make sense."

They reached the head of the line, and Fenneth ordered two gornog meals, and handed the talented Tannis a chit.

Once seated at a table, a young man delivered their gornog meals, and the two women dug in.

"Ah, Fenneth, I almost forgot how delicious this meat is. My taste buds are singing, and all is well with the world."

"I might not describe gornog meat the same way, but I agree with the sentiment."

A voice ran out. "Kat. Is that you?"

Kat glanced behind her, and beamed at the newcomer. "Kaleen. What a surprise. What are you doing here instead of in Shendea?"

"Lord Rhognor gave us leave to attend the ceremony for the heir. We arrived last evening's turn."

Kat stood and hugged Kaleen. She turned to Fenneth. "I want you to meet Kaleen. She runs a Rifellan female guard unit in Shendea. We met… " She faced Kaleen again, puzzled. "Where did we meet? The last few turns in Shendea, filled with distress nearly obliterated my sense of time. I can't remember."

Kat registered the sympathy of touch in Kaleen's hand on her arm.

"I am aware of the heartache of Lady Halfin's passing. I am sorry I could not be with you when you encountered such sorrow. But to refresh your memory, we met at the Ponti Inn."

"Thanks for reminding me. So much happened later in my journey." Kat realized she forgot to introduce Kaleen to Fenneth. "My apologies, this is my friend Fenneth."

The Rifellan flashed a smile. "You are in healer's robes. Are you assigned to Lord Murwenna?"

Fenneth rose and took both of Kaleen's hands in her own. "I am indeed. We are well met, Kaleen."

Kat gestured at the table. "We're about to enjoy some tea. Why don't you join us?"

"I would be delighted, but I am scheduled to work with my guard unit and need to meet with them. Perhaps you would join us for the evening meal at the keep dining hall?"

"Perfect. I'll meet you there." She hugged Kaleen again.

As Kaleen left to join her guards, Fenneth turned back to Kat. "Sit, Kat. I will order tea." She laughed as Kat opened her mouth to speak. "I understand. You wish to drink Kar-ri-san."

"Actually, Fenneth, I intended to say I'm not ready for tea yet. I wish to return to my room and unpack my purchases—and re-examine Wink, my teeny dragon posing as a pyrock. Plus, I think Murwenna might need you."

"You are probably correct. She does appear to want my presence more often now. I will accompany you back to where we met after the morning meal. You are able to find your rooms from the keep entrance?"

Kat nodded, and they smiled at each other and set off through the laneways of shops and stalls.

❦ ❦ ❦

Once in her rooms, Kat peered at Wink, who, rolled in a furry ball, slept soundly. *Poor little dragon—she's tired. Perhaps making flame requires loads of energy.*

After unpacking her purchases, Kat grabbed her diplo pouch and extracted her writing materials. She placed the cathnog pen and the Kaylin ink on the desk and withdrew her journal pages. *The Rifellan market is the most exotic so far. Gotta write down everything. By the time I arrive home, I'll bet this'll be enough material for multiple games. Especially now I'm the proud owner of a small dragon.* She chuckled to herself.

As she finished with her journal and placed the pages in her bag, the list of words fell out. *Darn. My list of cool daily words has been seriously neglected. I haven't added any for ages.*

Kat yawned. She stretched and yawned again and glanced at the comfortable bed. *Ooh a nap. Perfect.* She pulled the tassel in the corner of the room, and, when the apprentice knocked, Kat poked her head out the door. "Would you arrange for someone to call me when the evening meal begins?"

When the young male assented, she closed the door and headed for her bed.

Dropping clothes on the chair, she threw back the bedcovers, fell on the soft mattress, and pulled the comforter up to her nose. "Ahh."

Kat woke, stretched and rose from the bed. *I need to wake up. A cold shower should do the trick.* She headed for the personal. After, clean and ready for a fun evening, she gazed thoughtfully at her wardrobe offerings. She decided against her Rifellan leathers, and instead chose the culotte skirt and a fitted top and tied her sunset scarf around her waist, once again concealing the dagger on her belt.

At the sound of a knock, Kat opened her door, and a young apprentice advised her of the start of the evening meal.

"Thank you."

She followed him out, closed her door, and headed for food.

❦ ❦ ❦

Even before she reached the hall, Kat caught the sound of laughter and the buzz of animated conversation. She stopped at the huge open doors, and scanned the room. To her left, she caught Kaleen beckoning her to the table she shared with a number of women and men. Kat sat in an offered chair and acknowledged the others as they introduced themselves. A handsome man with dark hair advised her he was Tiewellan, sibling to Lord Murwenna's bond mate, Janella.

"I met Janella, and her hair is light-colored. You are her sibling?"

Tiewellan appeared uncomfortable. "I am not a sibling of her blood. My parents perished in an accident, and Janella's parents fostered me in their home."

"I'm sorry about your parents, but how lucky you found a home."

"Well, yes, it would seem so. They would hardly turn me out, as royal blood ran through the veins of my female parent."

He sounds arrogant. Hmph. Kat frowned and turned to Kaleen. "I must ask something. Why is Murwenna referred to as Lord and not Lady?"

"Lady is an honorific given to all females of importance, including the bond mates of all Lords and Thanes. Murwenna inherited the title of Lord as the leader of our land, which transcendes the title of Lady."

"Thanks. Now I understand. So, Kaleen when did you leave Shendea?"

"Three turns ago. My last visit to Rifella occurred over two paths ago, and I am most appreciative for the opportunity to visit my home."

"Rifellan warriors sacrifice much acting as guards in the lands of Pridden, don't they?"

Kaleen's expression appeared rueful. "We do, but this is who we are, and these are the services we are called on to perform in Pridden."

Tiewellan sneered. "Enough injured party thoughts. You are required to do your duty, and we do not need to listen to you complaining of such. This is a time of celebration, not self-pity. I shall order more near-ale." He rose and sauntered to the counter.

Kat gaped at him. *He's rude and insensitive. And he swaggers. I'll bet he suffers from delusions of adequacy. Even my necklace is cooler around him.* She shook her head with contempt.

The rest of the evening passed in laughter and amusing anecdotes. They drank enormous quantities of near-ale, ate wonderful food, and sang rather bawdy songs of conquest and love.

Kat flirted with a gorgeous Rifellan warrior seated on the other side of Kaleen, but kept herself in check with intermittent cups of Karri-san. She enjoyed the flirt, but Tiewellan kept interfering. Laughing louder than the rest of the company, he consumed two ales to everyone else's one. He touched her arm, and she shook his hand off. He put his hand on her shoulder, and she shrugged it off. She leaned away from him, and spoke again to the Rifellan guard beside Kaleen. But Tiewellan persisted and grabbed her hand. *Can't he notice I don't want him touching me?* She flung his hand away and shook herself free of him. He didn't take the hint when she leaned even further away from him.

Arrogant jerk. Creep. Can't he understand I don't want to be mauled by him.

Finally she reached the end of her patience. She rose from her seat. "Kaleen, my thanks for a fun evening, but I must return to my room. I need to plan for my journey through Rifella."

Kaleen rose and gave Kat a hug. "I experienced a fun evening with you too, Kat. I do not return to Shendea until after the celebration, so we are sure to meet again."

Kat thanked all the others at the table, and when she reached the exit to the hall, she groaned. Tiewellan followed her. *Doesn't he learn?*

"Kat, I will escort you to your rooms."

"This is not necessary, Tiewellan." She turned and stalked away from him.

He ran after her. "But yes. You are a woman alone, and you need an esh—cort."

Terrific. He's drunk and arrogant. She drew her lips in a thin line. "I'm telling you, I do not need you. Kindly leave me alone."

"No, no, no. You need me to help you." He grabbed her by the wrist.

"Let me go." Kat spat out the words. "If you don't, I will hurt you."

"Listen. You musht. You are beautiful, and you teashed me all night. Now you musht be nishe to me."

"You're drunk. You're an ass. I said. Let. Me. Go." Kat bared her teeth at him.

"No."

"Enough is enough." Kat twisted her arm to free herself, made a fist, and punched him.

He cried out in pain and clutched at his nose, blood streaming down his face.

Kat turned away, and hurried to her room, leaving Tiewellan moaning, dripping blood, and vomiting in a corner of the hallway.

As Kat unlocked her door and let herself into her room, she shook her head.

What an idiot. I must talk to Mouse tomorrow. He can't blame me for this.

CHAPTER SIX

Mouse spent the day studying various routes for him and Kat to follow in their first pass of Rifella. *I need better maps. Perhaps when I am at the evening meal with the Rifellan guards, they can help me*. At midturn, he ordered a light meal and some near-ale to his room. He wrote out a list of what would be needed for the first phase of Kat's journey through Rifella. He wrote a second list, translated into Kat's rune writing.

A knock at the door summoned him to the guards quarters.

Mouse tucked the list for Kat in the inner pocket in his grey cloak. He would drop it at her quarters after his evening with the guards. He planned to send a borrowed pyrock to Eduardo with an up-to-date version of his journeys with Kat on the morrow. As he headed to the guards' rooms, he mused on his travels with Kat to date

I cannot believe Eduardo understood how much challenge I would encounter in this assignment. Kat is an extraordinary woman, but her social skills are rough, and her tendency to loose arrows before determining if they are necessary, is daunting. She is quick to anger, but also quick to forgive. He grinned to himself. *Beneath all the bluster does beat a kind heart.*

He laughed aloud. He remembered the expression on her face when she mentioned how her pyrock shot flame.

He knocked at the door of the hall of the guards, which a blonde giant of a man flung open. “Sire Mouse, enter. I am Wolfdrang.”

Mouse shrank back into his grey persona. “We are well met, Wolfdrang.”

“Come in. Come in.”

Mouse coughed when Wolfdrang clapped him on the back with a massive meaty hand.

All those in the room, dressed in well-worn Rifellan leathers, welcomed him, pressed a near-ale into his hand, and sat him at a table. A hearty stewed meal of some unknown creature arrived at the table, brought by three young apprentices. Questions and answers eddied around Mouse like a whirlpool.

“We heard you are an excellent guide, Sire Mouse, so we are eager to learn what challenges you encountered guiding the Lady Kat. Rumor exists she tends to be willful.” All the guards requested similar information during the evening.

Finally, Mouse, not eager to arouse suspicions about the real purpose of their journey, amused the group with a few humorous tales about Kat’s tendency to trip over Priddanese customs. The room, afloat in male bonding, laughter, and many ribald stories of female conquests, touched Mouse. *I would find this so delightful to relax with these men and enjoy the camaraderie of being a man of action and power.* He sighed. *Alas, only Mouse can sit in this seat.*

He turned to Wolfdrang. “I regret I must leave promptly, but the Lady Kat and I are committed to continue our journey. We wish to return to the keep before the birth of the heir. You said you might be able to supply some relevant maps of the area in which we intend to travel?”

"Yes, of course." Wolfdrang led him back to an office filled with maps and drawings of places around Rifella. He rummaged through piles of parchments on his desk. "Here, these two should be all you will need this first trip. I will complete some other copies so when you set out on your final journey to Glowen, you will possess what you need."

"These are perfect. My thanks for the maps and for a most enjoyable evening. You serve with a fine group of men."

Wolfdrang roared with laughter and gave Mouse another thunderous clap on the back.

By Caleesh, he possesses the strength of a cathnog. If I were merely Mouse, I would be black and blue on the morrow.

❦ ❦ ❦

As Mouse headed down the path toward the central part of the keep, something flew at him. Startled, he stopped, and a messenger moth landed on his shoulder. Few others lingered about, but Mouse preferred to listen to the message privately, so he hastened through the hallways of the keep to his own room. As he closed the door, he dropped the maps on his desk and held the creature to his ear. He recognized Galdin's voice. "Come at once, I will give you some additional instructions. But before you leave, attempt to gain an audience with Murwenna to discover what she plans for the celebration of the heir. I order you to discuss this with no one."

Mouse would not ignore what Galdin demanded and what else he ordered Mouse to do. Disobeying might prove perilous to both him and Kat.

Deciding on a course of action, he brought the moth to his lips and whispered, "If I can attend Murwenna this night, I will leave after meeting with her and will be with you in two turns. I will learn what I can from her about the celebrations."

He opened his window and threw the moth into the night.

Mouse headed straight away for the dining hall. *With luck, I may be able to find help.*

A few last-minute diners sat in the hall, and Mouse sighed in relief when he spied Fenneth among them. He hurried over.

"Fenneth, may I disturb you?"

"Yes, what do you need?"

"I am informed of a family emergency which I must attend and am required to leave Rifella immediately. I will return three to four turns from now, but I cannot put off my journey. I need two things. How quickly can I meet with Lord Murwenna before I leave?"

"She is not yet abed, and I can, since this is an emergency, take you to her now."

"Excellent. My second request is Kat's initial journey through Rifella cannot be delayed until after the celebration, so I need to locate another guide for her for the three or four turns I am away. Who would you recommend?"

"I believe the best person would be Praetor Arrogol. He is more familiar with Rifella than any other. I will take you to Murwenna now, and you should request her to assign Arrogol to guide Kat during this first journey."

"My thanks Fenneth. You are most helpful. I will follow you."

Fenneth led Mouse out of the hall and through the various corridors to the quarters of Murwenna.

I dislike leaving Kat with another guide. She will no doubt assault me with questions when I return. "Where have you been? Why? Who did you meet?" I dread the inquisition.

CHAPTER SEVEN

Fenneth knocked on the door to Murwenna's quarters, and announced to the guard who answered she needed to speak with the Lord immediately. Soon, Murwenna called to Fenneth to join her.

With Mouse close behind her, she entered the room. "Murwenna, I bring Sire Mouse with me because an urgent matter in Morden requires his attention, and he needs to speak with you before he leaves."

"Urgent?" Murwenna, stretched out on a long sofa piled with pink pillows, shifted her very pregnant bulk so she might face Mouse, wincing as she did so. "What do you need?"

Mouse bowed his head to her. "Lord Murwenna, my deepest apologies for disturbing you so late in the evening. I am required to be in Morden as soon as possible." *I hope she does not ask who calls for me.* "Lady Kat is on important business for Lord Eduardo, and needs to perform her initial journey through Rifella before the celebration of the heir's arrival. If she does not achieve this, her full journey will be regrettably delayed. For reasons to which I am not privy, Lord Eduardo withheld the information regarding this."

"Sire Mouse, both Lord Eduardo and Lord Rhognor advised us of much of the reason for Kat's journey, and we do understand. What aid do you wish me to give you?"

"I enquired who might take my place as her guide for the initial four or five turns, and I received suggestions that Praetor Arrogol would be the perfect choice."

"Hmm." Murwenna called out, "Janella can you come in here?"

Murwenna's bond mate entered the room. "I overheard." She moved to a chair beside the chaise, sat, and patted Murwenna's arm affectionately. "Arrogol would be the perfect choice. He will guide Kat as capably as Mouse, and he is strong and able to help her should any untoward situation occur. I believe you should release him to perform this chore."

"I concur." Murwenna turned again to Mouse. "Be seated, Sire Mouse." She motioned to a bent-wood chair near the foot of the sofa. "We need to discuss the rules of this substitution." She waited until Mouse seated himself before she continued. "As you are aware, the birth of the heir will likely occur within the next six to seven turns, and I wish Arrogol to be present for the occasion. This means his accompaniment of Lady Kat is limited to less than six turns, after which I expect him to return with her to the keep. The celebration will be held approximately three turns after the arrival of the heir. This will enable Rifellans from all over Pridden to return home for the celebration. Some will not be able to appear due to the protection services they offer in other lands in Pridden."

"I understand, Lord Murwenna. I appreciate your help."

"I expect you to return before the celebration takes place. As Lady Kat's guide you are also her representative from the other lands, and will need to resume your post as her guide."

"I will definitely be back prior to the celebration, Lord Murwenna. I give you my word." *Thank Caleesh she did not ask questions about my emergency.* "I need to request a further favor, my Lord."

"What do you wish?"

"I did not meet with Kat this evening, and I must leave now. Would someone please inform her I cannot be here and Praetor Arrogol will be guiding her on the first part of her journey through Rifella?"

"I will. Janella, would you ask Melindar to come here?"

Janella left the room and returned moments later with Melindar, Murwenna's sibling.

Mouse started. Melindar was her sibling's duplicate. He glanced from one to the other, barely noticing the grins on their faces. "You are womb mates?"

Murwenna laughed aloud. "We are. We both enjoy perceiving the expressions on the faces of others when they view us together."

Mouse watched Melindar more closely and caught her smile tinged with something other than amusement. She appeared almost angry.

Murwenna addressed her sibling. "Melindar, would you send someone to advise Lady Kat that Sire Mouse is called away on urgent business, and Praetor Arrogol will accompany her through Rifella for the next four turns."

"I will request Tiewellan pass the message to her."

"Thank you, sister." She faced Mouse again. "If you require a faster horse, Sire, please be sure to request one from our Horse-Master."

"I thank you, my Lord, but I suspect most of your steeds would be too large."

"Perhaps. You are certainly not a large man, but I suspect you are most capable and are able to manage our horses without challenge."

"I believe, my Lord, you give me too much credit." Mouse bowed his head, and backed out from her presence. "Thank you again for your assistance."

❦ ❦ ❦

After taking his leave of Murwenna, Mouse headed for the stables and saddled the horse loaned to him by the keep's Horse-Master. The animal, more compact than most Rifellan steeds, stocky, and built with strong legs and a barrel chest, assured him it would convey him easily to Morden and back. He exited the keep and headed for Arrogol's home, in the direction the Horse-Master suggested.

Outside the home of the Praetor, he looped the reins of his horse around a small fence, and proceeded to the house. At the Praetor's door, he knocked. and he assumed the attractive woman who answered was Olwyn.

"You are Lady Olwyn, bond mate to Praetor Arrogol?"

"I am Olwyn, but Praetor Arrogol and I are bond mates-to-be. Our bonding ceremony will be celebrated after the birth of Lord Murwenna's heir."

"Forgive my assumption. I would request an audience with the Praetor. I am Mouse, the guide for the Lady Kat."

"Enter, Sire Mouse. You are welcome. May I prepare tea for you?"

Mouse accepted gratefully. He studied her as she prepared the drink and brought the cups to the table. *She is a beautiful woman. Her red hair compliments her cinnamon skin.*

Arrogol joined them. "Sire Mouse, my friend Ballinor mentioned he met you in Roothlan. Olwyn welcomed you, I perceive."

As he sat, Mouse caught him admiring his beautiful mate, and Olwyn's glance at Arrogol seemed filled with love. *Murwenna's match for them is brilliant.*

Arrogol turned to Mouse. "Why did you come to meet with us?"

"I apologize for coming to your home so late in the turn, but I require a favor from you. Lord Murwenna gave me permission to request this of you. I am called for an urgent meeting to Morden and cannot delay my visit." Mouse rubbed his eyebrow. "However, Lady Kat must complete a short journey within Rifella prior to the heir's arrival. She and I are tasked to travel throughout Pridden, which we will not be able to accomplish unless she completes this short journey within the next four to five turns."

"What is the favor you wish to request of me?"

"Would you agree to be Lady Kat's guide for this first trip, until I return from Morden?"

Olwyn stepped forward. "You cannot request this of Arrogol. He is required to be present during the birth of the heir."

"Lady Olwyn, Lord Murwenna made this most clear to me when I requested a guide. She did approve I would be allowed to approach Praetor Arrogol for his help. I am convinced she considers him the best possible substitute for me. She is aware this journey is commissioned by Lord Eduardo. She agreed to this. I only need you, Arrogol, to agree as well."

Olwyn frowned. "I am not comfortable with you performing this request so close to time of the birth, Arrogol."

"Olwyn, I will be fine, and Murwenna realizes I am one of the few men who can achieve this in a timely manner. Remember too, this request ultimately comes from Lord Eduardo."

Olwyn regarded both Arrogol and Mouse, still frowning. "I dislike politics, but this appears to be a situation where politics reign. Be careful, Arrogol."

He smiled down at her. "I will."

Mouse pulled three pieces of parchment from the bag over his shoulder. "Arrogol, I prepared a route for this initial journey. I also prepared a list of items Lady Kat should pack for this section of Rifella. Please give her this list, which is written in runes. She is only able to write and read runes, but the second list is written in Priddenese for your information."

Arrogol accepted the lists and the map. "I will take care of your Lady Kat and make sure she completes the journey in safety, Sire Mouse. I spoke with my Rifellan brothers-in-arms from Shendea. They speak well of you."

"I thank you, Arrogol. Lady Olwyn, I thank you for the tea. I must be off if I am to return in time for the birth of the heir." Mouse left the house, and paused only to wave at his hosts. He unhitched his horse, mounted, and rode for Morden. *Now to complete the process of becoming the smaller and more terrified Mouse.*

⚘⚘⚘

Melindar approached Tiewellan at his quarters. When he answered her knock, she stepped into his room.

He smiled at her and gathered her in his arms and leaned in to kiss her. "Melindar" He breathed her name.

She put her hand on his lips. "Wait. Before I forget what I came to tell you." She stroked his cheek. "Murwenna summoned me to a late-turn meeting with herself and the little grey man called Mouse. He needed to leave for an urgent meeting in Morden, and Arrogol will be guiding Kat on a short journey through Rifella. Murwenna suggested I advise you to convey the changes to the Lady Kat."

Tiewellan experienced a red rage as he felt the blood rise up his face. "Advise her? I will do no such thing. She is an arrogant woman, and struck me when I attempted to assist her."

"Assist her?" She pushed him away. " I believe you intended to seduce her. How easily you forget you are bound to me. I am losing patience over your dalliances with other women, Tiewellan. Do not forget how much you owe me."

"I can never forget you." He grabbed her hand. "She drank too much near-ale, and then made advances to me. She is a foul woman. I will tell her nothing."

Melindar stared at him, her eyes cold as ice. "I care not how you perform your duties. I performed what I needed to and advised you of Murwenna's request. Perform yours or not. This is no business of mine."

She turned and stalked from the room.

Tiewellan grabbed a mug from the table in his room and threw the full cup against the wall. The delicate beaker shattered in small pieces. *Melindar thwarts me as well. This is Kat's fault. I shall avoid her.* He struck the table with his fist. *But I must soothe Melindar. I need her.*

CHAPTER EIGHT

Mouse failed to appear for the morning meal. Kat remembered he planned to spend time preparing for their initial journey. *We're supposed to be back before the heir is born, and he's such a stickler for protocol. So where is he?*

Kat returned to her room, and checked on Wink. The small ball of fur, almost hidden in the warm bedding in her cage, stretched, and opened one eye when Kat stroked her.

"Hi, my little dragon."

The eye closed, and Wink shifted and slept, snoring as usual.

Kat grinned to herself and closed the cage. *Time for some meditation. Three days since my last one, and I miss the peace.* She sat in a comfortable chair, wrapped in a shawl, and let her brain empty of thoughts. People in the hallway talked as they went by, and she drifted. After about twenty minutes she opened her eyes and stretched. She rose from the comfortable chair and sprang to her feet.

Kat walked over to her desk, gathered her writing materials and sat. She recorded fuller descriptions of the people who'd crossed her path so far in this trip through Pridden. *Shendeans are tall people, but are heavier than the Mordens, who are also tall. I guess the Shendeans carry more fat because of the extreme cold where the majority of them live. The Dizerths, who are little people, are also quite plump.*

She also practiced her Pridden writing techniques, but, after an hour, she returned to her journal entries. Kat stretched, easing her cramped muscles. *Incredible, when you don't use proper writing, in a while, your hands almost forget.* Back to the inhabitants. *The Mordens are tall but almost stringy. They remind me of the bit from Shakespeare about a man who has a "lean and hungry look." Perfect description of Mordens in general.* She sipped Karri-san tea from the cup beside her. *Baklai are short and stocky. The Rifellans are the most beautiful—tall, bronze, buff, and most attractive. Yum.*

She stretched again. *Crap.* She extended hands and pulled on her fingers which cracked as she worked at them.. *I miss my computer.* Placing her hands on her head, she twisted her waist from side to side..

Kat stowed her journal, the cathnog pen, and her ink, and rose from the table. She started for the door, stopped, and snapped her fingers. She grabbed a couple of chits Fenneth gave her the previous day in case she wanted to buy something, and, with a spring in her step, set out for the market.

❦ ❦ ❦

Though she walked only as far as the entrance to the market place in the keep, Kat's muscles loosened enough to inspire her to walk farther. She visited the stall where she bought her beautiful scarf, but didn't find any as glorious as the one she bought the day before. She wound her way to the weapons seller.

He greeted her. "Lady Kat. You are back. Is your new long bow to your liking?"

"I didn't get a chance to practice as yet. I tested the bow a number of times, and I find the pull comfortable but resistant enough to challenge me. I adore my little dagger, which I'm wearing now, under my scarf belt."

He grinned at her. "I discovered in my travels, women always gain a sense of delight when they possess a small but effective weapon they are able to conceal." He beckoned her over to a back corner of the stall. "Did I show you these?"

Kat stood entranced at the display of tiny blades, with gem-encrusted hilts, beside a collection of small leather sheaths, decorated with painted and polished designs. "Oh, wow. They're gorgeous." *But what would I need one for?*

He chuckled. "They are fine works of art, which double as defensive weapons. They are designed to fit inside your boots."

"Oh. I've gotta have one." She pulled out a chit from a pocket. "Will this cover the cost?"

"Indeed. I will simply mark the amount of the purchase on the chit and present the bill later to the keep. Which one do you want?"

Kat scrutinized the tiny blades available and chose one with a hilt covered with deep emerald stones, similar in color to the one on her pendant. As her hand closed on the dagger, her stone warmed against her skin. *They like each other.*

"You chose one of my best. You possess an eye for quality, my Lady. Now you should choose a sheath to go with this blade."

This took much longer, as the array of sheaths dazzled her. At last, she found the perfect one. The leather, soft and butter-colored, caressed her hand, and the design consisted of three gold stars, which appealed to her. "This one." She handed the starred one to the stall owner.

"Fine. Now if you will seat yourself over here and remove your boot, my Lady. We will wrap the sheath around your ankle."

"Right. Which boot should I remove?"

"Which is your dominant hand?"

"I'm not sure. I shoot a long bow with my right, but I write with my left." She held up her hands to demonstrate.

"You are probably comfortable with either, but we will set this up for your left hand. Be seated and remove your left boot."

Once she did so, he placed the small blade in the sheath, and attached the sheath on the outside of her left ankle with soft leather strands. He replaced the boot. "Are you comfortable? Nothing scrapes on your ankle?"

"I'm very comfortable."

"Excellent. Now reach down and remove the blade from the sheath."

Kat did so, and the weapon slipped easily to her hand. "How simple."

"Now replace the knife, taking care not to cut yourself."

Kat did so, and the tiny dagger fitted perfectly in the sheath, almost as if familiar with the way.

She gazed up at the stall owner. "Wonderful. Thank you so much. I love it."

"I am glad this suits you so well. And I hope this is one you will never need to use."

"If I do need to, I'm sure my little stinger will serve me well."

The stall keeper laughed. "Little stinger. An excellent. name."

Kat's stomach grumbled. She thanked the stall owner and headed deeper into the market, following her nose toward the aromas of food.

Kat spied Melindar and Janella at a table when she entered the food area. She waved at the two women, and Janella gestured for her to join them.

Kat sat at the table. "What do you both recommend for my midturn meal?"

Janella responded first. "Ask for the pellotta. While the dish contains no animal flesh, the plant foods are delicious in themselves, but the spicing is what makes the meal famous in Rifella."

"So is Rifella famous for their spices?"

Melindar snorted. "Rifella? Spices? You forget, Kat, we are a warrior race. Our people spend more time concentrating on their physical capabilities than on the flavor of the food they ingest."

"Your people are beautiful physically." Kat swallowed, remembering Liandock and Ballinor and Bardu. *Whew. They don't need to be spicier.* "So where do these spices come from?"

"From Glowen. Those people may be stupid in many ways, but they make the best wine in all Pridden and they can perform amazing culinary feats with flavor combinations."

Janella patted Melindar on the arm. "You are being too harsh. The Glowens are not stupid."

"They most certainly are. They are self-indulgent, live only for pleasure, and do not possess any sense of what is important in life."

Janella sighed, and faced Kat. "Melindar is being unfair. The island on which the Glowens live is lush with vegetation and glorious flowers, and their crops flourish. Their Orenberry wine is the finest in all Pridden, and their island is always warm and receives plenty of rain. They are blessed with abundance in everything which we find is—"

"While we in Rifella receive limited moisture, and possess harsh deserts where little grows." Melindar snorted again. "Our people work hard. True, they are talented shipbuilders, but few on Pridden require such vessels. So we need to hire ourselves to other lands as guards and protectors."

"I understand." *Melindar is a cold fish compared to her sister. I wonder if she's good at her job?* "Melindar what exactly are your duties within the keep?"

"I am my sibling's chief counsel. I sit at the head of the Counsel of Seven. We make necessary decisions about our economy, our relationships with the other five lands in Pridden, and all the internal matters covering, food, metal, wood, ship-building, and so on."

"Yours is a most important role in Rifella."

"Leadership always is."

What an odd thing to say. Murwenna is the leader here. Kat turned back to Janella. "I assume you must perform specific duties to assist Murwenna as her bond mate?"

Janella beamed. "My duties, as you refer to them, are not always specific. I support Murwenna in her life. I most often act as a confidant, and I believe I help her to be balanced in her life as Lord—"

"Murwenna is most upset that all Rifellans will not be at the celebration. She wants all her people to attend."

Kat, surprised, glanced at Melindar. "But they accepted contracts to protect other lands and towns. They need to keep those commitments."

Melindar almost spat at Kat. "You must never say such a treasonous thing again."

"Treasonous? I don't believe my statement to be treasonous, but merely a fact of life for Rifella's warriors." *I'd better watch what I say around her as she's weird.*

Janella laid her hand on Melindar's arm. "Kat is right. They view their duty as a fact of life."

Melindar took a deep breath. "I suppose you are correct, Kat. Murwenna is most irritable at the moment, because she is confined to her rooms, and I bear the brunt of her temper.

Fenneth determined working with her guards became too challenging for her, so she insisted my sibling stop such severe exercise. Because Murwenna is curtailed, she tends to be short-tempered."

"I understand." *Perhaps Melindar is not cold, only worried about her sister. And, frustrated.*

Janella stood. "Forgive me. Although this is most pleasant, I suspect Murwenna needs me with her."

Melindar pushed her chair back and rose as well. "I will accompany you. I need to report to my sibling on the state of our metal production."

The two departed, leaving Kat at the table drinking a final cup of Karri-san. *I like Janella, but Melindar's an enigma. Something about her I don't care for.*

CHAPTER NINE

Kat yawned. She fiddled with her pen, and tapped the back end against her teeth. Wink, after being fed, refused to stay awake, and was little use as a conversational companion. *I don't want to traipse through the market again. Where the heck is Mouse?* She sighed, put her pen back in her diplo bag, and yawned again.

I wonder if Mouse is getting an early evening meal? She stood, stretched, yawned once more, and headed for the public dining room.

Standing at the open doors, she recognized Fenneth, seated alone and reading some documents.

Kat walked over to the healer. "Fenneth, may I join you?"

The woman glanced up. "Kat. I would be delighted." She patted a chair beside her. "Are you alone?"

"Yes."

A serving woman approached the table, acknowledged their orders, and returned shortly with their meals, and Kat's Karri-san tea.

"I can't find Mouse anywhere, and I'm sure we should be traveling."

"Did no one tell you? Sire Mouse left in the darkest part of the night for an urgent situation in Morden. Murwenna met with him before he left. She agreed she would assign Praetor Arrogol to be your guide for the next few turns until Mouse returns."

"No one told me." *What the heck's going on?*

Fenneth's eyebrows twitched. "How odd. I am most positive Murwenna requested Melindar order someone to inform you of the change of plans."

"I spent the midturn meal with her, and she never mentioned anything."

"I suspect she assumed whoever she charged with the task did their job." Fenneth scowled. "She will be irate when she discovers whoever she told, failed to follow her orders. I would not want to be in their place."

"So what do I do?"

"I believe under the circumstances, we should attend Praetor Arrogol now. He is no doubt expecting you to contact him." Fenneth rose and extended her hand to Kat. "We are both sated, so I will take you to Arrogol's home."

❦❦❦

Fenneth knocked on the plain wooden door, and Kat inspected the exterior of the Praetor's home. The building attached to the keep, larger than most of the surrounding ones, and built with simple lines, said to all, a man of strength and means, resides in this place. The home overflowed with discreet wealth. The gardens around the structure, lush with simple flowers, beautiful and elegantly formal, did not scream for attention in flamboyant overdone colors or odd shapes—the entire house and garden stated, "I am enough".

The woman who opened the door possessed extraordinary beauty, and her posture indicated confidence in her own attractiveness. Murwenna, a woman of beauty in her own right, presented the perfect example of power and strength. But this woman exuded a sexual energy that demanded attention. *Wow. Arrogol's reward for providing sperm for an heir is a major bonus.*

Fenneth stood to the side and gestured at Kat. "Lady Olwyn, I bring the Lady Kat to meet with Praetor Arrogol."

Olwyn lifted an eyebrow a mere fraction. "Do come in." She turned and called out. "Arrogol, Fenneth brings the Lady Kat you mentioned."

Arrogol appeared from another room. Kat's knees almost buckled and her mouth dropped open. She quickly closed her delinquent lips and swallowed.

He wore the leather leggings of the Rifellan guards but the red-blonde hairs on his bare chest glistened in the fading afternoon light inside the sunny room. "Lady Kat, I wondered why you did not call on me before."

Fenneth stepped forward. "Our apologies, Praetor. But the person to whom Murwenna gave the task to advise Lady Kat of the changes in plans, did not fulfill their order to do so. Not until our meal this evening, did she realize Mouse would not be her guide this time."

"I understand. Well, we need to discuss many things, because we must depart after the morning meal on the morrow." He turned to his future bond mate. "Olwyn, would you request our apprentice bring tea for Kat and me to the table, so we can discuss the route and equipment?"

Olwyn eyed Kat. "I will bring the tea myself, Arrogol."

Arrogol moved to a cabinet and opened the doors, which spilled charts on the floor. "If you wish to."

Fenneth moved toward the exit. "If you will pardon me, Lady Olwyn, Praetor Arrogol, I must leave you. Lord Murwenna is in need of me."

Olwyn led her to the door and smiled at Fenneth. "I understand your duties are many at this time."

They hugged goodbye and Olwyn headed to prepare tea.

Kat called after her, "Olwyn, may I please request Karri-san tea from you?"

Olwyn stiffened, and paused. She smirked at the request for Karri-san. "You resemble a Rifellan." She paused. "But you are definitely not one of us." She left the room.

Oops, I don't think she liked me dropping the word Lady.

Arrogol waved toward a table with two chairs. "Sit, Kat, I will bring the route information which your guide gave me."

Kat sat, mouth dry, scrutinizing his every move as he gathered maps and pieces of parchment.

Olwyn returned with a tray of cups of tea and small edible cookies. She indicated to Kat which cup contained Karri-san, which Kat thankfully grabbed and drank. Slowly the heat generated by the vision of Arrogol lessened, and Kat, now able to concentrate on the maps, leaned over the finely drawn lines.

As Arrogol covered their travel route, he leaned toward Kat, staring directly in her eyes. "You will enjoy this village. The warriors will appreciate a woman of your charm." He smiled at her, a smoky look to his eyes, used by all men when flirting.

Kat, unable to resist, licked her lips. "I do believe, Arrogol, you possess charm of your own." She glanced in Olwyn's direction, and halted a further remark when she caught the venomous expression on the woman's face. *Uh oh. If looks…*

Olwyn drew her lips into a thin line. "Arrogol, I do not understand why you need to guide Kat. Surely Murwenna possesses many others who can fill this position."

"If another existed, Murwenna would have suggested him. She did not—therefore, she decided I am her best option."

At that moment, the conversation was interrupted by mewling noises from beside the hearth. Curious, Kat rose and walked over to a basket filled with bedding. Inside, curled six furry creatures, similar to domestic kittens, except their fur blended with the spots of leopards. "They're adorable." She reached in and picked one up to cuddle. "What are they?"

Arrogol eyed her and grinned. "They are a species of cat we use to control the pests who live around stables, but, they are fierce when full grown. If you like them, take one"

Olwyn sputtered in protest. "You cannot give them away without thought."

"Olwyn, be sensible. You are aware we are having challenges getting rid of the young ones."

Kat gazed forlornly at the sweet furry creature. "Thank you for the offer, Arrogol, but I can't carry animals with me on my travels." *I miss having a pet. I miss Shade.*

Olwyn raised an eyebrow at Kat. "Arrogol is correct about these creatures. They are not intended to live inside with a family. These ones are only here because their parent was killed." She glanced at Arrogol, a speculative expression on her face. "Arrogol, I believe since Murwenna chose you to go on this trip, I will give you my permission as well."

Arrogol turned to her, peering from under heavy blond brows. "Since when do I need your permission to do anything?" He grinned.

She walked from the room, and turned back to him. "Since you wish to keep the bedroom door unlocked." She flashed him a brilliant smile.

Arrogol gazed at her as she sauntered from the room. He shook his head. "Females." He grinned at Kat. "Sometimes Olwyn thinks she is the ruler of this household, although we are not yet bonded."

Kat's mouth curled in a wry smile. *She doesn't think this.*

She knows she's the ruler of the household.

They returned to the task of mapping their route, and Arrogol handed Kat the rune list from Mouse. "Prepare your luggage tonight, and, before you head for your morning meal, request an assistant deliver your bags to the stable."

Kat agreed and left for her own rooms. *Damn Mouse for leaving like this. But, traveling with Arrogol should be more than interesting.*

CHAPTER TEN

Once in her room, Kat consulted Mouse's list and packed all she anticipated she would need. Her diplo bag contained everything she would require to keep up with the records of her adventures through Rifella.

She moved Wink to the traveling cage. Her leathers, dusted and ready, hung in the closet and waited to be worn. Extra clothes, including one outfit dressier than the rest, plus shoes, she packed in the largest duffle. A few last minute items would rest in her backpack along with pyrock treats and Karri-san tea.

Everything is ready. Now to bed. With those thoughts, she climbed in the bed and burrowed beneath the comforter.

⚘ ⚘ ⚘

Kat crept along the corridors of the keep, unaware of what wakened her. She peered down the dimly lit hallway and saw an indistinct figure in the distance. Her stone grew cold against her chest as she approached the unknown person, and a trickle of fear pricked at her skin. *Who are you?* She tried to ask his name, but no sound escaped her. The tall, almost formless figure, clad in jet black robes, concealed his features as he moved toward her. A feeling of fingers seemed to clutch at her throat.

Kat backed away, but the distance between them shrank. She stopped, hypnotized by those fathomless Stygian eyes. Her legs felt glued to the ground. She attempted to breathe. Without warning, he grabbed at her with a pale skeletal hand, tipped with shiny, pitch-colored nails.

I can't stop him. He's going to kill me.

"No. Stop. No."

Kat sat up, gasping for breath, drenched in icy sweat.

A nightmare?

She touched a nearby globe to light the room. Shadows still lurked in the corners, so she bounded out of bed and lit every globe. Her quarters now ablaze in light, she scanned every alcove. *Empty.* Only now did her ability to breathe normally return. Her stone was warm again. *Why another nightmare?*

She hurried to check on Wink. The little creature leaped around her cage, agitated. *I probably woke her.* With trembling hands, Kat scooped the pyrock from her rumpled bedding in her cage. "I need you to take a message to Wynneth." Consulting the Pridden writing from her diplo bag, she composed a message advising Wynneth about her dream. She inserted the parchment into a tube, and attached the missive to the foreleg that Wink extended for her. "Thank you, Wink. Go to Wynneth." The little animal raised her leathery wings, hopped in the air, and popped out of existence.

Waiting less than patiently for Wink's return, Kat paced her room. *Am I too early for tea?*

A couple of minutes later, Wink returned with a pop, landed on the desk and held out her foreleg. *Wow—fast.* She took the tube from Wink, fed her, and redeposited her in her cage. Within seconds, the pyrock fell asleep.

Wynneth's brief message read, "Go now to Fenneth. She is aware."

❦ ❦ ❦

Kat waited until the first tendrils of dawn lit the sky, and then found her way to Fenneth's quarters and knocked on the door.

"Come."

As Kat entered, the healer embraced her.

"My dear Kat, I expected you. Wynneth's pyrock said you experienced these dreams before. We must advise Murwenna of them. Come. Sit. I ordered tea."

Kat sat and sipped the tea. The Karri-san mixed with some peppermint-like herb, soothed, and within minutes, the tension drained from her body. "Fenneth, I can't spare time to meet with Murwenna. I agreed to join Arrogol at the stables after my morning meal."

Fenneth rubbed her brow. "Yes. You must keep this appointment with him. As I consider the problem, I would prefer we delay advising Murwenna until after the birth of the heir. I do not wish her to receive unnecessary stress now." She patted Kat's arm. "Are you ready to leave?"

"I prepared everything after my meeting with Arrogol."

"Fine, I will join you for your morning meal."

"Absolutely." Kat smiled. "May we stop at my rooms first? I need to arrange for my bag to be delivered to the stables."

"An excellent idea."

❦ ❦ ❦

Later, seated in the dining hall, Kat with her backpack and diplo bag on the chair beside her, and her quiver and bow over her shoulder, the two women enjoyed a meal of journeyklim. Kat sipped regularly from the huge mug of Karri-san.

Fenneth chatted about the planned celebrations for the birth of the heir. She raised her head and beckoned to someone. "Melindar is here. I will ask her about keeping Murwenna informed." She beckoned Melindar to the table, and when Murwenna's sibling joined them, Fenneth relayed the information about Mouse missing, and Kat unaware of the situation.

Melindar appeared horrified. "I requested Tiewellan convey the information to you, Kat. My apologies. I am aware he is busy at the moment, but I did not realize he failed to inform you promptly. Please do not pass this information to Murwenna. She does not need any further stress at this time." She addressed Fenneth. "You should take Kat immediately to Praetor Arrogol to make the arrangements with him."

"You need not fear, Melindar. I did so last evening. Arrogol will meet with Lady Kat after her morning meal."

"What a relief." Melindar rose from her seat. "I came here to arrange a meal for Murwenna. She will be waiting. Impatiently, I suspect."

Kat eyed Melindar as she spoke with one of the apprentices. *Hmm. I wonder if he did forget. Or perhaps it was deliberate because I refused him?*

"When you have completed your tea, Kat, perhaps you should head toward the stables."

"I'm almost finished." She smiled to herself. "Fenneth, traveling with Arrogol should be fun. He is a most compelling man, and I find myself attracted to him."

Fenneth gasped in horror. "Kat, do not for one moment consider indulging in a relationship with him. Olwyn is a strong woman and highly vindictive. Their final bonding ceremony will take place twenty turns after the birth of the heir. If you interfere with a bonding, the keep will be thrown into chaos. Not only will Olwyn seek her revenge, but Murwenna will discipline you and him."

"I'm only thinking how much fun it would be. I'm not considering anything physical." *Like hell I'm not.* "Relax. I'm—I'm joking."

"Do not joke about such things. The consequences would be dire. I quake at the thought of what might occur."

The two women rose, and Kat shouldered her backpack and the diplo bag, and she headed for the stables.

If I do indulge - it'll be our little secret. How can it harm anyone?

CHAPTER ELEVEN

The moonless night, ink-black and silent as a tomb, provided Mouse with the cover he required.

He departed from Arrogol's home, and rode in silence across the grasslands, headed directly for the Torrenton Forest.

He concentrated on traveling the entire journey through forests and grasslands. To remain anonymous, he forded streams to avoid man-built bridges, and always used these routes, except when Galdin demanded he travel on Morden business. Ensuring this anonymity, he continued to use animal trails rather than man-made roads.

He dove deeper into his Mouse persona, shrinking into himself, and embracing the small grey man whom Galdin regularly terrified.

Riding through the forest, he bypassed well north of the villages of Restin and Tangata. The first pinks and lighter blues of dawn rose in the west, and he crossed the Farralawn River into Morden. He paused briefly to allow the horse to drink her fill, replenished his own water, and headed for the trees. By midturn, immersed deep within one of Morden's many forests, he was forced to travel more slowly. Only small animals inhabited this particular woodland, and the resultant growth grew thick, which demanded Mouse travel with care. Luckily, he spotted burrows easily, and, riding close to dense foliage, he did not worry about his mount stepping into a hole.

Mouse brought food easily consumed during the ride, but his steed's flanks heaved, and sweat covered her. Both of them needed to stop for a more substantial meal and rest. A fine mist cooled them. Close to the north-eastern edge of the forest, he dismounted, gathered some dry kindling for a minuscule smokeless fire, and heated the stew he brought from Murwenna's keep. The tired mare cropped at fresh grass and drank from a nearby pool of rain. After, dowsing his fire, and burying the ashes, he led his mount into a deeper patch of foliage, and secured the reins to a tree, doing his best to keep her sheltered by the branches spreading from the massive central trunk. He gathered leaves and living branches and created a tiny shelter for himself. Wrapped in his cloak, he slept.

An ice-cold nose on his cheek startled him awake. A rat-like creature, seeking warmth, poked at him. Mouse crawled from the shelter and, standing upright, shook his cloak free of leaves, dirt, and rain, which caused the warmth seeker to squeak in outrage and scurry off.

He did not meet the night, cold and black, with much enthusiasm. But with both he and the horse rested, they needed to travel to Galdin's keep in the dark as much as possible. Horse and rider emerged from the forest and headed for the shallowest part of the Totowanga River. His horse initially shied from entering the rushing water, but Mouse held firm, and, reluctantly, the creature started across, eyes rolling frantically. Mouse soothed and urged the animal, and once across, the horse snorted and shook herself.

Mouse leaned over and patted the horse's neck. "I understand. The river frightened you. Sorry."

Mouse turned the mare downstream and slid from her back. He led her to a pool supplied by nature, and formed between two downed trees. The animal needed no urging to drink from the fresh clear, river water, while he topped his canteen. After the now calm animal consumed her fill, he remounted and set off for Morden's keep. Pridden's star rose in the sky, and the stark outline of buildings and massive iron gates loomed ahead. He had arrived.

Completely immersed in Mouse and his thoughts filled only with fear, he recalled his terror of Galdin. *I hope my master is pleased with how swiftly I came at his command and will forgive me any delay.*

As he neared the gates, an enormous guard, dressed in a metal breastplate and holding an iron lance, stepped toward him, barring the way. "Who goes there?"

Quaking, Mouse dismounted and stepped forward. "I come at Thane Galdin's order. I am Mouse."

The tall guard sneered at him. "Mouse." He snickered. "You are well named." He turned and sauntered to the gates, signaling to two other guards to open the entranceway. He glanced behind at the terrified Mouse, who remained stock still beside his horse. "Come on, man. I do not need to wait all this turn for you. If Thane Galdin ordered your presence, you should attend him immediately."

Startled, Mouse did a double take and scurried after the guard, dragging his horse by the reins.

❦ ❦ ❦

Mouse, held in place by Galdin's guard in a black assassin's uniform, shivered with fear as he waited outside the enormous metal-banded door. An icy trickle of sweat ran down his spine. *I am sure he is furious. I failed to bring the woman to him as soon as he desired.*

The door swung open, pushed by the in-room guard, who grabbed him and dragged him into Galdin's presence.

A tall, thin, man robed in black, lifted one pale hand. His long fingers, tipped with sharp ebony nails, glistened in the dim lights of the room. Two of those fingers beckoned to Mouse and the guard to approach.

Mouse now sweated profusely despite the cold chill in the room. With leaden feet, he forced himself to move to the gold, embossed seat, which Galdin considered his throne. Thrust to his knees by the black-clad guard, Mouse bowed his head. "Master."

The voice that emerged from the terrifying man in front of him issued from some gaping dark drains of the underworld. "You keep me constantly waiting. Why do you keep the woman from me?"

"I tried, my Thane. She is a difficult woman to control."

"I do not need you to control her, you inadequate grey rat. I need you to bring her to me. Here. Now."

"Master, I did try, I give you my promise. I am not aware of what is occurring. I thought you sent the assassins for her in Kaylin, but Lord Eduardo and many of his guards, plus others, rescued her. Then in Shendea, I attempted to join your assassins again, but Hesginn interfered and nearly cost the woman her life. This time, Lord Rhognor and his guards and the Magicians' Guild came to her rescue."

Galdin leaned menacingly toward Mouse. "Someone got between me and my prey. When I discover who is to blame, I will enjoy my revenge."

Mouse huddled further into his grey robes. *Please spare me.* "Master, I do not understand what is happening with this woman. No matter what situation she finds herself in, she manages to prevail in unaccountable ways. At times, it appears almost as if she possesses some type of hidden powers of her own."

Galdin straightened in his chair. "Powers, you say?"

"I am not positive of this, my Thane. She frees herself of the most extraordinary situations."

"Hmm. You may be of some use after all. You must continue to attempt to bring her to me. And in the interim, find out all you can about this woman and her powers."

Ohh. He is not going to kill me. I am safe. For now. "Yes Master."

"You are correct, Mouse. I will not kill you now." He stood and approached the cowering grey-cloaked man. He lifted a finger and touched Mouse on the forehead.

The small grey man screamed. *The pain. My head.*

"No, I will not kill you now, but you needed a reminder of what I will do should you even think of betraying me." He turned and strode to the door behind the throne, and glanced back at Mouse. "You may go now. You will still send me reports via the messenger moths." He left the room, slamming the door shut behind him.

Mouse remained kneeling on the floor. *Close. So close.* He rose, shaking, and headed toward the principal door. He stumbled so often the assassin guard grabbed him by the arm and threw him out the room.

He headed for the stables to reclaim his horse, and hastily saddled the beast, threw himself into the saddle, and galloped through the keep and exited the enormous outer gates.

Deep down in his innermost being, a small seed of hope blossomed.

I am alive.

CHAPTER TWELVE

When Kat reached the stables, the baggage now loaded on the pack animal, Arrogol and another male, who resembled a Baklai, waited beside their horses.

"Tardiness is unwelcome on this trip, Kat."

She glared at Arrogol. "I needed to meet with Fenneth before leaving, and I also required a morning meal. Do not assume I am careless about appointments."

Arrogol bowed at her, sarcasm in every movement. "I would never suspect you of such a thing, Lady Kat."

Kat harrumphed, and gazed expectantly at the Baklai. His dark, brown, almost black eyes unnerved her and reminded her of the Kaylin Horse-Master.

"I am Bannigus, Lady Kat. I am the Horse-Master for Rifella. Praetor Arrogol requested I accompany both of you on this trip, as we will pass through the Great Hellesmouth Desert. Traveling through the desert is best done with more than two people."

Arrogol walked over to Bannigus and clapped an arm around his shoulders. "I would never travel through the Hellesmouth without this man at my side."

Kat recoiled from the man. *He reminds me too much of Haydar.* "This Hellesmouth sounds like a dangerous place."

"The desert can be. But with Arrogol and me as your guides, you need fear nothing." He smiled at her.

He smiled? Haydar never smiled. Perhaps without the influence of the Kaylins, he's normal. "I will take your word for this. If I am later than expected, shouldn't we be on our way?"

"Yes." Arrogol turned to Bannigus. "I arranged for a mid-turn meal from the keep so we can eat without stopping. I would prefer to arrive at Tirenna before dusk."

Is he going to rush through every moment because we must be back at the keep in a few days? "Why?"

"Brantors."

"Enough said, Arrogol. I'm all for avoiding brantors."

Before the three set off, Olwyn appeared, accompanied by a band of female mercenaries with whom she rode. Arrogol stood tall and displayed a magnificent body for Olwyn. Kat still sensed the heat generated by his frank gaze, and despite the playful conversation she and Fenneth indulged in, she doubted she would accept his implied invitation to move closer. Whenever Kat remained near the delicious Arrogol, Olwyn fixed her with the glare of a snake eying its dinner. He intrigued her, but Olwyn spooked her. The woman convinced Kat she would leave Rifella free of the taste of the gorgeous Arrogol.

The Rifellan woman reminded Kat of the Tasmanian devils she once saw in an Australian zoo—smaller than their males, but seventy times as ferocious and one hundred times as dangerous.

I suspect Rifellan warrior women are not to be trifled with.

With all preparations complete for the journey through Rifella, and before the group departed on their own journey, Olwyn handed a huge horn to Arrogol.

"Good journey, future mate. Return unscathed." She shot another hooded spike of displeasure toward Kat. "Beware of crosa spawn." She spat the last words out.

Kat swallowed. *Whatever crosa spawn are, I'm pretty sure they're unpleasant. I don't fear men, but women can be terrifying.*

Arrogol and Bannigus completed the preparation of the four horses for travel by loading Kat's baggage on the pack animal. The two biggest ones obviously belonged to them. They picked a smaller one for Kat, but the horse still reached a height of seventeen hands. Bannigus tossed Kat up in the saddle as if she weighed as much as a thistle.

The saddle affair nestled around her, nearly as comfortable as an overstuffed sofa, but Kat hurried to fasten the straps to hold her in place, because the ground appeared far away.

Both Arrogol and Bannigus, leaped on their enormous beasts with as much ease as if they climbed into their beds. Of course they both stood much taller than Kat, and their muscles possessed muscles.

Once in the saddle, Bannigus removed Kat's quiver and long bow from her luggage, and handed them to her. She placed the quiver, complete with her long-bow arrows, across her back, and inserted the bow itself in an attachment at the front of her saddle, beside her diplo bag. She knew she prepared them well, because she copied what Arrogol and the Horse-Master did with theirs.

Her two guides gazed at her, speculation on their faces.

"I observe, Kat, you are familiar with brantor hunting." Bannigus's face showed respect.

"No, but Mouse and I did encounter some on our way to the keep, and although I also own a spring bow, I assumed the long bow would be more efficient against these creatures."

Arrogol led the group, followed by Kat, and Bannigus took up the rear with the pack animal attached to his saddle.

They rode a similar trail to the one she and Mouse had traveled to reach the keep. They moved through the grasslands and paused briefly beside a simple bridge over the Tyrol River to water the horses.

"What is the name of this bridge, Arrogol?"

"The bridge." He grinned at her with puzzled expression. "This is not grand enough to be given a name of its own."

Kat shrugged. "Whatever."

They crossed the bridge and proceeded through more grasslands on the other side.

The journey carried on in peace, but Arrogol handed packets of food to the other two. "I would prefer not to stop to eat. The horses are watered, and we filled our canteens, so this way we will arrive at Tirenna well before star set."

They rode without difficulty through the grasses, and Kat enjoyed the ripples of grains whispering in the light breezes as she travelled. She remembered the sound of waves rushing up the shore of a sandy beach. The ebb and flow of the wind caused the grasses to swish and sway as they moved, like the waves on a body of water.

A strange noise of creatures moving at speed through the grass reached Kat's ears. She stopped her horse. "What's that?"

Arrogol paused for a brief moment, and, kicked his horse into a gallop. "Ride, Kat. As fast as you can."

She rode, aware as she did so, the gem on her necklace reacted by lying against her skin like a block of ice.

The sound of hoofbeats behind her meant Bannigus and the pack animal were fleeing as if pursued by devils

Without any other warning, hundreds of dog-sized brantors surrounded them. Kat pulled her bow free, reached for arrows, and fired shot after shot. Bannigus rode past them, brandishing a long whip, which cracked among the brantors, downing some and causing others to flee.

Too many brantors appeared, and the three riders were soon overwhelmed by the numbers of the foul creatures. They came from all sides, with growls and gnashing of teeth. All Kat could see were hundreds of horns and claws and dripping muzzles. *I can understand dying by a cathnog, but killed by a bunch of disgusting looking rats?*

Like a rescue by the cavalry, a substantial party of men on horseback surrounded them, producing unpleasant and discordant sounds on whistles. The harsh jarring vibrations irritated everyone's ears, but the brantors most of all, who began squealing and thrashing out at everything around them. Soon the air filled with the clamor of the screeching of whistles, the shrieks of brantors, and the bugling of horses, wounded and frightened. The horsemen who blew the whistles herded the brantors before them, still fighting among themselves, and appearing to possess but one thought: kill, or be killed.

Kat, trembling, paused as Arrogol and Bannigus stopped their mounts, and watched in amazement as the horsemen galloped past the three of them, and drove the brantors forward to a clearing surrounded by a wall of gathered brush. A huge cart, drawn by four enormous horses, each at least eighteen hands high, rumbled behind the whistling horsemen. They appeared bigger than Clydesdales. A number of men dropped from the cart, gathered the carcasses of the brantors, and tossed them on board.

Within minutes, the men in the clearing dispatched the dying creatures, and threw them up on the cart, along with the dead. Kat and her group caught up to the horsemen. The whistles silenced, and, with the grassland now clear of bodies, the massive cart headed toward a village on the horizon.

Liandock's necklace reacts with major emphasis from brantors. I don't believe it likes them.

Arrogol slowed and pointed toward the buildings ahead. "Tirenna."

Kat's shivering ceased, and, her breathing reduced. She slowed her horse to a walk. "Their people are the ones with the whistles?"

"Yes. The Tirennians, through their ways of cooperation, passed on some excellent examples to Rifellans everywhere. Their villagers hunted and slaughtered the brantors for many paths. They designed the blowing instruments to produce a sound which profoundly irritates the creatures. The animals become confused and enraged and attack one another."

Bannigus continued the tale. "They kill a number of their own, and their confusion gives the Tirennians the opportunity to drive them to a pen constructed of bush and trees, and then they can deal with the remaining few. This is a wonderful illustration of men working in harmony and in cooperation with each other."

Cooperation? What's he getting at?

Arrogol added. "This example inspired the training and operation of Rifellan guards and Rifellan armies."

Kat rolled her eyes. "You mean this is an instance of teamwork in action?"

"Yes, Kat. This teamwork, as you call our way of working with each other, Rifellan guards have used for many paths to hone their effectiveness in the field. We owe much to the Tirennians."

"I suppose I can see teamwork is effective in situations such as these. But…"

"But? Kat, we Rifellans use this type of cooperation in most of the things we accomplish in our land. Rifellans learned to work together in many situations. Almost everything we do depends upon our cooperation with each other. No *but* exists."

I think the brantors demonstrated more teamwork than the men.

CHAPTER THIRTEEN

The Tirennian team who gathered the brantors, escorted the three travelers to the village. Once in Tirenna, the head of the village, Prefect Pentramore welcomed them and assigned them rooms within the primary inn for the town. Constructed of a lustrous wood, the rich color of burnt sienna, the inner corridors, lined with woodcut scenes of horsemen rounding up brantors, glowed with the polish of many loving hands. Kat admired the way they used different cuts and colors of wood to create the most artistic representations of their hunts.

However, covered in dust from the encounter with the nasty creatures, Kat headed gratefully to her quarters, where she settled Wink. She seized the opportunity to shower the dust of the hunt from herself and changed into clean clothes.

Kat poked her head out the door of her room and, spying an apprentice, requested his help. "Can you please arrange for my leathers to be cleaned this evening?" She handed him the clothes in question.

"I will do so, my Lady." He took them from her and moved to complete the task.

Before he ventured far, she called to him again. "Can you also show me the direction to the dining hall?"

He turned back to her and pointed out the way.

"Thanks."

⁂

Before Kat arrived at the hall, the hum of laughter tickled her ears. The happy sounds delighted her, and she smiled to herself. The residents of Tirenna celebrated a successful hunt. As she approached the entrance, Arrogol joined her, with Bannigus close on his heels.

He grinned at her. "Well, I find the dust devil I escorted here turned itself into a most attractive female." His eyes sparkled, and he bowed his head as he reached for her hand to escort her to the hall.

Kat experienced a flush of heat. *Does he realize what he's doing? He's gorgeous... irresistible... I want—*

Arrogol and Bannigus walked her to a table for eight, and, they were seated. Prefect Pentramore joined them along with two Tirennian hunters. Meals ordered, a serving woman brought flagons of near-ale for all. Pilar, one of the Tirennian hunters, an accomplished comedian, kept them entertained with wild stories about previous hunts.

Kat, although fascinated by the tales he passed on, expressed concern. "Don't the hunters suffer injuries? Brantors are gruesome and nasty animals."

"Of course hunters are wounded from time to time. And sometimes they do not survive their wounds. But we wear armor similar to Rifellan guards." He glanced at Arrogol. "Are you planning on visiting Pakanna?"

Arrogol nodded.

Pentramore beamed at Kat. "When you visit Pakanna, you will observe how our armor is created and will understand how the slight embellishments are designed to protect us from below, rather than from man height. We also provide specific armor for the legs of our horses." He grimaced. "If brantors bring a horse down, this does not bode well for the hunter."

Kat shuddered at his words. She well remembered the vile appearance of those creatures.

"Please do not worry, my Lady. We hunted the brantor for more paths than I am able to recall. Our experiences in the past taught us well. We do not lose hunters often in these times."

Some person's loud entrance to the dining hall attracted Kat's attention. Tiewellan, sibling to Janella, entered the hall and chose to approach their table.

Oh no. Not him.

He bowed his head to the Prefect, but only enough to acknowledge the man's position in the village. He glanced over at Kat. "Ah, Kat. I was aware you traveled to Tirenna, and so decided to bring you some excellent cheer for this evening." He held up a beautiful blue bottle. "Orenberry wine." He leaned toward her. "Since you are no longer at the keep, at least you can indulge in something better than mere near-ale."

Crap. I'll keep away from his wine. I'll bet he's roofied the damn stuff. The Tirennians don't look happy either.

He plunked himself down beside Kat, who drew back from him as much as possible. As she did so, she brushed up against the gorgeous Arrogol, and she experienced another wave of heat. *Whew, I must grab more Karri-san.* She rose from the table to obtain another mug, when Tiewellan grabbed her hand.

"Leaving so soon, Lady Kat?"

Kat glared at him and shook off his hand as if something repulsive gripped her. "I need to visit the serving counter." She attempted to instill as much ice and disgust in her reply as possible.

Arrogol began to rise as well, but she shook her head.

Kat approached a serving woman at the counter. "Would you give me a mug of Karri-san tea, please?"

"I will bring the tea to your table, my Lady."

"No… " An idea surfaced. "I will carry it with me." *If Tiewellan attempts anything more, I can always spill hot tea.* She chuckled to herself, imagining a mug of hot beverage in Tiewellan's lap. *It'll also serve him right for failing to tell me of Mouse's leaving.*

The woman left to fill her order, and Kat glanced back at her nemesis and squinted at Arrogol and Bannigus with curiosity. Arrogol, now seated in her place, carefully kept a place for her between he and Bannigus. They conversed with Tiewellan, who appeared uncomfortable. *I wonder what they're saying to him?*

The serving woman returned, and Kat lifted the full mug of steaming liquid and, carrying the tea with care, made her way back to the table.

Arrogol half rose from his seat beside Tiewellan. "Can I help you with the mug? I would not wish you to spill such a hot beverage."

But Bannigus took the mug from her and held out the chair between him and Arrogol. "Lady Kat." He bowed his head.

What is going on? These two are acting as if I'm royalty and need protection. Weird. She sat and took a few sips from the mug. *Ouch. Hot.* However, the heat of Arrogol faded to a manageable level. *Good old Karri-san.* She took a gulp. *But with these two hovering over me, I can't spill tea on Tiewellan by accident now. Darn.*

Prefect Pentramore kept the table entertained with stories of dangers of brantor hunts, and humorous anecdotes about recent recruits for the hunt. "…and as we approached the gate, Aenid, exhausted from the hunt, fell from his horse, landing face down in the dirt. When he stood, the egg he transported so carefully in his pocket, spread over the front of his shirt and his face." The entire company at the table roared with laughter.

I don't think, Tiewellan is amused. He didn't laugh, and seems grumpy.

The man rose, and moved from the table on unsteady legs. *Goody, he's going.*

With food consumed and many near-ales later, Kat yawned.

Pentramore appeared perturbed. "My Lady, my apologies, I am boring you."

"On the contrary, Prefect, I find your stories most stimulating." She yawned again. "I experienced a long day, and I need my bed."

Arrogol rose. "We all do. Please excuse us, Prefect, as we must depart early on the morrow."

As the party broke up, Kat dragged her feet to her room. Tired, and not paying attention to her surroundings, she whirled when a male hand grabbed her arm. Simultaneously, she snatched her dagger from below her scarf, and stopped her thrust barely in time. "Crap. Arrogol?"

He grabbed her wrist and moved closer to her. "Who did you expect?"

"I'm so sorry. I didn't want to kill you. I thought Tiewellan, the rat, crept up on me again."

"Ah. I noticed your reactions when he sat at our table. Bannigus and I decided the time was needed to speak a few words with him about you." He grinned. "I do not believe he will be annoying you again."

"But he's the brother of Janella. Aren't you politically unwise to threaten him?"

"This may show signs of being the case, but his own sibling, Janella, finds him tedious, and I suspect she believes he is untrustworthy. Plus, I am the male parent of the heir. Seed always ranks highest."

Kat laughed. "Arrogol, you are a most political animal. You possess a brilliant and talented mind. You're not only a pretty face and a terrific set of legs."

The blue cornflower eyes grew smoky. "I notice too. I watched you consume three cups of Karri-san at the meal." He purred at her. "I suspect you need some Arrogol for dessert."

Kat stared at him, fire building up in her body. "But… but Olwyn."

"We are not yet bonded, and the ensuing turns before the bonding allow for us both to sample elsewhere and satisfy ourselves, so no others tempt us once our bonding is complete."

Kat opened her mouth to object.

He placed two fingers on her lips. "You tempt me now, Kat. Both of us should explore this temptation."

His mouth reached for hers, and the kiss, long and deep, made Kat ache for him. She turned from his lips, and fumbled at the lock. Opening the door, and joined in his embrace, she dragged him in. Not that he needed much dragging.

Her mind consumed by the heat raging through her body, she ripped off his shirt, shed her skirt and blouse, and fell upon the bed. He stood to remove his boots and pants. Now naked in the faint light of a single globe, the red-blonde hairs on his magnificent chest glistening, he removed her underclothes. Lying beside her, he stroked and kissed and licked, leaving her gasping with pleasure.

Kat's body became a mass of flaming need. "Arrogol. Now."

His only answer a growl of pleasure.

The heat built up, and Kat, beyond sensible thought and lost in sensations of pleasure like some lotus-eater of the past, could contain herself no longer. She arched her body toward him, and he joined with her, moving so that he stimulated her once anew. The rhythm they found, ancient and natural for all people, stirred them both, and he threw back his head and howled like a satisfied wolf.

Her heart pounding, and her body sweating, she sank back among the pillows.

He grinned at her and reached down and licked between her breasts. "Mmm, salt and sweet." He kissed her neck, and rolled off her.

He lay spread-eagled and spent, and she drifted off to sleep. At some point in the early hours of the morning, she rolled over in bed. No one there. *Hmph. He snuck out of here like some one-night stand. Left me the wet spot. Not cool.*

She drifted off again.

Rifellan men...

CHAPTER FOURTEEN

A shaft of sunlight in her eyes and the light fluttering of curtains in a breeze, woke Kat, and she stretched luxuriously. Liquid muscles and a profound sense of well-being suffused her body. She cuddled in the warm comfort of her bed and remembered. *A little love-making is the best tonic ever. Still? Would've appreciated a bit more.*

Smiling to herself, she slipped from her bed and headed for the personal. *Better shower and pack. Suppose I shouldn't keep them waiting.*

She emerged from the shower, donned her leathers, and tugged the tassel in the corner of the room three times.

By the time a knock at the door heralded the arrival of her morning meal, Kat, packing completed and Wink fed, sat at the desk, concluding her journal entries from the previous day. "Come."

The young man brought the tray of journeyklim and Karri-san, which he placed on the desk.

Kat thanked him. "By the way, would you please arrange for my luggage to be collected and delivered to the stables?"

"I will, my Lady."

She thanked him again and dived into her meal. As she finished eating, a further knock indicated another apprentice, who gathered her luggage. Her duffle on the way to the stable, she attached Wink's travel cage to her backpack, and eased the straps over her shoulders. With the diplo bag slung across her body, she picked up her long bow and quiver and headed for the departure area.

❦❦❦

As Kat approached the stables, she caught sight of Arrogol and Bannigus, but started at the appearance of Olwyn riding toward them. *OMG not her. What if she guesses?* Kat eavesdropped. While she pretended not to see what they did, she eyed them narrowly.

Olwyn slid from her horse, and hurried to Arrogol. He grabbed her around the waist and kissed her with passion. As he released her, Olwyn glanced over at Kat, a speculative expression on her face, and shifted her gaze back to Arrogol. "You sampled?"

"I did." He gazed down at her and ruffled her hair.

"Will you do so again?"

"Doubtful. I am ready for our ceremony."

They smiled at each other, and the air crackled with sexual tension.

As if he only now remembered that she waited close by, Arrogol turned to Kat. "I did not see your friend Tiewellan, Kat. I assume he departed early this morrow." He grinned at her.

Glancing from Arrogol to Olwyn and back again, Kat attempted a weak smile. *Oh crap, they're discussing me as if I'm a planned test. Damn them both.*

Arrogol headed over to Bannigus, and they both examined the horses and verified the straps on the pack animal's load guaranteed security.

Olwyn strolled over to Kat and smiled triumphantly at her. "Remember Kat, a sample is only a sample, and is no guarantee of a full meal." She smirked and returned to her horse.

A group of women on horseback rode up, all dressed in Rifellan warrior leathers, and dusty from what appeared to be a lengthy journey. They crowded around Olwyn, greeting her as their leader.

Kat watched them as they chattered among themselves, spoke to the stable master about their horses, and headed for the inn. She presumed they intended to consume a morning meal. Olwyn turned and wiggled her fingers at Kat, smiling coyly.

Bugger. They planned all that, and I thought I held control.

⚘ ⚘ ⚘

Kat rode in silence. She fumed over what she considered a massive slight by Arrogol. *He used me.* But as she considered the situation, she indulged in an internal giggle. *This is the first time a man beat me at my own game. He's smarter than he looks.*

He and Bannigus rode behind her, but she paid scant attention to their conversation. From the few words she caught, they exchanged ideas regarding the best way to travel to Pakanna,

Arrogol rode up beside her. "We will take the path to the right so we are able to avoid any possible confrontations with brantors."

Kat nodded and mumbled a reply. *I'm not going to let him off the hook. Must appear to be insulted.*

"What is your problem, Kat?"

She glared at him. "Don't start with me, Arrogol."

"I thought you understood."

"You used me."

He grinned. "We used each other. I conveyed the situation with clarity. I assumed you did not expect anything further?"

"You idiot. You're the one who doesn't understand. I'm not looking for anything permanent in the least." She banged on the saddle horn. *Ouch*. "I did not anticipate, however, being used as a one-night-stand."

"I do not understand the phrase you use, but I suspect the meaning." He shook his head in obvious frustration. "You and I both wished dessert, and our coupling provided a perfect finish to the evening. We indulged in mutual pleasure, and neither of us used the other. I explained my agreement with Olwyn, and I advised her this morrow of what we enjoyed."

"I overheard you. Her behavior came across as odd. I anticipated her anger."

He grinned again. "Lady Kat. You misjudge both of us. Had I been tempted with a lesser woman than you, Olwyn would be most insulted. She approves of you and is much pleased to know I still wish to bond with her. And our bonding will be permanent." He paused and peered at her. "We enjoyed a mutual night of pleasure. What made you believe you were used?"

"Olwyn."

"Olwyn? How?"

"When she spoke to me after, she struck me as insufferably smug."

This time Arrogol roared with laughter. "Of course. Olwyn is always smug. You are the only woman she considered might be competition for our bonding."

Kat stopped her horse and scratched her head. "You people are weird."

At his puzzled glance, she explained. "Strange."

"An interesting word. Your world must be odd indeed if you consider our attitude toward coupling as—weird." He rode on, shaking his head.

❦ ❦ ❦

Kat continued to ride in silence through farmland, which grew greener and more lush than any area encountered thus far in Rifella. *Olwyn pushes my buttons. I've always been able to attract men, but I retained control in physical situations.* She snorted to herself. *What neither of them realize is, I don't want or need Arrogol in my bed again. As he said, I got my sample. So they think I'm odd.*

She smiled, and kicked her horse to catch up with Arrogol. "Hey there. How soon will we be at Pakanna?"

He peered down at her. "You now understand our mutual entertainment?"

"I thought the sampling discussion was closed. The fact is, I'm competitive, and Olwyn's words made me suspect I lost the competition."

He grinned at her. "Only in your own mind, Kat." He stopped his horse and indicated Bannigus should catch up to them. "You are more familiar with this region than I, Bannigus. When do you anticipate we will reach Pakanna?"

Bannigus gazed around at their position and regarded the height of the star in the sky. "We are not far. I believe we will be in time for a late midturn meal."

At the same moment, a rather loud gurgle in Kat's stomach startled her.

Bannigus hid a smile behind his hand. "I do believe you are in need of sustenance, my Lady."

Kat remained silent and shook the reins to encourage her horse to speed up. Over her shoulder, she sniffed at Bannigus. "I do believe it's impolite to comment on the vagaries of someone's body challenges."

Bannigus chuckled, and hung his head. "I understand my Lady."

Nobody's taking me seriously any more.

They proceeded on, and the small neat farms they passed, increased in number. Each plot of land sported some rows of flowers, but also a variety of vegetation of different shapes and sizes. Some plants resembled tomatoes on vines, while a few others consisted of masses of green leaves.

Beside the small neat houses, all with roofs thatched with long grasses, stood well-constructed pens in which a number of small, pig-like creatures, rooted and grunted among the vegetation in their feed bins. Most of the homes also boasted a stable for one or two horses.

They neared the village of Pakanna, and half a dozen men rode out to greet them. "Arrogol, welcome back. Are you and Bannigus ready for new armor?"

The man in question agreed, and back slapping and conversation filled the air. Almost as one, the six turned to Kat and waited for introductions.

"Lady Kat, this is Prefect Merrindock, who is the head of the village of Pakanna." Arrogol faced Merrindock. "Let me introduce the Lady Kat, who travels through our land under the auspices of Lord Eduardo of Kaylin."

Merrindock smiled and bobbed his head at her. "Well met, Lady Kat."

They all rode to the village, and Merrindock arranged for an apprentice stable hand to care for their horses and another young man to escort them to their rooms at the local inn.

"Settle yourselves in your rooms and join us for a midturn meal. We waited to eat, knowing you would be arriving soon."

❦ ❦ ❦

Kat set up Wink's cage in her capacious room, decorated with fearsome heads of brantors. A comfortable room, but better suited for a male guest with the rather gruesome trophies adorning the walls. Kat beat the dust from her leathers and dressed in loose leather pants, a neat shirt, and wound her rainbow scarf around her waist to resemble a skirt. Unencumbered with bags, she exited her room and, following cheerful noises of people enjoying themselves, located the dining hall with ease.

During the light meal, Kat, seated beside Merrindock, took the opportunity to ask about the making of armor. "I've seen the armor your people create, and I'm impressed about the strength, despite being cast from leather. How do you manage to do this?"

"The process is simple. We in Pakanna enjoy a history of many paths in creating strong, but light armor."

"Excuse me, Prefect." Kat swiveled in her seat and asked a passing wait person for a beaker of Karri-san tea and turned back to Merrindock. "I forgot to request tea with my meal."

"Of course, Lady Kat."

"Please call me Kat. The honorific Lady is so formal and unnecessary."

"I will do so. Pakanna, involved as it is in the manufacture of materials of war, tends not to stand on ceremony either. As to your curiosity about our armor, since your tea is almost finished, I will escort you in person on a tour and answer any questions you may wish to ask." He stood and indicated she should follow.

Arrogol called out to him. "Bannigus and I would enjoy the tour as well. We are both familiar with the general construction of our armor, but never received the opportunity to discover the specifics."

Merrindock indicated they should follow and led them through a number of connected rooms, stopping first to demonstrate the breakdown of the brynosh stalks. "We soak these for one half a turn and after, drain the excess water."

Kat watched, entranced, as the assistants added a thick gooey substance, similar to glue, to a vat of already-softened brynosh.

Merrindock explained they received the goo, which he called panwon, from Tirenna. "Not everything about a brantor is consumable. The horns, claws, and hoofs are boiled for six turns and produce this mixture, which helps the brynosh become hard as stone."

He led them to the next room. "Here, we mold the leather on a form, which we produce ahead of time from a mold of a specific customer. The leather is soaked in brine and allowed to dry. We produce a second piece of leather, also hardened over the form. Brynosh mixture is spread between the two pieces of leather to a thickness of a small finger, which become glued together, and these are set in the sun to dry and harden for five turns. For complete armor for a customer, we produce forms for the chest, the back, the shins, and the legs of the horses."

He led them further on. "In the next room, you will notice a series of holes are drilled at the top and down the sides of the back and chest pieces of the dried leather/brynosh pieces. We call them greeve-pieces. These other forms we call gee-legs, which are for the warriors shins and for the horses, also possess holes drilled down either side. Leather stripping wound through all the holes are to enable us to tie the protection pieces in place so they fit with comfort, without falling off the wearer."

Kat gasped at the finished product. "They appear so heavy. How can the hunters move fast enough to take down brantors?"

Merrindock glanced down at Kat. "You will be surprised, my Lady, how light-weight the armor is. Here, hold one yourself." He handed her a set of small armor.

Kat picked up the front and back set. "You're right. They weigh almost nothing."

"This is a set for a woman warrior. Let me put this on you so you can experience the true value of this protection." He slipped the two pieces over her shoulders, and tied three straps on each side.

Kat laughed with pleasure. "This is amazing. I can't believe I'm wearing anything extra. I'm so impressed." *If our cops back home could wear this body armor, they wouldn't believe the strength and ease of wearing. Of course, this mixture may not stop bullets.*

Kat allowed Merrindock to loosen the side straps and slip the armor off her shoulders.

She picked up the two pieces and examined them with care. "These feel lighter than two pieces of leather on their own. How can you achieve this?"

Merrindock's face appeared sheepish. "I am unable to explain this. We believe the brynosh, prepared in this way, somehow changes the weight of the leather. But this is only a suspicion. Brynosh is one of those plants with many abilities. We learned to accept those benefits without question."

Arrogol and Bannigus, who followed them through all the stages of the preparation, stepped forward. "Prefect, Bannigus and I are in need of new armor. We should purchase a complete set for each of us, and two sets each of the horse armor."

"One of our apprentice armorers will help you. Our stores include prepared armor which will fit you well."

Kat touched Merrindock on the arm. "Excuse me Prefect, but from what I saw, preparing a full set of armor appears to take many turns to produce. How are you able to supply Arrogol and Bannigus without waiting?"

"Ah, not as odd as you may think. We keep a series of twenty forms pre-prepared, which means we carry at least three of each size of completed armor. The forms cover both males and females, for adults and for younger ones. We also possess some forms for those of small height. If someone who is not an existing client, wishes armor, they send us their measurements via pyrock, well in advance of their visit. When they arrive in Pakanna, their armor is waiting."

"Astonishing. I do believe Prefect, you Pakannas are all artists."

Merrindock reddened. "Thank you Lady Kat. You flatter us."

Arrogol walked over to Kat. "You are embarrassing the man, Kat." He kept his voice low. He peered over his shoulder and motioned to Bannigus. "Kat, Bannigus and I will see you for the evening meal."

Kat nodded her agreement at him but turned to Merrindock. "Prefect, I suspect I may require a set of armor myself, since my journey through Pridden remains lengthy. If you take my measurements now, can you prepare a set and ship them when I need them?"

"We would be honored, my Lady. If you will follow me, I will bring you to the chief armorer."

She followed Merrindock back to the preparation rooms.

❦❦❦

Kat joined Bannigus and Arrogol in the hall for the evening meal, and, as usual, the food tickled her taste buds. "What is this meat?"

Bannigus glanced over at her. "I assumed you ate brantor in Tirenna."

"I did, but this is so different, and the texture is wonderful. The dish is savory and sweet at the same time."

"Brantor is an unusual meat because the flavor responds in different ways to various spices. Every village which prepares brantor meals possess its own unique way of cooking the creatures, and each recipe identifies with the village which is responsible for the dish."

"Do all the villagers use spices from Glowen?"

"For the most part, yes."

"Bannigus, do you also consume brantor meat in Baklai?"

"No. We raise our own version of a small creature which we find pleasant to eat, and we receive many vegetables from Glowen. We eat more vegetables than any of the other lands in Pridden."

Kat sensed a yawn coming on, so she did her best to hide her mouth. "Pardon me, bed calls. I didn't sleep much the previous night."

Arrogol rose. "The evening wears on. We all need to attend our beds." He took Kat's arm. "Let me escort you to your room, Kat."

"Fine. I meant to advise you I ordered a set of armor, and the Prefect will come to you for a chit for payment."

"I will supply him with one. I suspect having a set of armor makes sense for you." He led her from the hall, and they strode to her room.

At her door, Arrogol leaned toward her lips.

She drew back." No."

"I am still given leave to enjoy another sample, Kat."

She put her hand on his chest, stopped him, and smiled sweetly. "Not necessary, Arrogol. One taste sufficed. I require no further need of your ministrations."

She turned, unlocked her door, slipped inside, and shut the heavy wooden barrier firmly.

A second one-night stand? She chuckled. to herself. *No way. I'm in control now.*

CHAPTER FIFTEEN

When Kat woke the following morning, she stayed snuggled under the covers. She'd packed everything the night before. *I think I'll join my guides for breakfast.* She bounded from her bed and performed her usual morning ablutions, and donned cleaned leathers.

I'm glad I ordered a set of armor. I suspect my niggling feeling about needing this in the future is warranted. She pulled the tassel in the corner of the room once, and a young man responded within minutes. "Would you deliver my duffle to the stable please?"

"Yes my lady."

"My thanks. I will be taking my morning meal in the communal hall, and, once finished, I'll head straight to the stable. I'd appreciate having my bag waiting for me."

"I will make sure your bag will be delivered, my Lady."

He picked up the duffle and departed the room.

Kat stowed all her writing materials in her diplo bag, fed Wink, and tied the travel cage to her backpack, which contained some last minute items. She attached her long bow and quiver to the side of the pack, and slung one strap over her right shoulder. The diplo bag hung across her body. Taking a final glance around the room to make sure no items remained unpacked, she left and walked toward the dining hall.

At the entrance, she peered in and, spying Arrogol and Bannigus, walked over to their table. On her way there, she asked a wait person to bring journeyklim and Karri-san tea to her.

Slinging her diplo bag over the back of the chair, and resting the back-pack on the floor beside her, Kat sat. "So, where are we off to today?"

"Our primary destination is the edge of the Great Hellesmouth Desert. To reach it, we must cross the Tyrol River, and we face a lengthy trek through the Brondish Forest. The trees in this forest grow close together, so the horses cannot travel fast."

"Do we need to worry about nasty creatures in this forest?"

Bannigus smiled at her. "No. Only small and benign animals live in the Brondish, and the majority of them are shy, and avoid people as much as possible."

"Excellent. I suspect far too many vile animals in Pridden decided to view me as prey."

"Did you encounter kithras in Kaylin?"

Kat shuddered. "I did, and I hope never to be in their company again. Mind you, brantors are almost as bad."

Arrogol grinned at her. "But at least brantors are delicious to eat. Kithras are not suitable for anything, and their odor always makes me nauseous."

Kat thought a moment. "Now I think of them, you're correct. When they died, the stench grew stronger." She shuddered again.

Arrogol rose from his seat. "I believe we should be on our way to the Hellesmouth Desert. I want us to travel through the forest and be camped for the night before we attempt the crossing. The Hellesmouth is no place to travel through after dark."

Kat and Bannigus got up and followed Arrogol to the stable.

✾ ✾ ✾

They left the perfection of the laid-out farms of Pakanna behind and traveled for some time through scrubland. A line of bushes and stunted trees appeared at the same time Kat caught the sound of water gurgling ahead. The rough pathway they followed veered to the right, and the posts of a more substantial bridge appeared.

"This is the Tyrol Bridge." Arrogol waved at the structure in front of him. "As you can observe, this one is far more substantial than the one we used when we left the keep and thus warrants a name." He flicked the reins to move his steed forward. "On the other side of the bridge, we will encounter a number of more liberal pools, which will enable us to water the horses and refill our canteens. There are two extra canteens attached to your saddle. Make sure they are filled as well. You will need them crossing the Hellesmouth."

The three of them clopped across the bridge, with the baggage animal tied to Bannigus's saddle. At the promised pools, they filled all their canteens, consumed water themselves, and allowed the horses to drink their fill. The droplets of water glistening on the muzzle of her mount, fascinated Kat. It looked like a painted picture.

They remounted, refreshed from their brief stop. The bushes and trees did grow thicker and closer together on this side of the river.

The trails left by small animals made travel difficult, so they rode in single file, with Arrogol in front, followed by Kat, and Bannigus and the pack animal bringing up the rear. They were able to plow through, only by physically pushing their way against the heavy brush.

The number and type of trees changed, and the brush thickened even more. Arrogol stopped his horse and reached back to Kat, a pair of heavy gloves in his hand. “Put these on. They will help you to brush the insects and needles of the trees from you and your animal. Keep the needles cleared as much as possible, as the sap on them is sticky and retains dirt. When we are through the forest, we will need to wipe down our animals and ourselves.”

Kat reached forward and grasped the gloves, and began the onerous task of keeping herself and her horse clear of the sap-soaked needles. “Ugh, they are sticky. Is this why we brought extra water?”

“No, the water in the canteens is only for drinking. We will locate some pools of water at the edges of the trees. While not potable, the water is fine for washing off the debris from this forest.”

“Got you.”

By the time they exited the forest, the sky exhibited the beginnings of the night’s wash of color, from the deep blue overhead, fading through aquamarines, pale blue, pinks and red. As Kat gazed at the horizon, the sky reached a pale yellow, topping the still bright sun.

Arrogol motioned to Bannigus to catch up to him, as the path widened and masses of underbrush thinned. “Ahead of us is the tree line before the entrance to the Hellesmouth. We will set up camp in the clearing near those pools. Remember the water in them is not drinkable. Cut some branches for shelters, and Kat and I will locate sufficient wood for a fire.”

Kat’s eyes widened at his words. “Me?” *I didn’t have to do stuff in Kaylin, and even in Shendea, Mouse performed all these tasks. Why now?*

Arrogol glanced back at her, surprise in his eyes. “Yes, you as well. We are about to cross one of the worst sections of Rifella, and we must work together to prepare our camp for the night." He gestured to the clearing. "Bannigus will set up the shelters, and while he is doing so, you should gather plenty of kindling, and a couple of full sized logs. When Bannigus completes the shelter, use the efficient blade you hide beneath your belt—" He paused when she breathed in suddenly. "Yes, I saw it when we enjoyed our sampling. As I said, use your blade to cut a number of branches to cushion our blankets from any rocks."

"I can do it, but, no one asked me to before. I thought you two are my guides, so I'm surprised by your order.

Arrogol appeared puzzled. "We are your guides, Kat. Not your servants. We must act in concert to create a comfortable camp for the night. The Hellesmouth is hot, long, dangerous, and unforgiving. We must ensure we obtain a full and comfortable night's rest. Remember what I said. Rifellans work at their best in groups, and a group is what saves a life in the Hellesmouth."

"Fine. I understand the need for a team in this instance, but I still do not agree, they work in every situation."

"Work with us, Kat, and we will cross the desert in safety. Now climb down from your horse and lead the animal over to the trees. Remove the saddle, and you may use the soft leather to pillow your head, if you wish." He demonstrated with his own animal, and moved his saddle next to the beginnings of the shelter.

Kat followed suit and she deposited her bow and quiver beside the saddle.

Arrogol began to unload the pack animal. He smiled at Kat, who regarded his actions with puzzlement. "The horses must also rest from their burdens. A long and slow journey lies ahead of us, and our animals must equally be refreshed when we start out."

Kat shrugged. *They usually don't unload the pack animal, because the bags aren't that many.* She helped him stow the baggage on the ground in a mound, which they covered with a section of canvas-type material. "I thought you said the animals in this region are small and benign." *Surely a small critter can't harm anything.*

"They are, but they are also curious, and we need our luggage to sustain us, not supply creatures who are able to support themselves." He grinned at her. "You do not appear to be knowledgeable about living outdoors."

"I'm not. Which is why I was taken aback by your orders to perform the tasks you gave us. I much prefer to be comfortable indoors. I dislike camping. Intensely."

"You might need to change your attitude about this, Kat. Our world is not one luxurious inn after another. Traveling through Pridden often requires living off the land."

Kat shrugged and, drawing her dagger, began to cut branches from the trees. *I guess I got spoiled in Kaylin.*

They each completed the chores assigned them by Arrogol, and, as dusk descended, they sat beside the fire to consume a meal, a shelter behind them, waiting for tired bodies.

Kat slipped pyrock treats to Wink, and placed the travel cage, covered with a spare scarf atop her backpack. They cleaned their plates and cups in the sand and poured water from the nearby pond over them.

By the time the dark of night descended, Kat slipped gratefully between two blankets on her bed, cushioned by the leaves of sweet-smelling bushes.

Wow, almost as comfortable as beds at the inns. I kinda miss Mouse, but these two are good guides. I feel safe, and I trust them. Mmm.

CHAPTER SIXTEEN

A shrill bird call woke Kat from a satisfying and dreamless sleep. Despite sleeping on the ground, she passed the night in reasonable comfort. Bannigus and Arrogol allowed her limited privacy for a quick wash in the muddy pools, which refreshed her. Other personal needs took place inside the tree line, protected from view. When she emerged, Arrogol and Bannigus, their luggage loaded, worked at saddling their horses.

Kat rolled her blankets and grabbed her saddle. *Heavy, and the damn horse is so high.* She gathered herself and flung the saddle up to her mount's back. The poor horse responded with a grunt as the saddle landed with a crash.

Arrogol eyed them both. "You might ask for help when necessary, you realize?"

Kat scowled at him. "I'm only pulling my weight." She snorted and smiled sweetly.

He grinned. "We appreciate you doing so. However, I am certain your animal would be served better if she is able to survive this trip."

All three mounted and set off for the tree line. The shimmering heat of sand dunes stretched to the horizon through the last few stunted plants. At that moment, three odd animals appeared and stepped in front of the travelers. The creatures stood on two limbs, but when they dropped to all fours, they appeared just as comfortable. Their bodies, sinewy and loose-limbed, were covered in white hair that stood out from their skin, giving the impression they wore fur coats. Their faces astonished Kat the most. Their eyes, brown, intelligent and almost benign, contrasted markedly with their teeth. They revealed fangs almost too massive for their mouths, with each tooth long, pointed, and razor sharp in appearance. *What are they?* Kat's stone lay warm against her skin. *Guess they're okay.*

Arrogol turned to Kat. "These three are the busta. They will accompany us across the desert to the edge of the crystal fields where we will continue on to Geronna. There, they will leave us to return to this place."

He reached into his saddle bag and brought out three sacks with straps which he tossed to the busta.

Bannigus offered more information. "Cranna"— he pointed to the largest one—"bonds to Arrogol. Carrog"— he indicated the middle one—"bonds to me. For you they bring Casseg. She will, we hope, bond to you, though she is aware this may be the only bonding in her life."

"What do you mean bonds?"

"We are entering the desert of the Great Hellesmouth, home of the crosa. None of us would make the journey across without the busta, nor would the busta be able to survive without us. "

"Why?'

"The crosa lie beneath the sands where they breed and lay their eggs, deep within the cooler sands of the Hellesmouth. They wait, and as soon as any creature steps at the edge of their lairs, the sands give way, and nothing can crawl out without help. The crosa will pounce upon the victim and paralyze the unfortunate creature with one bite. The victim is stored with the eggs to provide live food for the young when they hatch."

"Eeeww."

"However," Bannigus continued, "Busta find crosa eggs much to their liking. When they fall in the sand trap, they are able to overcome the adult crosa. Only by working with Rifellans can they get out of the sand traps to take the eggs back to their shelters."

"How?"

"The rope ladders tied to the side of your saddle, allow them to escape."

I'm creative, but I would not be able to imagine this astonishing symbiotic relationship, no matter how hard I tried. This is perfect for my game — I can't wait to return home. Truth is stranger than fiction.

"Arrogol, what happens if Casseg only bonds once in her life?"

"Many busta do not bond more than once. So they cannot add to the stores of crosa eggs, they are required to fulfill functions around their homes that are less dangerous, but important for the survival of the troupe."

"Like what?"

"Repairs to their homes, tending to the young, and other useful things."

Whew. I didn't want her to be destroyed if she couldn't get crosa eggs any more.

The horses, each preceded by a busta, moved in slow procession across the hot dunes, when Bannigus's busta paused and emitted a sound like a horn.

Arrogol dismounted. "Kat, we must now walk and lead our horses across the sands."

"Why? What's wrong?"

"Nothing as yet. We cannot afford for any of our horses to fall into a crosa trap. They are too heavy for us to extricate. So we must walk well in front of them to protect them."

Kat slid off her saddle and held the reins of her mount.

Bannigus followed suit.

The three travelers moved gingerly across the sands, led by the busta. *Casseg comes across as female, compared to the other two. I wonder if this is deliberate?*

Kat hoped Casseg would bond with her. *I'm vehemently opposed to becoming crosa dinner.*

Without a word of warning, the sands gave way, and, Arrogol's busta slid down the sands into the crosa trap. Fine grains flew in all directions, and Cranna hooted as he disappeared covered in pouring sand, down a shaft. All those above ground, froze in place. A chorus of shrieks, snarls, and growls rose from the trap, and sand sprayed upwards. Now, all quiet, Kat waited for Arrogol to throw down the rope for Cranna, but he and his horse stood waiting with composed patience. A hoot sounded from the sands. Arrogol lifted the horn Olwyn had given him, and blew a reply. Confirming the security of the rope ladder to his saddle he tossed the rope down the trap, and he and his horse took two steps back. Moments later, Cranna's head appeared above the sand, which was still pouring down the chute around him, and he scrambled up the balance of the rope and rose to his feet beside Arrogol's mount.

With one of the bags Arrogol had distributed earlier, strapped on his back, Cranna regarded Arrogol and hooted at him again. The sack bulged with booty from below the desert. Arrogol tossed a water container to the busta, who drank, washing the blood from his muzzle.

He returned the canteen and handed the backpack to Arrogol, who secured the pouch to the saddle, moved around the trap, and set off once again.

The three bustas hooted and growled at each other. *Post battle debriefing?*

The heat of the desert and the constant plodding in the shifting sands tired Kat. She felt as if she trudged through treacle, and found trouble keeping her eyes open. Kat led her mount off course and Casseg's warning hoot came too late. Even the icy feel of the brilliant emerald on the chain about her neck failed to reach her in time. As the sands gave way under her feet, her mount neighed, retreated, and pulled the reins from her hands. Kat screamed in terror as she slid down the sands, which collapsed beneath her, sliding her down toward the yawning pit, but caught sight of Casseg above her, rocketing after her, jaws open and screaming and hooting in defiance. Sands poured down, capturing Kat in a moving dry river. She glanced below her and gasped at the horrifying sight of the crosa, a gruesome thing that ambled slowly toward her, as she thumped down on a mound of sand from the desert above.

The crosa, huge and bloated, was completely covered in sharp thorny spines, erupting from bulging pimples over its entire body. The head, black and shiny sported a mass of eyes, similar to a spider, with two sharp ebony horns on either side. The four fangs on either side of the mouth frightened her more, because they dripped a scarlet venom, which hissed as the liquid fell on the floor of the trap. *Thank my stars the crosa can't move fast.*

Casseg landed on the floor of the trap on top of an equally large mound of sand. She uttered a fierce growling hoot of challenge as she hit the mound. The crosa opened a repulsive mouth and hissed, sending a spray of venom toward Casseg. She switched direction, knocked Kat out of the way, and leaped on the neck of the monster, on a disgusting mound of flesh. Positioning herself behind the head of the crosa, Casseg sank fangs deep into the neck of the foul animal.

The crosa screamed and thrashed, but appeared unable to dislodge Casseg from her perch. At last, the shrieks and the flailing ceased, and the crosa lay dead on the floor of its lair.

Casseg eyed Kat, lifted her head, and hooted. She began to gather the crosa eggs and stow them in her bag.

The rope ladder appeared, and Casseg, still gathering eggs, motioned to Kat to ascend. She needed no further urging. She grabbed the ladder and, skin still prickling with excess adrenalin surging in her system, climbed to safety.

Her limbs so weak, by the time she reached the surface, Arrogol needed to drag her away from the mouth of the trap. Her knees buckled, and, exhausted by her brush with the crosa, she clung to her horse. At the sounds of the bustas greeting each other, Kat turned as Casseg climbed, triumph in every movement, from the trap, with a bag holding her booty.

Kat glanced up at Arrogol and saw the worry etched on his face.

"Are you alright, Kat?"

"I am, thanks to Casseg. No matter how much you told me, I wasn't prepared for what happened."

"Not many people are. Few realize how intimidating the crosa can be. Do you understand better how important a group of busta and men can be when crossing the Hellesmouth?"

"Will you stop ramming teamwork down my throat? I don't want to hear about this again."

Arrogol gave her a wry smile. "We shall agree to disagree. Rifella can be a harsh land, but is part of us. We cannot conceive of any situation in which working together is not a valuable asset."

Kat shrugged. "Whatever."

The busta completed their mutual hooting and grunting, and Cranna hooted again at Arrogol.

He nodded. "Cranna suggests we must continue our journey now to exit the Hellesmouth before nightfall."

They took up their positions again and set off slowly through the hot shimmering desert.

Kat, paying strict attention to the location of her busta, followed Bannigus. Arrogol, with the pack animal now secured to his horse, walked behind her.

Kat's limbs ached from her experience. *Crap that was close. Arrogol's right about one thing. Rifella is a harsh land.*

CHAPTER SEVENTEEN

The group reached the edge of the Hellesmouth as dusk descended, and the sands no longer shifted beneath their feet. A few pint-sized bushes grew from the hard sand, and the odd bit of lichen flourished under trees whose twisted and gnarled branches indicated little available water. However, the dunes ahead of them undulated with shifting colors and light, which reflected from thousands of crystalline shapes. They lay in cubes, rhomboids, shafts, ovals, and some flat ones exploding from a single source, like a mass of flower petals. *Wow, these aren't cut by jewelers. They're gems in their natural state.*

Arrogol gazed around him. "This is a perfect place to camp for the night. The ground is firm and smooth, and we can dig for water."

The three busta approached him and hooted a conversation. Arrogol turned to Bannigus and Kat. "The busta leave us this night to return to their homes. They plan to skirt the perimeter of the Hellesmouth, to avoid the sand traps. A longer journey, but much safer. Without our help, they will not take the chance of becoming crosa fodder. They are well pleased with the number of eggs they received for protecting us, and thank us."

Kat walked over to Arrogol and put her hand on the horn attached to his belt. "Do you mind?"

"No. Do what you believe is necessary."

She took the horn and, facing Casseg, blew a single note. The busta hooted back, and jumped up and down with the other two. “I hope they know I’m thanking Casseg for saving my life.”

“Busta are a most intelligent species. They are not animals, but a different civilization, and they understand with precision what you mean.”

The busta waved to them and set off along the edge of the desert, keeping among the diminutive bushes.

Kat’s eyes followed them as they disappeared in the dusk, but she turned her attention once more to gather wood she would use for their fire. Deciding upon a saddle for a pillow once more, she helped Bannigus set up the camp, while Arrogol dug for water.

After allowing the sand to settle to the bottom of the pool revealed by his digging, he filled their canteens, and led each of the horses to drink their fill.

Night fell fast, and, shivering in air much cooler than the evening before, Kat snuggled beneath her blankets.

❦ ❦ ❦

Kat opened her eyes to a brilliant dawn, the sky streaked with vermillion, and crimson, trimmed clouds. Both men snored on, so she set her blankets aside and tip-toed to the pool, which had refilled overnight. Keeping one blanket over her to conceal her actions, she washed herself, relishing the temporary sense of cleanliness. *Oh for a personal.*

She filled a tin with water and set the container on rocks around the fire and brewed a cup of Karri-san. While waiting for the water to boil, she fed Wink, and stowed everything else in her backpack.

Arrogol and Bannigus, also risen, completed their ablutions, and prepared the morning meal for the three of them.

When they began to re-saddle their horses, Kat requested help from Arrogol. "I don't want to cause my mount any distress." She smiled coyly at him, batting her eyelids.

Arrogol rolled his eyes, and saddled the animal for her.

Once ready, Arrogol handed out three pairs of dark masks with slits in them. "When we begin our trek across the crystal dunes, be sure to wear these masks. Our star in this area is strong, and the light shining from the crystals can be almost blinding. These masks reduce the amount of light that reaches our eyes, and thus protects them."

Kat put her mask on and, understood instantly what he meant. The slits reflected the light in a much reduced manner, and, rather than squinting to protect her eyes, she could relax and view things with comfort.

Arrogol then handed them each four pieces of thick blanket, and leather ties. "Wrap the blanket around each of your animal's hooves, and secure them with the leather strips. The dunes appear gentle, and the colors of the crystals are beautiful. However, they are more rugged than they seem, and hard and sharp crystals, can cause much pain if they become imbedded in the hooves of our mounts. The blanket padding will prevent this, and allow our horses to travel in comfort."

Kat bent down to cushion her horse's feet, and the animal waited with equine patience for her to complete the job. Once she tied the last blanket on, her horse bent down, nickered and blew at Kat's hair.

Kat looked up. "Oh, you like that do you?"

Arrogol chuckled at her. "You speak to horses?"

"Where I come from, we do. I suppose this creates a kind of bond with the animal."

Arrogol snorted.

"She is not alone in her thoughts, Arrogol. The finest horsemen in Baklai always speak with their charges. This is why we are so successful as riders and trainers. You are aware of our reputation for superior skills with our horses?"

"Your reputation is beyond reproach, Bannigus, but I never realized you spoke to your steeds."

Bannigus shrugged and secured the pack animal to his horse.

Arrogol flicked the reins and eased his horse forward. Kat followed, and Bannigus and the pack animal, took up the rear.

Arrogol called to the other two. "Avoid, if you can, the piles of crystals, and travel in the sand as much as possible. In this way, we will be able to avoid many of the sharpest objects."

❦ ❦ ❦

The star, now high in the sky, heated up the sand and the crystals, and Arrogol called a rest. "The going is slow, but we all need water." He released the spade from the pack horse, and dug in the sand beside a massive number of crystals. About a foot down, the hole began filling with water.

They each brought cups to drink from, and also filled their canteens. Kat took a cup to Wink, who raised her sleepy head and lapped at the water. She consumed half a cup before dropping off to sleep once more. *Wow, this is the thirstiest she's been.*

Bannigus led the four horses to the hole and allowed each of them to drink their fill.

Kat moved some crystals aside and sat on the sand in the shade created by her horse. She and the others chewed on strips of dried brantor meat. She gazed around her and spotted a fist-sized crystal of the most glorious robin's egg blue, interspersed with bands of a deep golden citrine. *This is gorgeous. I'll give this to someone as a gift.* She tucked the sparkling jewel in a side pocket of her backpack, where she used to tuck Breen.

Arrogol rose from his seat. "Everyone up, and let us continue. This part of our journey may be slow, but we are not far from our rest stop for the night."

Kat sighed with relief when she detected the beginnings of bushes and other greenery, because the trip had seemed to last forever.

Arrogol pointed to a small wooden building in the middle of some bushes. "Our destination. This is a traveler's hut which housed many others before us. Remove the saddles from your mounts and take them and all your bags inside as well, so the horses may spend the night unencumbered."

All bent to their tasks. Carrying her heavy saddle, Kat thought the burden lighter than when they first set out. *I guess I'm developing muscles.* She dropped the saddle in the corner of the hut, where Bannigus and Arrogol deposited theirs. The one large room held three cots, with leather strips as mattresses; a pot hanging over a stone hearth; cupboards to the side; and a door at the end, which Arrogol identified as the personal.

"This hut is blessed with a tank attached to the side, which fills with water whenever the rains fall. A pump in the personal will bring sufficient water with which to wash yourself. You should find this refreshing, though not as fine as one at an inn."

Before either Arrogol or Bannigus could move, Kat threw her backpack on one of the beds and rushed into the simple personal to clean herself as well as possible. *The heck with teamwork here. I'm the woman, and I need to wash the dust from my lady parts. Now.* By the time she emerged, Bannigus's fire in the huge stone hearth, heated a pot hanging from the top stone. The pot bubbled and gurgled, cooking something that reminded her of the delicate taste of tarragon.

"What are you cooking? The aroma is divine."

"We are most fortunate. This is the time of the path when the eethnaire flourishes. When we combine this root with dried brantor, we produce a fine and flavorful stew." He served them in rough bowls from the cupboard, and placed the full steaming dishes on a makeshift table, with a bench down either side.

Yum. Kat ate her way through a third helping. The other two managed five each.

Well fed, they all pitched in to wash the dishes and prepare for bed.

Kat slid between the blankets on her choice of bed, reached in the side pocket of her backpack, and brought out the crystal she found.

The blue reminded her of something… someone? She replaced the stone in the backpack and gradually drifted into a half sleep. The snoring from the two other beds lulled her, not musical, but rhythmic and soothing.

Without warning the steps of animals scurrying across the roof, woke her. She bolted upright. *What was that?* She lay back down. She recalled Arrogol saying no nasty creatures were about. She began to drift again and the tiresome animal on the roof scuttled across again.

This time as she drifted into sleep, she recalled the color of Liandock's eyes. *One gold, and one blue. Perhaps I'm meant to give him the stone.*

CHAPTER EIGHTEEN

Kat lay in bed listening to the morning sounds of birds and leaves tapping against the wooden structure. Snoring sounds issued from one — no, both — of her companions. *At least their snores are bearable.* She yawned and stretched as much as possible in the confines of the narrow cot, got up and nipped into the personal. By the time she emerged, her two guides were demonstrating their kitchen skills, preparing journeyklim for them all. She suspected they made use of the woods outside as their personal.

Bannigus handed her a bowl of her favorite morning meal. "Lady Kat, when you are finished eating, we will saddle and load the horses, and leave for Geronna. We should arrive before the midturn meal."

"If Geronna is so close, why didn't we continue last evening?"

"If the possibility existed to arrive while the star still shone, we would not have stopped for the night. However, the route can be challenging after dusk."

"I thought you said no dangerous creatures lived in this part of the woodlands."

"None exist. However, as you will find on our way today, many plants grow in the area which are poisonous to the touch. They are difficult to avoid after dusk. You would not appreciate the irritating rash they cause."

"I'm sure I wouldn't. Thanks."

Kat swallowed the last of her meal, and gulped a double cup of Karri-san. *The heat of Arrogol's presence faded.*

The three washed their dishes and tidied the hut, ensuring they left it in the same state as when they entered. Kat joined the other two outside and they saddled the horses—Kat with a little help from Bannigus—and Arrogol loaded the bulk of the baggage on the pack animal. With no handy rocks to stand on, Bannigus tossed her up to her saddle as if she weighed as little as a her pyrock. *Bannigus is not at all like Haydar. He's helpful.*

They set off for Geronna, this time with Arrogol in the lead, and Bannigus trailing, with the pack horse's reins attached to his saddle.

Arrogol stopped his horse and turned back to Kat. "Do you see the spiky plant with the blue leaves?"

"Yes."

"The name is prickle-fur. If you got closer to the ground, you would find small blue hairs on the leaves. Many visitors to Rifella are fooled by thinking the hairs are soft to the touch." He grimaced. "Close up, they resemble tiny blue barbs, which dig into the skin, and release a toxic acid. This only irritates at first but progresses to create a fiery red itch which drives many insane."

"The plants are beautiful. I can understand why unsuspecting visitors might mistake the barbs for fur. Aren't the horses affected?"

"Animals do not appear to be impacted. I suspect their own fur or hair protects them."

"What are the small round red things on the bushes? Are they flowers or berries?"

"They are berries, but, as you notice, the bushes are full of them. Only one animal devours them, a scaled creature called a kamelona, and they cause these animals to develop a deadly poisonous saliva. Kamelonas possess lengthy curled-up tongues, and when they spy prey, they release their tongues, firing their saliva at it. The result is a quick but painful death."

"Wow. What size are the adults?"

"The body is only this long." He held his hands about six inches apart. "The tail is about three times the length of the body, and allows them to maintain a sturdy perch on tree branches."

Kat shuddered. "I promise to leave them alone."

Arrogol grinned at her. "A wise move. Now we should move as well, because if we do reach Geronna before the midturn meal, we will be in time to obtain rooms, and to refresh ourselves before eating." He shook the reins and his animal moved forward.

Kat clicked at her horse and followed. The air, scented with the sweet fragrance of the blossoms of the prickle-fur and the brilliance of early star shine, warm on her skin, prompted her to hum a few bars of a song she recalled from the Keep.

Arrogol turned in his saddle and gazed back at Kat, an amused grin on his face. "This is the first time you made a tune. Am I to understand you are happy?"

"This turn is beautiful, and life is fine. How can one not be happy?"

"You are correct." Arrogol began to sing the same song, but with a deep melodic baritone.

Unbelievable. Awesome looking, and a terrific singer too. Olwyn's got herself an excellent mate. Because she didn't remember the words, Kat began to hum again, and when another voice joined in, she glanced behind her, startled.

Bannigus. His voice is pleasant too, although he's more of a tenor.

They finished the song, and Arrogol began another—this time a song of war and mighty warriors.

The song stirred the blood. *Good thing I drank extra Kar-ri-san this morning.*

When Arrogol completed his song, Bannigus began one from Baklai. More a ballad, the words spoke of horses and foals and the bonds they shared with their riders. The way to Geronna passed pleasantly, and Kat spied the rooftops of the town in the distance. The three lapsed in silence and quick-ened their steeds to reach their destination sooner.

A tall and burly man stepped from the stables as they rode up, and greeted Arrogol by name. "Welcome, Praetor. Leave your horses with us, and one of my apprentices will deliver your luggage to your rooms."

Arrogol dismounted, and slapped the man on the back. A huge meaty sound. "Nonsense. Bannigus and I can take our own luggage."

The man displayed horror on his face. "Praetor Arrogol? Take his own baggage from my stables? You jest. My stable would never live down such an insult to a guest."

Arrogol roared with laughter and held up his hands as if in surrender. "You win Benden. I will not fight you for the privilege of carting my luggage to my rooms."

As the two men made fun of each other, Kat examined the town, and the inn in particular, with curiosity. Unlike many villages she visited, Geronna's buildings sported only fine wood in their construction, with intricate carvings on the frames and lintels which added to the beauty of the town. While no stone construction appeared evident, each building enjoyed decorations of gem stones from the crystal dunes.

The designs the citizens used fascinated Kat. They reminded her of the abstract paintings by Piet Mondrian, all squares and geometric shapes. Most homes, however, used only a single crystal color.

"Bannigus, why do people use only one color of crystal on their homes?"

"This may appear unusual to you, but each color is used for a family. For example, quite a number of homes use blue crystals. They all descend from the same bloodline."

"Fascinating."

"This is something peculiar to Rifellans in the south. If Praetor Arrogol's family used these crystals, they would all be yellow citrine. The homes of his kin in the northern area of Rifella do not decorate the exteriors of their homes with crystals, but within each home, you will find a fine example of citrine, mounted in a place of honor."

"I remember seeing a yellow crystal carved in the shape of a bird. Beside the carved bird though, sat a pale pink one in the shape of a flower."

"Pink crystal represents Lady Olwyn's family. Their future home would need to include both colors."

"Thank you Bannigus. Do your people use stone or wood for your houses?"

"We are blessed with bountiful forests, so wood is our building material of choice."

"You don't use crystals for decoration?"

"No, our land is rich in forests and grasslands. So we possess wood and horses." He smiled. "Our people, in addition to being adept with the latter, are also master carvers. Our furnishings are fine works of art."

"Indeed." She cast her eyes with impatience at Arrogol, who still exchanged stories and laughter with Benden.

"Bannigus can you pry Arrogol away from his friend. I'm desperate to find my room. I want to clean up and put on fresh clothing before our midturn meal."

Bannigus smiled at her and went and spoke to Arrogol.

A young apprentice led them to their rooms. Kat entered, and walked over to the desk where she set Wink's cage on the dresser. She indulged in a lengthy shower to eliminate the grit and sand from The Great Hellesmouth. Dressed, she headed for the dining hall, situated outside, but attached to the inn.

Approaching the door, she spotted Bannigus and Arrogol, but before she joined them, a small blue animal, resembling a lizard, decorated with brilliant green spots rushed toward her.

The innkeeper called to her. "My Lady, do not move. That is a kamelona, a dangerous creature."

Kat glanced down at the tiny scaled entity. "Why it's beautiful." *It looks like a weird type of chameleon. It can't be dangerous. My necklace's warm and toasty as ever.* The animal approached her foot, glanced up at her, ran up her leather trousers, and settled on her shoulder. She and the kamelona regarded each other curiously, and her new blue friend reached over and butted a small head against her ear. Kat grinned in delight. "Hello. Who are you?" The kamelona tilted its head and reached around to peer at her face, blinking at her. *Her green spots remind me of Shade's eyes.* "Aren't you adorable? I'm going to call you Brade." As if in approval, Brade butted her jaw this time, emitted a gravelly croak, and wound her long tail around Kat's neck.

Arrogol, Bannigus and the innkeeper stood stock still, and stared at Kat with astonishment.

Kat frowned at them. "What?"

None of the three spoke.

"I'm in no danger. She likes me."

The innkeeper, at last, shrugged. "I suspect the kamelona chose you, and you are indeed safe from the poison. Kamalonas are odd animals, and she appears to have chosen to be your guard. This is a rare occurrence, but does happen." He eyed Kat with a puzzled frown on his face. "Why do you refer to the animal as female?"

Kat felt unconcerned. "I'm not sure. I just believe she is."

Arrogol and Bannigus kept a fair distance between them and Brade. "So, she is your protector. I pray this means she will refrain from spitting at us."

"Of course." *For some reason, I'm convinced she won't injure them.* Kat turned and peered at Brade. "You won't hurt them, will you?"

Brade gave another croak.

"She said yes. Both of you are also safe." *OK, so I don't understand what she said but I feel safe with her, and my teeny lie will make them less jumpy.*

Arrogol twisted an eyebrow at Brade. "I am much more comfortable being aware of this."

As the innkeeper showed them into the dining hall, all conversation halted. Mouths dropped open, and every eye focused on the blue animal on Kat's shoulder, sitting as if on a small throne, with a long blue tail wrapped around Kat's neck.

Arrogol chose a table for six, and he and Bannigus sat opposite her.

I don't think they trust Brade. They'll become used to her.

They ordered their midturn meal, and conversation resumed.

The innkeeper checked with his guests about food quality and the service of his apprentices, and Kat asked what she should feed Brade.

“I am not sure, My Lady. I suspect they are quite capable of feeding themselves.”

⚘⚘⚘

After the meal, Kat made for her room to feed Wink.

Brade, appeared curious about Wink’s squeaks, and reached out to sniff at her. They butted noses. Wink squeaked and Brade croaked at her with her gruff voice. Wink turned to Kat and chirped for food, so Kat fed her. Brade rasped at her. Kat shrugged and offered the kamalona a treat. The food disappeared down a red, toothless maw, and she croaked for another. She possessed a bigger appetite than Wink, and managed to consume four pieces.

The cot the previous night, while adequate, did not supply Kat with as deep a sleep as in a proper and comfortable bed. She yawned and prepared for a quick nap. Brade unwrapped her tail and headed for the dresser, where she settled next to Wink’s cage, curled in a ball, and slept.

Hmm. I think they like each other. I wonder if they’re related?

CHAPTER NINETEEN

Kat woke, startled, convinced, an earthquake surrounded her. She jumped off the bed and stood staring at her blue companion. Brade croaked in her gravelly voice trying, it seemed, to advise Kat to feed her. She gave Brade a few pyrock nibbles. *I'm not hungry yet, but tea would be perfect.* She scanned the room for the typical tassel, and tugged three times.

While waiting for her tea to be delivered, she gathered her writing materials and set them on the desk in the room. *Karri-san first, and after I add some new words, I'll journal about Brade.*

A knock heralded the arrival of her refreshment, and at her "Come," the apprentice entered.

A short dark man held a tray with a substantial mug of Karri-san.

"You're not Rifellan, are you?"

He ducked his head at her. "No, my Lady. I hail from Baklai."

"I find a number of Baklai work as apprentices in Rifella. Is this common?"

"Yes. Baklai is not a wealthy land, and since we share a border with Rifella, many of our young people seek to work and learn a trade here. Opportunities to become trainers of horses are limited, and raising foodstuffs is not a lucrative position."

"Aren't you competing with young Rifellans for these positions?"

"No my Lady. Rifellans much prefer to apprentice as warriors and guards. Many availabilities throughout Pridden exist for these positions."

"My thanks for the tea. Is the dining hall open for an evening meal?"

"Yes, my Lady. A number of travelers are attending to their feed already."

"If you view Praetor Arrogol or Horse-Master Bannigus at their meals, will you please inform them I will join them shortly?"

"Indeed." He bowed his head and left her room.

Kat headed for her table and sipped from the cup, blowing on the tea to cool it. She opened her journal to add information about Brade. She wrote about her beautiful blue color with the splendid green spots, and chuckled to herself when she wrote down the reactions of fear from other people about the cute creature. Finally, she drained the last of the tea from her mug, and prepared to head for the dining area.

She glanced around the room, eyes settling on Brade. "So, are you coming, or what?"

One throaty rasp, and her blue friend leaped to her shoulder, winding her long tail around Kat's neck. Kat wrapped a gauzy scarf around her throat, concealing the kamalona from general view.

❦ ❦ ❦

Kat entered the hall, and scanned the room, spotting Arrogol and Bannigus at a table for six, accompanied by two strangers, both Rifellans. Arrogol raised his hand and gestured for her to join them. On her way, she stopped a waitperson and requested he bring food and Karri-san tea to her as soon as she seated herself. She strode to the table and plopped herself in an empty seat beside Bannigus.

He introduced her to the two strangers at the table. "These warriors, Tythan and Bodeth, are with the guard unit here in Geronna." He paused as Kat acknowledged the two men. "You appear much more refreshed, Lady Kat."

"I am now. I needed a sleep after our midturn meal. I'm afraid I slept poorly last evening. The cot in the hut was not that comfortable, and various creatures kept running over the roof all night."

The three Rifellans laughed.

"What's funny?"

Arrogol explained. "Your dress and your appearance are much like a female in a guard unit, but you would not be able to survive such a calling." He chuckled anew. "Rifellan women of the guard are not troubled by creatures on the roof, nor do they complain about disagreeable sleeping accommodations."

Kat humphed. "A likely story. Women everywhere appreciate comfort. They keep their silence when men like you would mock them. Plus women are less likely to complain. As to the creatures on the roof, you in Rifella are used to such things. Much of what you encounter is new to me. I will, eventually, become more accustomed."

Arrogol snorted. "Females in other lands are not as strong as our guards."

"Brave words, Arrogol, from one who never experienced the challenge of birthing."

Arrogol glared at her.

Tythan laughed and slapped Arrogol on the back. "The Lady Kat makes a valid argument. You are aware my mate is a strong and capable woman, but I noted her pain when she birthed our first offspring. Not something I would wish to experience." He shook his head, as if remembering. "True, she never complained about her travels as a guard, but she did request a padded roll which she now places on her cot whenever she is on duty. She says she is more rested each morrow."

Kat frowned at Arrogol. "You are not being fair, Arrogol. Like all strangers, I will learn to live with the challenges of being in Rifella."

Disturbed by the voices around her, Brade poked her head out from the scarf and croaked.

The two Rifellans stared, wide-eyed, at the blue animal, and Bodeth warned Kat. "You are aware, are you not, Lady Kat, of the reputation of kamalonas?"

"I'm safe with Brade. She is my protector."

Tythan turned to face Bodeth. "Do you remember our first kamalona sighting?"

"I remember the experience well."

Tythan shook his head. "You are blessed with luck if the blue creature on your shoulder chooses to protect you, Lady Kat. The one we encountered took a dislike to the Morden prisoner when we transported him to a cell in Restin. The saliva of the creature proved unfortunate for him, as the poison from the kamelona was swift and fatal."

"From what I'm aware, Morden might be inclined to retaliate."

"No, Lady. The kamelona performed a valuable service for us, and Rifellans did not, therefore, need to punish the man. Thus Morden accepted an animal as responsible for his demise, and a trial and the subsequent penalty by our land, proved unnecessary."

"It sounds like Morden would have objected if you had punished him. Are relations between your two lands fragile?"

"Not with the Mordens from the south, but, they are with those from the north. The Baklai formed a treaty with our land a number of paths ago." He grimaced. "Morden's Thane covets the Baklai horses, and we are their only protectors. We suspect if we did not defend our little neighbors, they might no longer exist. The Thane finds our support of Baklai is an anathema to him."

Bodeth nodded in agreement, his face grim.

"Have Rifella and Morden always been enemies?"

"Not at all. Many paths ago, a Lord ruled the land of Morden, but the current Thane's male parent, attacked and killed him. The deceased Lord left behind two male offspring, who all expected to eventually regain the Lordship of Morden. However Galdin's parent sent his assassins to locate and eliminate the young males. They were assumed killed. Their fate is unknown, and they or their bodies remain undiscovered to this day."

"So Galdin is the current Thane of Morden?"

"Yes, and under his rule, Morden changed from a land of productive people to a land divided. The southerners are much the same people as before. The northerners, faced with the rise to prominence of the Assassins' Guild, became suspicious and cruel. Even their appearance changed. They tend to live indoors and in a series underground passages, so their skin is so pale they appear to possess no color."

Perhaps this Galdin is responsible for all the trouble in Pridden. Am I supposed to find proof of this for Eduardo?

Kat stroked Brade. "So these creatures are of help. But, do they often attack Rifellans?"

Bodeth gazed at the ceiling. "Now I think of this, I am not aware of an attack on a Rifellan." He turned to Tythan. "They appear to attack Mordens more often, do they not?"

His fellow guardsman agreed. "They do indeed. How interesting we did not understand this before." He peered at Brade. "Our thanks to you, Brade."

Brade's only reply, a hoarse croak.

Tythan eyed his companion. "Since when did you speak to animals?"

Bodeth chuckled. "I deem it advantageous to be polite to one who possesses such power."

Arrogol regarded Brade with a wry smile. "Perhaps we should include kamelonas in our guard units."

Kat chuckled. "I suspect you would be unwise to embrace them as guards. Brade does not appear to be intelligent. She does her own thing."

"I made a humorous suggestion Kat." He stretched. "Without the benefit of a brief sleep after my midturn meal, I find myself in need of a bed." He yawned. "Kat, we shall meet you at the stables on the morrow. I suggest you partake of your morning meal in your rooms, and call on an apprentice to bring your packed bag to the stable. We head for Brevista first thing. While the journey is not lengthy, the route via the Merrithan Forest is a slow one."

"Fine. I need to do some writing before I pack my bags. I will meet you on the morrow." She rose with the others, and headed for her rooms.

Galdin. *Kat shivered. I don't like the sound of the man's name. Is he the cause of all the trouble on Pridden?* She sighed. *I hope Eduardo is right and I can help. I often feel so out of my depth here.*

CHAPTER TWENTY

A raspy croak near her ear roused Kat, and she opened one eye. Her vision filled with a blue head, decorated with brilliant green spots. *Brade's markings are the same color as the stone on my pendant.* "Are you hungry?" At the same moment a plaintive squeak from Wink issued from her cage. "Ah, you're both hungry."

Kat fed them. "I'll need to carry a more substantial number of treats if you're going to eat so much, Brade."

Kat tugged once on the tassel, and ordered journeyklim from the apprentice when she appeared.

By the time the apprentice arrived with her food tray, she had dressed and was completing her packing

She sat down to eat, and Brade reached over to sniff at her bowl of journeyklim. Curious, Kat spooned a small amount on a separate plate. The kamelona lapped at the meal and cleaned the plate within minutes.

"I'll be… you can eat journeyklim from now on, and leave Wink's treats for her." *Wonderful. This solves the food problem.*

Kat tugged on the tassel, and when the apprentice arrived to remove the empty dishes, she requested someone to convey her bags to the stable. Within minutes of the serving woman's departure, a young man appeared, hoisted the luggage, and exited Kat's room.

She slung her backpack, with Wink's cage attached, over one shoulder, her diplo bag over the other, and carried her bow and quiver in her hands. Waiting only long enough for Brade to leap to her shoulder and wind her tail around her neck, she made for the stables.

Arrogol and Bannigus, still involved in saddling and bridling their own horses, ignored Kat, so she dragged a stool over to her mount, and wrestled her saddle on the animal's back. Bannigus did not appear to enjoy the sight of Kat's struggles and came over to help her. Even he needed the stool to accomplish the task.

"Although I'd be willing to load the baggage, I suspect, with your experience, Arrogol, you'll do a better job." She handed the bags to Arrogol.

Arrogol glanced at her with a smug smile.

He's preening because I paid him a compliment. Men. Really. He is good at what he does though.

She moved the stool back beside her mount, and stretched up with her foot to reach the stirrup. Instead of putting his hands around her waist to help her, as Bannigus did, Arrogol placed his substantial mitt under her buttock and pushed her up to the saddle. She glared at him as his hand lingered too long, but he only grinned.

Sometimes guys are such little boys.

Bannigus led the trio toward Brevista. Kat followed, and Arrogol brought up the rear, with the baggage animal attached to his saddle.

The three approached a thick tangle of bushes and trees, which Bannigus identified as the Merrithan Forest. The trail through the forest, narrow, with small bushes growing in the pathway, made passage difficult for the horses. Birds twittered at their approach, and the brush filled with rustlings and the occasional snap of a branch under the hooves of their steeds.

"Do dangerous things live in this forest?"

Lucky for him, Arrogol refrained from pointing out Rifellan guardswomen would not be upset by the noises. Instead, Bannigus answered her question. "No. Only minor tree dwellers who consume the fruits of the trees around them. We do not often view these inhabitants. as the growth is so thick and shaggy, the forest so dark, and little star-shine reaches the ground."

"Why would anyone want to live in Brevista if the trees grow so close together?"

"The trees supply the wood which the Brevistans harvest for the shipyards at Orkanna."

"I heard the Rifellans build ships?"

"Only three lands possess shallow coastal areas which allow for shipbuilding and safe haven for boats: Rifella, who own a major harbor is able to handle the construction of siz-able sailing vessels; Glowen, whose shoreline is gentle and perfect for the construction of smaller fishing vessels; and Baklai, who purchase small ships from Rifella to allow them to trade horses with Glowen for Orenberry wine, and their harbor offers safe berth-age for boats."

"I understand." Kat nodded and scratched her head. *I'm beginning to figure out how these lands work with each other.*

The three rode on in silence, each wrapped in their own thoughts. Kat assumed both the men thought about their eventual return to the keep. Her own consisted of home, the odd systems within the lands, and also what kept Mouse from this initial journey. *I miss Mouse. He's a lot less challenging to travel with than Arrogol.*

Despite the brief stop for food at midturn, which the inn at Geronna supplied them, Kat's stomach grumbled. *I need to eat.*

Arrogol halted his mount, and pointed. "Brevista."

Kat squinted through the trees at a clearing and buildings. "Yum. Food."

The three horses pushed their way through the last of the trees and rode up to the stable. Kat groaned and slid out of her saddle to the ground.

An apprentice rushed up to them to help. "Lady, Sires, we will place your mounts in stalls, and deliver your baggage to the inn. The evening meal is underway, so you may wish to attend the dining hall now, which is in a separate building to your left."

Bannigus murmured assent, but Kat after thanking the man, glanced over at the direction he indicated, and her attention riveted on a pale Morden beating a much smaller male.

Kat rushed over her hand clenched. "Stop." She could feel the heat in her face.

As she neared the pair, the Morden turned on her, glared, and raised his hand to hit her.

Arrogol moved toward him, but Kat blocked the man's hand and thrust a fist at his throat. He choked and Kat, without thinking, dashed to the watering trough, filled a bucket, and drenched the attacker. His choking ceased, but now he gasped for breath, and his face twisted in rage.

"I told you to stop. You're a bully."

He did stop.

Kat snarled with rage. "Do you observe this creature on my shoulder?"

He gave a faint nod.

"If you charge, you would never reach me, because this animal would spit poison at you. Death be would instantaneous."

He appeared taken aback by the ferocity on Kat's face and growled at her. "You interfered and came between me and my servant. You possess no right to do so."

Kat still shaking with anger, whirled around to question the small man, a Baklai in appearance. "Are you his servant?"

The short brown man hung his head. "I am, your Lady. I sold my services to him when I failed to find employment, and my family faced the danger of starvation."

She glared at the Morden. "How much did you pay him?"

Kat gasped, astonished at the pittance he mentioned. She asked Arrogol to give a chit to the Morden to free the Baklai from his service.

"Lady Kat, you want me to give him a chit?" Arrogol's voice dripped ice.

Kat smiled as sweetly as possible. "But I don't carry chits with me, and we can replace yours when we return to the keep."

Arrogol sputtered. "But…"

Kat continued to smile. "You did suggest, Arrogol, we are a team?"

He blinked, sighed, and withdrew a chit from his pockets. He scribbled something on the parchment, and handed the paper to the Morden.

The man snatched the chit from Arrogol with bad grace. He grabbed his horse's reins from the post to which they were secured, swung into his saddle, and rode in the direction of the Morden border.

Arrogol rounded on Kat. "Why do you strike out before questioning?"

Kat stared at him. "Didn't you catch him raise his hand to me? Do you think I would wait for him to strike me first?"

Arrogol frowned and swallowed. "I suppose not. However, you did not wait for me to intervene."

"Men. I do not need to be rescued in such a silly situation. I'm more than capable of defending myself." *If danger lurked, the stone on my pendant would be the first to warn me.*

Arrogol put up his hands. "Kat, I shall not continue to argue. I understand this is one battle I shall not win."

Despite the fact I can take care of myself, I can't really fault them for wanting to rush to the rescue.

The Baklai approached Bannigus who stood grinning in the background. "Sire, I am grateful for all your help. I would accompany your group and serve you instead."

Kat stared at him. "No this not necessary for you to do. We will accompany you to the river so you may return to your family."

Arrogol walked over to him. "What is your name?"

"I am called Hamrid, sire."

"Excellent. You may come with us and perform chores for us."

Kat frowned at him for his suggestion to Hamrid. "But—"

"Kat if we leave him at the river, he is still without work and unable to support his family. He may work for us until he earns sufficient funds to return home and aid his family."

"But—"

Arrogol smirked at Kat. "You did mention, did you not, something about teams?"

Kat grumped. "I'm hungry. Instead of standing around talking, I suggest we attend the dining hall."

Arrogol roared with laughter. "I agree. Hamrid you may join us."

Kat led the way to the meal building. *He's so annoying. I hope Mouse comes back soon.*

CHAPTER TWENTY-ONE

The travelers, now four in number, consumed their meals, and headed for their rooms. Hamrid insisted on bedding with the horses, as a proper servant should. Kat, stifled a yawn, rolled her eyes, and ignored Bannigus's argument with him. As they rose from the table, Arrogol advised them to meet early on the morrow. "We head for Restin, but the journey is long, so we must make camp for one evening."

Kat groaned to herself. *I hope my cot is softer than the last time*. She headed for the inn and made her way to her room. She fed her animals and call for an apprentice. "Can you clean my dusty leathers overnight and return them to me early on the morrow when you bring my morning meal?"

When he left, she prepared herself for bed, wearing a cool nightdress. She approached her bed, when a husky croak interrupted her. Brade butted at Wink's cage. Kat, curious, walked over and unlatched the door. Brade sauntered in, nudged Wink, who peeped a sleepy chirp at her, and the pair curled up together.

Kat shook her head in amazement. *What an odd pair. I'm glad they're friendly toward each other.* With that as her last thought she slid beneath the covers, curled in a fetal position, and slept.

❦ ❦ ❦

A knock at her door roused Kat from a deep and satisfying sleep. She leaped from the bed and donned a robe, calling to the apprentice, "Come." The young male hung her cleaned and freshened leathers on a hook and placed a tray with her meal and drink on the small table. She thanked him, and requested he arrange for someone to deliver her bags, which she would place outside her door, to the stables,.

She consumed her meal and the huge cup of Karri-san, and then packed and placed her biggest bag in the corridor. Dressed in her leathers, she gazed around the room. Her writings she tucked in the diplo bag. All else she stowed with care in her backpack.

She opened the door to Wink's cage, and Brade sauntered out. "Okay. Time to leave. Up you go." She indicated her shoulder. The kamalona, hurried to the journeyklim plate and cleaned the last few remnants. Licking her nose, she hopped on Kat's arm, scrambled to her shoulder, and curled her long tale around her neck. Kat fed Wink and picking up her small bags set off for the stables.

❦❦❦

"You are most prompt this morrow." Arrogol, without a request for help from Kat, picked up and tossed her saddle on her horse's back. She nodded her thanks and fastened the girth, giving the horse a punch in the stomach to force the animal to exhale. She shook her finger at the horse. *You won't catch me hanging upside down.*

Hamrid, the Baklai, helped her with the bridle, and took over the chore of loading the packhorse. *He's small, but, wow, he's strong.*

Kat pulled the stool up beside her horse, and before Arrogol stepped toward her to help, she glared at him. Instead, Bannigus tossed her up on her saddle. Once seated, with her backpack attached to the side, along with her long bow and quiver, she caught Arrogol's smirk.

He knows I avoided his groping. Don't care, I'm in terrific spirits today.

Hamrid arranged the luggage on the pack animal to create a seat on the top of everything. Kat overheard him insisting to Arrogol he did not require a separate horse.

He's small, so I doubt he weighs much.

They journeyed around the edge of the Merrithan Forest, and the way proved easier and swifter. A pleasant day greeted them, with a fine breeze blowing, and the Pridden star warm at her back. The trail wound through high grasses, which whispered and hissed in the wind. Kat hummed the tune a trio played in the inn the previous evening. *All is well with the world.*

She received a surprise when another singer joined her. The harmony emerged two tones above her own. She glanced around, searching for the singer, and discovered Brade adding her voice to the song. All four riders stopped in surprise.

Arrogol, eyes wide, stared at the kamalona. "Is your blue friend singing?"

Kat, dumbstruck, shut her open mouth with a snap. "I believe she is. What a glorious voice."

Arrogol's baritone began the song again, and, without prompting, Bannigus added his tenor. Not until Kat began to hum the tune as well, did Brade join in. Hamrid added his voice, an astoundingly deep bass. The four began their journey once more, this time amid joyous music.

This is one of the most extraordinary experiences. How does a voice like this come from such a small creature? I'm so alive. And the voices on these men. I only wish I could reproduce this for the game.

Arrogol called for a halt at a small pool amid the grasslands. "We will rest the horses now, and the inn supplied us with a meal. We will not, however, take a lengthy break, I wish us to arrive at the camp area well before dusk."

Kat groaned. "Not dangerous animals?"

"No, but this is the time of the path when heavy rain showers occur most nights. We will be more comfortable if we set up our camp in the full light of this turn." He faced Kat. "I am aware how much comfort means to you."

"Enough," Kat snapped. "I do not appreciate the constant comments about my apparent lack of Rifellan warrior qualities. You are not amusing. On the contrary, you are annoying in the extreme."

Arrogol blinked at her. "You are correct. My comments are no longer valid." He grinned at her, chastened. "Indeed you do possess the qualities of a Rifellan warrior. I apologize."

Kat's mouth dropped open and she gawked at him. *He apologized?* "Who are you, and what have you done with Arrogol?"

Arrogol said nothing, but appeared baffled by her comment.

The moment passed, and all four climbed from their mounts and led them to the pool to drink. A number of jumbo boulders, strewn about the pool, served as temporary seats. Hamrid passed them servings of journeyklim and an unnamed dried meat, not unlike jerky. As they ate, he hastened to fill their canteens.

Bannigus eyed him, amused. "Hamrid, you are not a slave. We can each fill our own canteens. Sit and eat."

The small Baklai bobbed his head and sat to consume his own meal.

Canteens filled, meal demolished, all four mounted and continued to the camp.

❦ ❦ ❦

A few feet inside the entrance to the Torrentine Forest, Hamrid set about the preparation of the camp, under the direction of Bannigus, who, while not a Rifellan warrior, possessed greater experience camping. When Kat camped during her trip through Kaylin, because of the wagon, the amenities proved far superior to what she'd experienced in Rifella to this point. This camp proved different. Hamrid used branches of evergreen trees to cover the roof of a structure and a small lean-to for the horses, and thus ensured a dense covering to keep those inside warm and dry. More branches as the base for their blankets and for Kat's thick padded roll, which she'd purchased from the inn in Brevista, ensured a restful sleep during the night.

I do believe I'll be comfy.

Hamrid appeared to be everywhere, helping with firewood, and cooking a meal for them. He located some eethnaire, and returned from a trip deeper in the forest, bearing three odd looking animals slung from his belt.

They reminded Kat of rabbits with long tails. "What are those?"

"They are called blicks, my Lady, and are excellent for eating."

Later, seated around the camp fire, shielded by the branches of a beneficial and outsized tree, all agreed with Hamrid's assessment of blicks.

Kat peered at Arrogol and detected his eyebrow raised in a question. "You are right. Your decision to bring Hamrid along turned out to be a first rate idea."

Arrogol smiled. "I am satisfied to be right sometimes." He yawned. "We should sleep well this night."

Snuggled on her padded roll and wrapped in cozy blankets, Kat dropped into a deep, dreamless sleep. At some point in the night, she caught the patter of the rain on the leaves overhead. The hypnotic sound soothed her as she drifted back in the waves of half slumber.

I miss home, but I'm happy. I wonder when Mouse...

CHAPTER TWENTY-TWO

The raucous caw of some bird, a thin beam of sunlight in her eyes, and the sputter of the fire as someone added wood to the flames, wakened Kat to a morning smelling of fresh rain and the green odor of pine branches surrounding her.

She stretched and reveled in the pop and crackle of muscles. She needed movement.

A glance around the lean-to, confirmed Bannigus and Hamrid began their day earlier. Arrogol sat on his bedroll and indulged himself in straightening his own spine.

His yawn proved lengthy and loud. "Today will be a good day." He squinted at Kat. "You slept well?"

"I did. The three of you created a most pleasant and restful camp. And none of you snored loud enough to wake me. My thanks."

"You are most welcome. Although you are incorrect, I never snore."

Kat snorted. *Hmph. What about at the hut? The man snored like a pack of tigers.*

Arrogol obviously failed to detect Kat's snort. "We should rise and head for Restin. We must travel through the entire forest, and the going is much slower than via grasslands."

Kat rose and packed her bedding and rolled the pad for storage on the pack animal. She poked her head out the lean-to. "Men. I need a quick wash in the pool. I would appreciate privacy."

They all twitched at her announcement and hastened to busy themselves elsewhere.

Kat strolled to the pool, with a cloth and towel at hand, and proceeded to clean what she referred to, in private, as her FHPPs—face, hands, pits and parts. The pool, not deep enough to swim, allowed only a brief wash. Refreshed, she re-donned her outer leathers, ready for the day's journey to Restin.

They consumed Hamrid's breakfast with gusto, and Kat gulped a mug of Karri-san tea before they packed.

They rode off through the forest, and, when Kat glanced back, she saw only evergreen trees, grass and low bushes. *Excellent, we restored the camp site to the previous pristine quality*

⁂

The Torrentine Forest abounded with a combination of tall deciduous trees, which rustled their broad leaves in the breeze, and evergreens, whose needles rattled as they fell to earth. The star shone above, with outstanding brilliance, bringing light to the forest path, which glowed with old brown needles littering the way. Sparse growth between the trees gave the sense of space and air, and allowed a journey filled with energy.

Bannigus called forward to Kat. "The passage through the Torrentine may be lengthy, but the path is clear, and we shall make Restin well before dusk."

Wonderful. But this forest smells of pine, and fresh earth. She gazed around at her three companions. *They're a good group of men, and they work well together.*

Without the challenge of untidy brush and substantial rocks in their route, the easy rhythm of the horses soon had Kat nodding in her saddle. Warm and comfortable, in a half doze, she remembered sitting in Nick's office back home, with the sunlight pouring in through his windows. She drifted in a half dream imagining herself sitting at her desk doing rough illustrations for new games. A horse's hoof clopped on a stone, and brought her to full consciousness.

Bannigus rode up beside her. "I feared you might fall off your horse, as I thought you slept." He smiled and took a deep breath. "Not far now."

Soon the farms and houses of Restin appeared. The horses quickened their gaits, eager it appeared for food, water and a clean stable.

The stable master, with Hamrid's help, unsaddled and groomed the horses, ushering them to clean bedded stalls, with hay nets full, and water troughs waiting for them. Hamrid requested to sleep at the stable. Arrogol shrugged and nodded his assent.

Kat and the two men departed for their rooms, and took time to freshen up before heading for their evening meal. Conversations at the table lagged as they consumed their food, and Kat excused herself early.

Once in her room, she shook the dust from her leathers in the shower stall, then fed Brade and Wink. Once again, Brade butted at Wink's cage, eager to sleep with her friend. Kat slipped beneath the comforters covering her bed and dropped off soon after she'd fluffed her pillow.

❦ ❦ ❦

Someone banged on her door and woke Kat from a delicious and deep sleep. She sat up gasping. Wink and Brade both leaped around Wink's cage, croaking and cheeping in alarm.

Kat clutched at her stone. *Warm?* "Who's there?"

Arrogol answered. "Kat, you need to rise."

She jumped from her bed, grabbed a robe, and went to the door. "What's wrong?"

"Nothing is wrong, except we must leave at once for the keep. I received a pyrock from Fenneth, and she advised me Murwenna's birth pangs are started. We must leave now so I can be at the Lord's side when the heir is birthed."

"Will we be on time?"

"If we leave now and ride all night, we should be. Dress, pack everything, and an apprentice will be at your door soon to take your baggage to the stable. The innkeeper will bring some light food to the stable for us to consume on the way. "

"I'll be on time."

Kat rushed to secure Wink in her cage and partake the hastiest and coldest shower possible. She dressed, and by the time the apprentice knocked at the door, she was wide awake, with bags packed and ready to leave. She indicated to the assistant the luggage he should convey to the stables, and followed him with Brade on her shoulders and carrying the rest of her luggage. The horses, saddled and bridled by Hamrid, and with only her baggage to be loaded, Kat secured her backpack and Wink's cage to the pommel. Lacking the usual footstool, Bannigus threw her up to her saddle, without hesitation.

The innkeeper handed them each a package of food, and their canteens, filled with hot tea. Without further ado, they wheeled their mounts around and headed for the keep.

Arrogol called to them to make haste. "Ride swiftly, but we must slow to a walk on a regular basis to preserve the energy of our horses. I will lead the way."

The four set off at an easy trot. At specified times, Arrogol slowed his mount to a walk. When they cleared the edges of the Torrenton Forest, with only grasslands before them, Arrogol urged his horse to a canter. Kat much preferred the canter to trotting, even though Pridden saddles appeared closer to western style ones from home. When they broke into a canter, she experienced the ride as if she rocked in an overstuffed chair. *I never did lengthy cross country rides at speed. I wonder how long these beasts can take this?*

"We need to stop for a break." Arrogol slowed his horse to a stop and slid off the saddle. "At a small pool to our left, the horses will need to drink and rest a short while. Eat your food, drink from your canteens, and then refill them with cold water."

All dismounted and brought out their canteens and the food packets.

Kat groaned to herself. *I'm not used to riding for so long at any speed. My butt hurts and I'm chilly. We're not far from the desert here, but I'm kinda cold.*

Arrogol grabbed his mount, which cropped at the grass for a few brief moments while the riders ate and drank their fill. "Time to ride again." He mounted, waited for Bannigus to help Kat mount up, and then wheeled his horse around and set off once again in the direction of the keep. "We will not be long now."

They cantered again and slowed when the outlines of houses surrounding the keep peeked out in the faint light of the crescent moon, and the first tendrils of pink at the horizon. *Oh joy, we're almost back.*

Arrogol slowed his mount, and scanned the area to the east. "A rider approaches from the direction of Haligon."

"Who?"

"I believe, Kat, he is your guide, Mouse. I recognize the horse."

The rider joined them as they slowed to enter the outer gates of the keep. All the horses, including the one ridden by Mouse, sweated and lathered. The sides of the animals heaved as they breathed, and Arrogol dropped to the ground and called to the stable master. "You should call your extra stable hands. All these horses will need walking to cool them down."

Wide-eyed at the timing of the arrival of the five of them, he bobbed his head in respect. "Of course, Praetor Arrogol. Our healer requested I inform you when you appeared, you are wanted by Lord Murwenna."

"My thanks, I will attend my Lord." He turned his head toward Bannigus. "Will you handle everything here?"

"Yes Praetor."

Kat slid down from her saddle and strode over to Mouse. "Where did you go? Someone forgot to tell me Arrogol would accompany me on this initial journey. Why didn't you? Are you alright?"

Mouse held up both his hands as if to ward her off. "Kat, not now. I am beyond weary, and I rode for two turns without rest to be here on time for the entrance of the heir into this world." He rubbed his eyes. "I must seek my bed. I will meet you at this turn's evening meal." He stumbled toward the lodging area. "Oh yes. At the general dining hall." He yawned and continued to his rooms.

Kat took steps toward her own room and stopped. "Bannigus, I'm more weary than I anticipated. Would you please ask someone to bring my bags to my room?"

"I will, but Arrogol did request I do this for you when we arrived."

Grabbing her diplo bag, her backpack with Wink's cage attached, and her long bow and quiver, Kat yawned so broadly her jaw creaked as she moved to the inner rooms of the keep.

I wonder where in hell Mouse got to? He does seem tired, but he's been a good guide 'til now. Is he OK?

CHAPTER TWENTY-THREE

When Kat reached her rooms, she dumped her bags, taking time to put Wink's cage on a dresser. Both Wink and Brade chirped and croaked their desire for food, so she dispensed pyrock treats to both.

Dropping clothes everywhere, she took a quick shower and donned a temporary robe. A knock at the door indicated the arrival of her bag.

"Thank you for my luggage. Are you able to take my leathers to be cleaned?"

"Of course, my Lady." The apprentice studied them and raised an eyebrow. "From the state of your leathers, you rode hard. May I suggest you leave them with the cleaner over this night, and on the morrow, when I return them, I will receive your morning meal order."

"Perfect, thank you."

The young apprentice gathered her leathers and turned to leave.

"I wish to sleep. Would you please arrange for someone to bring a meal for me at midturn. Journeyklim and Karri-san tea will be sufficient. Oh, yes, one more thing. Would you please advise the male called Mouse, I will meet with him for an early evening meal?"

He bobbed his head. "Yes, my Lady. You will not be disturbed until midturn."

"Thank you." *If I dine early, I can enjoy a lengthy sleep tonight.* She closed the door behind him and staggered over to her bed. She snuggled beneath the covers and slept.

❦❦❦

A knock roused her from a deep sleep, so she donned a robe and dragged herself to the door. The young apprentice stood with her meal in hand.

“Terrific. Please put my food on the table, and you can fetch the dishes when I leave my room for the evening meal.”

He acknowledged her with a nod and departed.

As she ate her journeyklim, Brade stuck her nose through the bars of Wink’s cage and gave a hoarse croak. Kat unlatched the door on the cage and Brade scurried across to Kat’s plate of journeyklim, stuck her mouth in, and sucked up some of the mixture.

“Hey you’re being rude. You’re supposed to wait for your own plate.”

Brade gazed up at Kat, a bland expression on her face, assuming animals could summon such expressions. A blob of journeyklim sat on the tip of her nose. A tiny portion of her tongue whipped out, and the blob disappeared.

“Your tongue’s supposed to be poisonous. Can I eat my meal without danger?”

Brade picked her way over to Kat and butted at her hand.

“I guess you think I should know it’s safe for me to eat.” She shrugged. “Fine, I’m hungry.” She dug in her spoon and finished her meal. “Still alive so I guess the food’s OK.” She peered down at Brade as she unlatched the door to Wink’s cage. “You want in? I’m going back to sleep.”

Brade strolled slowly through the door of the cage and curled up beside Wink, who murmured a sleepy chirp. Kat latched the door and stopped only to gulp down Karri-san before she returned to her bed.

Tired.

❦❦❦

A series of gravelly croaks woke Kat, and she raised her head from her pillow to catch Brade attempting to open the door to Wink's cage. Her forelegs, a little too short to do this with ease, woke Wink, who uncurled and, with one eye open, uttered a plaintive peep.

Kat got out of bed, opened the cage door, and Brade bounced out and ran toward her and jumped on her shoulder. The kamalona butted at Kat's jaw and thrummed a scratchy sound at her. "Are you bored?" She twisted her back and hips to loosen cramped muscles. "Well. Time I dressed and went for my evening meal."

She ran cold water over her face at the sink, doffed her nightgown, dressed, and invited Brade back to her shoulder. They left for the community dining hall.

Kat paused at the entrance to seek Mouse and spotted him at a table with Bannigus and Hamrid. Bannigus waved her over.

She sat in the fourth chair and swiveled her head to address them all. "So, are you all recovered from lack of sleep?" Unable to help herself, she yawned.

Bannigus laughed. "Like you appear to, Kat, we all need a bit more rest." He pointed at Hamrid. "You will be happy to be told, Hamrid has been accepted at the keep as an apprentice. In this way, he will be able to repay Arrogol for freeing him, and to return to his family in Baklai with new skills and sufficient funds to ease their burdens."

Kat smiled at Hamrid. "I'm glad for you." *Arrogol did a fine thing insisting he come with us.* She faced Mouse. "You are aware Arrogol and Bannigus guided me on the first tour of Rifella because you were not available? The big question is, where were you?"

Mouse ducked his head. "I thought my reasons were important at the time, but they changed to simple duties I needed to perform. Had I known how trivial, I would not have left." He coughed.

Mouse is lying. What is he up to? Perhaps this means he senses he cannot speak freely in front of Bannigus and Hamrid.

He stared at her shoulder. "I see you obtained a kamalona. How very unusual."

"She is called Brade, and she chose me. I guess this means I and my companions are safe from her abilities." *Changing the subject. There's no question, he's lying. Why?*

Their food arrived and all conversation ceased. The master of the kitchen approached their table. "My Lady and Sires, our apologies for the simple fare. With a celebration in the offing, we are keeping all our finest victuals to be served later."

This is simple fare? "I find your dishes excellent in both flavor and quantity. I enjoy gornog stew every time I consume some." She ate another spoonful and moaned in pleasure.

The master of the kitchen thanked her and brought four additional mugs of near-ale to the table.

As they raised their mugs to drink, a young man rushed into the hall, excited and shouting. "The heir is here. The heir is here."

Soon the entire hall buzzed with chatter and happy conversation, and diners moved from table to table discussing the thrilling news of Rifella's new male heir.

As the volume of noise rose in the hall, Kat managed a series of discrete burps. *Gornog meat always fills me with gas, and, as usual, I ate too much.*

Another apprentice entered and called for the attention of the diners. "We are pleased to announce a winner of the lottery." The din decreased and all eyes turned toward the young man. "The Lady Kat is the one who predicted with accuracy, the time and turn of the heir's birth."

Everyone scanned the room for the lucky winner, and, after a push from Mouse, Kat stood and acknowledged her achievement, while the entire crowd cheered and whistled and stamped their feet.

The apprentice made a further announcement. "The celebration will be held in two turns hence, and Lady Kat will receive her winning chits during the festivities." More cheering followed this announcement. "Lord Murwenna urges you all to be rested for the feasting, singing, and dancing which will take place. Many of our fellow Rifellans are bound for the keep to join in, and we urge you to welcome them."

Conversation buzzed again, and a number of Rifellans approached Kat to congratulate her on her win.

When the crowd in front of her thinned, she stood. "Bannigus and Hamrid, please excuse me, I am still weary and need more sleep. Mouse, I will join you for the morning meal on the morrow."

"I appreciate this Kat. I too am still weary but need to complete a number of chores before I attend my bed. I will meet with you on the morrow."

So what did he do?

⚘ ⚘ ⚘

Kate woke in the morning to the sound of horses' hooves and the buzz of conversation from many people. *They're arriving for the celebration. When Rifellans throw a party, they go all out.*

The previous night, Kat forgot to open Wink's cage to give Brade access, but, she appeared to enjoy being about with all the sounds and odors of people arriving from all over Pridden. As Kat rose from the bed, Brade leaped to her shoulder and croaked and butted. The excited kamalona crawled from should to shoulder, urging Kat to leave her room.

Kat raised an eyebrow at Brade. “Down, little one, I have to get ready.” Brade leaped to the dresser and butted at Wink’s cage. *Odd, she almost seems to understand what I want from her.*

After a quick wash, Kat dressed in her culotte-type skirt and a blouse which Brith designed for her. A knock at the door, and when Kat called “Come.” the young apprentice from the previous evening, entered, carrying her fresh, clean leathers.

“Thank you. I do not need to give you an order for the morning meal, as I’ll be joining someone in the communal hall instead.”

He nodded his head and exited.

After he left, Kat walked over to her dresser, leaned toward Brade, and indicated her shoulder. The blue creature leaped to her favorite perch and anchored her tail around Kat’s neck.

⚘ ⚘ ⚘

When Kat entered the hall, Mouse, seated in a far corner, waved her over.

“Good morrow, Kat. I ordered food for you and plenty of Karri-san tea. I suspect you may need extra due to the prevalence of Rifellans, with their increased output of pheromones, who will be arriving throughout the next few turns.”

“Good morrow to you too, Mouse. Thank you for placing my order. So are you going to tell me what you left Rifella for?”

“Kat, your curiosity is quite unfounded. I needed to complete some routine items I neglected to attend to. Now is not the time to discuss this. We need to prepare far too much to indulge in idle conversation."

Kat squinted at him. *What's going on? He's avoiding answering.* "What's so urgent that needs our attention now?"

"First, we must plan our route from Rifella. With the celebration tomorrow, and our need to prepare for our lengthy journey to Glowen, we need to accomplish much."

"Fine. Let's take care of the travel route thing now."

"Are you finished your meal?"

She nodded.

"We will first advise Fenneth we are both returned, so she may pass the message on to Murwenna. After visiting Fenneth, we will go to your rooms and order tea to be sent. I possess all the maps we will need and lists of what we should pack. Remember, we will not be returning to the keep after this journey, but will make for Glowen instead."

He stood and picked up two bags of maps, and they left to call on Fenneth.

The meeting was brief, as the healer was much occupied with the Lord and her new heir. "I will pass this information to Lord Murwenna, and I will no doubt find additional items to supply to you, before you leave on the balance of your journey through Rifella."

❦ ❦ ❦

Mouse spread his maps over the table in Kat's room. Fresh cups of tea and some delicacies sat on the side.

Pouring over the documents, he pointed out the route to her. "We head first to Haligon, which contains the mines of the silver and gold metal our artisans use for their jewelry. When we leave, we will take the long trek via Rashnig, down to Farratown, and we will end our journey at the shipyards of Orkanna Harbor."

"I've been told about Rifella's harbor?"

"Rifella's harbor is the largest of the three in Pridden, and this is fortunate because of Rifella's standing in Pridden. This is a stable land, because their warriors are raised within strong customs of loyalty. All the lands, with the possible exception of Morden, understand they benefit from Rifella's substantial contingent of warriors, many of whom travel to other lands as hired guards." Mouse tapped on the map at the location of the harbor.

I never realized how strong Mouse's hands look. But they're not calloused like farm workers.

He continued on. "Rifellan warriors are strong and capable and plagued by few enemies."

"They're certainly strong and appear to be well-respected for who they are."

"They hire themselves to other lands, but Rifellan codes prevent them from interfering in disputes between lands, with the exception of Baklai. In return for Baklai's horses, they swore to protect the people. Elsewhere they only are involved when they have specific contracts. Most of the time, only the rulers of each land can afford them, and in these cases, they are sworn to protect the rulers, not the rest of the population. Unless, once again, these are part of their contracted duties."

"Does this system work?"

"Yes. Rifellans are such strong men and women, if they interfered in other lands, their very presence might curtail the freedoms of all the lands in Pridden. They are people of honor, Kat."

"They are unusual people." She leaned back in her chair and stretched her spine. "So what do we do in… Orkanna? A harbor you said?"

"We board a ship and sail for Glowen."

Oh no. Upchuck city. Not my favorite way to travel.

CHAPTER TWENTY-FOUR

Mouse agreed to meet Kat for the evening meal, and departed to complete some unknown chores, while Kat took the opportunity to enjoy some exercise by walking.

She was not ready to partake of a full midturn meal, but rather than get distracted by weapons or jewelry, she stuck to the area with food stalls. Aromas of fish cooked with unusual spices attracted her to a stall selling pieces of fried fish. They were served in a small parchment-like cup, and smothered in a dark brown sauce, which reminded her of lemon. Her mouth watered from the smell of the fish, but she only purchased a small serving. She paid with a chit given to her by Fenneth.

After a pleasant stroll in the area, she returned to her room, determined to complete some writing. Having eaten her fill of snacks at the stalls near the inn, she wanted only some Karri-san, and she tugged on the tassel in the corner to place an order.

As it arrived, she removed her journal pages and her pen and ink from her diplo bag, and began to add the happenings of the past couple of days to the parchment. In the middle of adding the information about the game of guessing the turn of the heir's birth, Kat paused, thinking about words. She'd missed a number of days of adding unique words to her list. *Wait a minute. Behemoth. If I remember correctly, the word referred to a monster of considerable size.* She wrote "behemoth" on the parchment. *Today this represents something monstrous—not of necessity a creature.*

Kat drank the last of her cup of Karri-san, now cold, and sat back and scratched her neck. Something grunted in her ear. "Sorry, Brade, but the end of your tail tickled me." Her windows were open a crack, but the air smelled stale. She rose from her chair at the same time as a knock came at her door. "Who is it?"

"Mouse. I am about to go for the evening meal."

"Wow, so quickly? Can you find us a table, and I'll join you soon? I need to freshen up a bit."

"I will do so."

Kat pointed at the table and peered at Brade. "Off. I need to dress for my dinner."

Brade released her tail, and jumped from Kat's shoulder and landed on the dresser. Hurrying in the direction of the personal, Kat caught Brade as she butted at Wink's cage and croaked at the pyrock. She paused to unlatch the door and allow her access to her friend.

She washed her face again, scrubbed the smell of fish from her hands, and, applied a minimal amount of makeup, then dressed in another Brith-made chocolate brown split skirt and a loose cream blouse. *I hope I am properly dressed, though the celebration will not begin until tomorrow.*

⚘ ⚘ ⚘

At the entrance to the communal hall, Kat scanned the room and glimpsed, to her delight, Irina and Bardu, the Praetor from Kaylin. They beckoned to her, and she hastened over to meet them. On the way, she passed Mouse, sitting by himself. "Come Mouse, join us."

He frowned, but, with reluctance, followed her to Bardu's table.

Kat hurried to Irina and hugged her, and then faced Bardu. "I'm so glad to meet you both again." She hugged Bardu.

Kat saw Mouse twitch an eyebrow at the Bardu hug.

"Mouse, these are my friends, Irina and Bardu. He is Praetor with Lord Eduardo's guards."

Mouse bobbed his head at them. "Lady Irina, we are well met." He turned to Bardu and did the weird man hand-clasp thing, which Kat had noticed seemed common among Rifellan males. "Praetor Bardu, we meet again."

Kat was familiar with the Rifella male version of a hand shake, which she'd inspected a number of times before. *Wish I could figure out how they do that.*

They all sat, and a serving woman approached the table to receive their orders.

As the woman left, Kat questioned Mouse and Bardu. "You said you met each other before. When?"

Mouse replied first. "I joined Bardu and his men when Drainin and the assassins in Kaylin captured you."

"Now I remember. After the fighting, right?"

Mouse shrugged.

Their meals arrived at the table, and they dug in. As they ate, Kat told them about her travels in Shendea, and those in Rifella.

Bardu asked about their visit to Pakanna. "Have any of the residents prepared new designs in armor?"

"I couldn't tell, and Mouse wasn't with me. He attended business elsewhere." She continued with her tale of the current journey. "The Great Hellesmouth proved the most extraordinary place I've traveled through. Those crosa are horrid. No wonder Rifella produces such excellent soldiers and guards. Your land is filled with difficult terrain and challenging plants and animals."

Bardu chuckled. "We do find most of the other lands quite tame in comparison."

Kat laughed, and grabbed the attention of a passing serving person. "I forgot to order Karri-san, would you please bring me some now?"

The young man scurried off.

Kat caught Irina as she eyed Bardu and made a subtle motion with her head toward Mouse.

Bardu acknowledged her with a slight nod of agreement. "Mouse. I am glad I encountered you. I would much appreciate your opinion on a new type of saddle my men and I designed. We Rifellans ride for long hours when patrolling, and some discomfort from our saddles is a constant challenge. Would you agree to come and view my design now?"

"Lady Kat and I are both spending many hours in the saddle, so if you can help with such a situation, I am most anxious to inspect your design."

He and Bardu excused themselves and departed from the hall.

Kat glanced at Irina. "Why are you smiling?"

"I am always grateful when Bardu understands my subtle hints. I wished him to depart with Mouse and allow us the opportunity to talk."

"Why? Is something wrong?"

"On the contrary. You are drinking less Karri-san these days. In Kaylin, you would have consumed three cups by now, yet you forgot to order, and now you drink only one."

"I'm aware I'm drinking less, and I wonder if the effect is cumulative?"

"I believe, Kat, you are becoming more used to Rifellans and our pheromones. You hugged Bardu, and would never do such a thing in Kaylin." Irina shrugged. "I suspect this is due to encountering Rifellans more often than in Kaylin. We are protectors for most of Pridden, including parts of southern Morden, although the Thane is not aware of our presence in the south of his land. Galdin possesses his own assassins, and does not wish us within his domain, so the only area where Rifellans are absent is the north of Morden. Elsewhere?" She shrugged again.

"So you think I'm reacting less to Rifellans because I'm in their company so often?"

"Yes. Tell me do you often use the distilled Karri-san I gave you?"

Kat gazed up at the ceiling, her forehead twisted, thinking. "Now I consider this, no. Not since my early days in Shendea."

"Excellent. A time might come, Kat, when you no longer need the benefits of Karri-san."

"If this does happen, this will be one less thing to worry about." She smiled and absentmindedly lifted her cup and drank. "By the way, I need your help."

"With what?"

"Well, the people of the keep played this game to guess the turn and time of the birth of the heir, and…well, I won the whole thing."

"How fortunate."

"No, Irina, you don't understand. I won a huge number of chits, which I can't use. What can I do with them?"

Irina rubbed her forehead. "Perhaps I can help with a suggestion. Because of our reputation for protection in other lands, many people from southern Morden and from Baklai seek refuge here. The challenges are, most of them are not equipped to earn decent wages because they are not blessed with many skills. As you can imagine, since our own people are well trained in the tending of horses, and farming, we possess little need for these, which are the only abilities the refugees share."

"I understand. We met a Baklai by the name of Hamrid, and he was forced to sell himself to a northern Morden, because his family were unable to support themselves and suffered from lack of food and adequate housing. Arrogol arranged an apprenticeship for him, so when he is trained, he will be able to help his family."

"Yes indeed." Irina patted Kat's hand on the table. "So, why not donate your chits to establish a center where such people are able to learn skills which are marketable anywhere?"

Kat clapped her hands in delight. "Irina. What a fantastic idea. I'll announce this when they award my prize. Thank you. Your idea is brilliant."

"You are most welcome." She gave Kat a mischievous smile. "I also need to impart some news which you may view as pleasant."

"I'm always open to happy news."

"My sibling, Liandock, will be with us on the morrow."

"He will?" Kat could feel heat creeping up her neck and face. "I'll be delighted to see him again. The stone he gave me proved invaluable, many times over."

Irina grinned. "From your color I suspect you will wish to discuss more than your stone."

Kat's face was on fire. "Uh, yes… I've missed seeing him. Um…and, I want to find out if he sent Shade to me."

"Shade? Who is Shade?"

"When I traveled in Shendea, a huge cat, black as pitch, decided to accompany me on my journey. No one else seemed to glimpse her, but she acted as my protector against a cathnog, and in some other situations. Her eyes displayed the color of my stone." Kat pulled her necklace from around her throat. "The exact same color, Irina." She tucked the pendant back under her clothes. "Before we left Shendea, I remained unwell because I had been bitten by a syeth, and my stone lacked luster as well. I needed to rest, and Shade lay beside me on my bed. As I lay there, too ill to move much, she gradually became transparent. When she disappeared, my stone, once again regained the deep emerald color, and my health had been restored." Kat's chest tightened when she thought of the loss of Shade. "I'm almost sure Liandock sent her to me."

"What an extraordinary tale. I do not know if my sibling manifested your cat. He may not understand this himself. He often manages to create things which appear to be beyond his ken, and he is unaware of how or why this happens. You should ask him when you speak to him."

Not the only thing I'll ask him. I'm dying to see him. "I will." Kat yawned. "I'm ready for my bed. From what I understand, the celebration on the morrow will be quite exciting, and I plan to be well-rested."

They rose, and, as they reached the entrance to the hall, Bardu and Mouse returned from the stables.

Mouse walked over to Kat. "You must experience the saddle Bardu designed. We will be much more comfortable in our travels. I ordered them for us, and I hope they will be ready when we leave in two or three turns."

Over Mouse's shoulder, Kat caught Bardu winking at Irina. "I'm most grateful, Bardu. Certain parts of my anatomy complain to me about the length of time we spend in our saddles."

"I am pleased to be of service, Kat." He turned to Irina. "Mate of mine, Arrogol and Olwyn invited us to stay at their home. We would be discourteous to linger here longer. Mouse, we shall meet with you on the morrow, perhaps for the midturn meal, but for certain for the celebrations after midturn."

They parted, and Mouse, accompanied by Kat, set off toward their rooms. "Kat, I shall meet you for the midturn meal. I suspect I may wish to skip the morning one. I need sleep more than food."

"Me too, Mouse. Yes to the midturn meal." She arrived at her room, unlocked the door and entered, as Mouse opened his own door across the hall.

Kat yawned again as she locked her door behind her.

Oh joy, Liandock's arriving tomorrow? I wonder what time?

CHAPTER TWENTY-FIVE

Kat entered her room, and fed Brade and Wink who demanded food.

She undressed, and removed a loose night dress from her closet, and made for the personal. *I want a luxurious warm shower which will help me sleep well.* In a guest room for an important person, the amenities at the keep provided particular luxury. The washing liquid, scented with a type of lavender, prompted Kat to take her time. Rinsing with a gentle shower left her with soft, smooth skin. On the counter of the facial basin, she squirted out a handful of body cream and massaged the lotion over her entire body. *I wonder what this is made from? No matter — the touch is marvelous and the scent reminds me of jasmine.*

Slipping the light night dress over her head, she wandered over to her bed and relaxed beneath the covers. She smiled to herself. *Tomorrow.*

In the middle of a yawn, a soft knock at her door, roused her from her half-sleep. She tiptoed to the door. "Yes, who's there?"

The voice on the other side reminded her of the purr of a lion. "A manipulator of metals and a blender of jewels."

Kat threw open the door. "Liandock." She leaped at him, wrapping her legs around his waist.

"Kat. I believe we should enter your room before we indulge ourselves." He laughed aloud and, carrying her clasped to him, moved into the room.

He reached out with his left leg, clad in laced-up leather boots and kicked the door shut behind him.

She rubbed her nose in his neck and breathed in the clean scent of him. The crisp musk of warm male combined with Rifellan pheromones lit the fire within her. “Ahh. I’m so glad you’re here. At last.”

“I did not expect such an enthusiastic welcome.” He licked her mouth and gently bit her lower lip.

She felt his hard body against her and she reacted without prompting, and flashed with heat. She squirmed against him, hot with desire.

“Slow down, woman. I would prefer you wait for me to join you in this pleasuring.”

“You’re asking me to wait when I’ve been without you for so long?”

“Yes. I wish us to enjoy a lengthy experience.” He loosened her legs from his waist and deposited her on the bed. He moved to a chair at her dresser, sat, and undid the laces of his boots. He removed them from his feet with painstaking deliberation.

Liandock stood and took off his leather jerkin and the golden hair of his chest almost glittered in the dim light of the room.

Oh glory, he’s doing a striptease for me. Whew.

At last, he dropped the leather kilt to the floor and stood, like a Michelangelo carving, exhibiting his entire magnificent body for her. He was not a small man.

He strode over to her, lifted her to her feet and pulled the night dress from her body.

They took each other in pleasure, ebbing and flowing, joined together in a dance of exquisite sensations, of heat and light, and finally soaring with ecstasy to the pinnacle of joyous gratification. Drained, they lay spread out and exhausted.

As perspiration evaporated, Kat shivered in the sudden cold.

"Sit, my Kat."

He pulled back the covers, laid her in the bed, and climbed in beside her, pulling the covers over both of them.

Kat mumbled as she cuddled into his warm body. "Good, the wet spot's on the outside."

Startled, Liandock roared with laughter. "You do say the oddest things."

He perhaps said more, but Kat slept.

❦ ❦ ❦

A heavy log pressed down on her chest, a raucous bird call outside the window, croaks and peeps from Wink's cage, and a knock at the door woke Kat in the morning.

The log turned out to be Liandock's arm, so she slid from under him, grabbed a robe and went to the door. "Yes, who's outside?"

"I am the apprentice for your room, Lady Kat. I wish to learn what you would prefer for your morning meal?"

"Thank you for wakening me. Would you please bring journeyklim for… um… for three, and tea to serve four."

"I will, my lady, and will return soon."

Liandock peered at her from the mound of covers, and yawned so broadly he did, indeed, resemble a lion. "What is happening?"

"You look so cozy surrounded by those covers, but now the time has arrived for you to remove yourself from my bed. I ordered a morning meal for us, but I would prefer we refrain from being viewed naked when our food arrives."

"I will remove my clothes elsewhere and wait until our meal is delivered." He left the bed, gathered his leathers and took them to the personal. He closed the door.

Within minutes, a knock signaled the arrival of their food. Kat hastened to straighten the bed clothes, and made space on the table for their meal. *The bed appears innocent enough, but the entire room has the scent of hot sex.* She blushed at her own thoughts.

Kat opened the door to allow the young apprentice access, and he deposited the tray with three plates of journeyklim and a substantial pot of tea with four cups.

Kat thanked him as she escorted him out the door.

Liandock exited the personal, wearing only his kilt, and settled in a chair at the table. "Why do you order three plates of journeyklim, and why four cups?"

"I preferred not to have rumors flying around the keep that I entertained someone here last evening. Perhaps they'll think I'm having a meeting."

"I suspected you might wish to keep our pleasure to yourself. We Rifellans do not require a need to hide our enjoyments, but I am aware you prefer to be private."

Kat patted him on the arm. "Thank you, Liandock. I appreciate your consideration. Oh, and the third plate is for Brade."

"Brade?"

Kat stood and walked over to Wink's cage, and unlatched the door.

Brade, released from captivity, rushed to the table and dipped her mouth into the third plate of journeyklim. At the same time, Liandock jumped from his chair and backed away from his meal. Brade raised her head and peered at him. She gave a rusty croak and dropped her mouth back to her plate of food.

Liandock shook his head and rolled his eyes at Kat. "Of all the things you do, I am not surprised you would attract a kamelona. I assume, since the creature is bonded to you, I am safe from its considerable defenses? This, I gather, is Brade?"

"Yes, you're safe because she likes me." Kat tried hard to suppress a chuckle. "She does not expect you to be a threat to me." Kat reached in the cage and extracted her furry friend. "My pyrock is named Wink." Kat fed the little creature a couple of pyrock treats, and as soon as Wink consumed them, she rolled back into a furry ball, dropped off to sleep and was soon redeposited in her little bed.

Kat continued her meal, and Liandock questioned her about her travels in Shendea and the limited journey she completed in Rifella. She covered the high points. "I must ask you something. While in Shendea, I received a visit from a gorgeous black cat with brilliant emerald green eyes. I called her Shade. What was odd about her is she remained invisible to others, except animals, but she defended me against a cathnog, and later attempted to come to my rescue from the Morden Assassins. She remained with me throughout my stay in Shendea. Did you send her to me?"

"Strange. A few times I experienced dreams you faced danger, but when I woke each morrow after a dream, I did not fear for you but rested at peace. I assumed they were only dreams."

"Liandock, one more thing. A short time before we left Shendea, I received a bite from a syeth, and continued to be most unwell despite drinking at least two vials of antidote. On my last night I discovered my stone to be lackluster, the color faded almost to a pale green. I remembered how you told me to replenish the brilliance to the stone." *Good grief,*

I'm blushing. "However, I suffered so much, I couldn't summon up the energy. I lay down to rest, and Shade joined me. As she stretched out beside me she began to fade from my sight. By the time she disappeared, my stone shone as bright as a star again and I regained my health and my energy. This is why I ask if you sent her."

"I am not aware of doing so, and I cannot tell you what other abilities your stone might possess."

They spoke some more, enjoying each other's company, when Kat glanced out the window and realized the midturn must be approaching. "I've got to shower and begin to prepare for the celebration. I did mention I might join Mouse for the midturn meal."

"I shall join you in the shower. I took a room at the keep because I arrived after dark the previous turn. I would not, in deference to my hosts, arrive at Arrogol and Olwyn's home at such a late hour. But I cannot return to my room smelling of my Lady Kat."

"Fine. I'll race you for the shower."

"No need to race. I shall walk without haste and still catch you." He chuckled.

Once in the shower, with a spongy type cloth filled with soapy suds, Kat washed Liandock's back, and experienced heat building in her body.

He took the sponge from her and washed her breasts and dropped his hand between her thighs. She shivered with desire, and snatched the cloth from him, before she became unable to wait.

Sponge in hand, she turned him and soaped his gorgeous chest, and worked her way down to her favorite place, which now stood proudly at attention.

He groaned and she plied the cloth with more vigor, when a loud knock at the door startled them.

All desire vanished. *I hope I locked the door.*

The knock came again. *Damn.* Kat stuck her head out the personal door and called out. “Um, who… um who is it?”

“Mouse. I am here to escort you to the midturn meal. Bardu and Irina will obtain a table for us.”

“Oh, Mouse. Well, um…I’m not quite ready. I’ll meet you at the hall. I need time to dress.”

“Fine.” She caught the sound of his footsteps retreating.

“Liandock I must leave. No time for a little extra dessert.”

“No matter, I will meet you later at the celebration.” He kissed her, exited the personal, dried himself, and dressed in his leathers. Leaving, he paused at the door, and turned to face her. “Relax Kat, your Mouse does not know I was here.”

Kat gulped. *He’s probably right. Anyway, why do I care if Mouse knows?* She dried herself and put her pendant back on. The emerald glowed with an almost blinding brilliance.

She stared at herself in the mirror.

And come to think of it, why does Liandock think I care if Mouse knows.

CHAPTER TWENTY-SIX

After Liandock left for his room, Kat completed her shower, and now pink, clean and cocooned in the bouquet of the jasmine lotion, she dressed in another Brith-manufactured skirt of brilliant yellow. She topped the skirt with a cream-colored wispy blouse, with threads of emerald running through the cloth. She loved the colors and until now, had not encountered an opportunity to wear the outfit.

The din of laughter and excited conversation enveloped her well before she approached the community hall. Scanning the room, she glimpsed Irina and Bardu motioning her over to a table for eight. She hurried to meet them. Mouse also sat waiting for her, and, as she approached, Olwyn and Arrogol joined them.

Arrogol gave a mock bow. "Lady Kat, we meet again."

Olwyn grinned at her. "Your outfit is most 'tasteful' Kat."

"Thank you. Brith, the seamstress at Eduardo's keep, sewed this. She is almost a magician when she creates clothes." *Is she mocking me? Arrogol said she respects me. She's got a funny way of showing this.*

Irina's face broke into a smile, and Kat turned as Liandock loped toward them. Her breath caught in her throat. The wild mass of untamed blonde hair, and the caramel-colored leather kilt, which appeared softer than the ones she'd seen him in before, dazzled her senses. His deep cream shirt flowed as he moved, and clung to his body, revealing the muscles of his chest. Loose sleeves, gathered below his elbows, draped from his shoulders.

Kat stared at him. *What is it about him that affects me so?*

They all stood, and Irina rushed from her seat to hug her sibling. “Brother mine.”

He kissed her affectionately on both cheeks, and then turned to Bardu and hand clasped with him. Next, he transferred his attention to Olwyn, whom he kissed chastely on one cheek. Last, he executed the handshake thing with Arrogol.

“Are you acquainted with Mouse?” Arrogol pointed at Kat’s guide.

“I am indeed.” He performed the Rifellan handshake with Mouse. “We met before you and Lady Kat departed for Shendea.”

At last he faced her. “Lady Kat.” He took her hand, turned it over and kissed her palm.

This is more than pheromones or sex. Every time I’m with him, I’m a puddle of emotions. What is odd is I have no desire to control him. “Liandock.” She shivered with her reaction to him. The rest of the world faded, and time stretched.

She shook her head and became aware of her surroundings. Irina grinned at her, and Olwyn, both eyebrows raised, cocked her head at Kat. Only Bardu, Arrogol and Mouse, discussing some unimportant detail, failed to spot what passed between Kat and the delicious Metal-Master.

She pulled her hand from his, as a number of serving women and men circulated among them, gathering food orders. The party seated themselves, and Liandock sat beside her.

Olwyn took the seat on her other side. “Kat, you appear to be acquainted with Liandock?”

“Err… yes. We met in Kaylin and he created some beautiful jewelry for me.” Kat pushed back her chair, and displayed her foot, bearing the silver anklet with the green gem. "I love the color, and the stone matches a pendant I wear." She moved her seat back to the table.

"I find more to you than I first thought."

Kat raised an eyebrow. "Few people understand the real me, Olwyn."

Olwyn nodded and grinned. She reached over and patted Kat's hand, who turned to face her, startled by the gesture.

The group completed their meal, and sat conversing and drinking tea, when a series of horns executing a wild allegro shattered the normal commotion. The horns rose to a crescendo and then lapsed into silence. Two men appeared to announce the beginning of the celebration in the enormous adjacent room.

As they moved to the other room, Kat stopped Olwyn. "May I ask a favor of you and Arrogol, Olwyn?"

"A favor? What kind of favor?"

"I won the chits in the game about the time and turn of the birthing of the heir."

"You are most fortunate."

"I know, but I can't make use of them, and Irina suggested I donate them to create an education center for Baklai and southern Mordens who, in order to survive, were forced to leave their lands."

"An excellent idea. What is the problem?"

"Olwyn, I'll not be here to bring the idea to fruition. Will you and Arrogol oversee the project? Please?"

Olwyn stopped and stared at Kat. "I suspect Arrogol will be pleased to agree. We will do it."

"Thank you so much, I will rest easier knowing the chits are put to good use."

Kat felt a hand grab hers, but she smiled as she realized Liandock was leading her to the celebration room.

By the time everyone entered the celebration hall, the heralds continued their narrative. "The ceremony will begin with the presentation of the heir." The largest herald blew on his horn again. "Once Lord Murwenna and the heir leave the chamber, we will announce the winner of the game. The celebrations will begin in earnest, with jugglers and musicians, singers and acrobats presenting their talents. Each man and woman will display their artistic efforts for your enjoyment. The celebration is expected to occur over two full turns."

During his announcement, the celebrants made their way to tables and seats around the outer ring of the chamber and jostled for positions beside friends, ready and waiting for the festivities to begin. Once again, Olwyn took the chair beside Kat. Disappointed because Liandock now sat across the table beside his sibling, Kat discovered Mouse on her other side. *At least I've someone to talk to. Wonder if I can persuade Mouse to tell me where he went?*

The uproar of conversation, quieted when gentle music drifted from the corner of the room. Murwenna entered, with Fenneth at her side, pushing the heir in a wheeled cradle. They circled the chamber, allowing all to view the beautiful blond baby.

Olwyn beamed with pride. "Arrogol produced a fine heir. He will also produce for me a number of excellent progeny who will carry on the duties of our two houses."

Once Murwenna and Fenneth left, another man entered carrying a huge bowl filled with the chits of the participants of the game. Although the chit was already drawn, the man recreated the scene, and announced Kat as the winner.

Invited up to the makeshift stage, the herald presented Kat with the bowl of chits, amid much cheering and whistling.

Nervously, Kat motioned for quiet. Her insides were quaking and she cleared her throat. "My thanks to all. This is such a generous thing you've done, and I'm most grateful. However, I'm not one who's in need, and many others are." *Boy, I hope I pull this off. I should have practiced my adlibs.* "I consulted with friends, and I wish to make a donation of this bounty to build a place of education. This is for those from other lands who are without skills to support them and their families. At this place, my hope is, they will gain the abilities necessary to survive and flourish." She swallowed again, feeling almost shaky.

People began to cheer, and she held up her hand again. *I think this is the first time I haven't blundered. They're really pleased.* "Since I cannot be available to oversee the construction, I have asked Praetor Arrogol and Lady Olwyn if they will perform this task on my behalf."

The crowd called and whistled with wild abandon as Arrogol and Olwyn made their way to the stage. Olwyn replied on their behalf. "Our thanks to you, Lady Kat, for your generosity." Kat passed her the huge bowl of chits, desperately hoping she wouldn't drop it. "Arrogol and I will be most willing to oversee this project."

When they returned to the table, Olwyn whispered in Kat's ear. "You depart from the woman I, in error, judged you to be. My apologies for my rudeness after your sampling of Arrogol, although you are indeed worthy of him. I am most fortunate your desires lie elsewhere."

Kat still shaking from her time on the stage, was disconcerted. *Does she know that Liandock and I...?* Kat took a hasty sip of the near-ale in front of her.

Soon, the sound level increased to the point where normal conversation became impossible, and laughter and cheering filled the chamber. Kat was only too pleased she was no longer the center of attention. The crowd became wilder, as musicians and acrobats and singers, moved across the stage, each entertaining the celebrants.

"Wow, Mouse, did you see what the acrobat wearing blue did? How did he managed to bend his body like that?"

The viewers left their seats to meet with other friends who were stationed outside Rifella. Kat stood and along with many others, filled a plate from tables of food and picked up two mugs of near-ale from serving counters throughout the room. Armed with food and drink, she returned to her seat beside Mouse. "I brought you a mug of near-ale. I think the one I drank before was really yours."

Mouse chuckled. "It was, Kat. But, you appeared to need it."

I finally did blunder. Oh, well. Mouse didn't seem annoyed. "Sorry, Mouse."

Eating and drinking and enjoying the variety of entertainment, the ruckus increased, and the temperature in the chamber continued to climb.

A musical group consisting of six tall blond Rifellan males took the stage and played a tune with a wild, pounding, demanding beat. Rifellan men reached for their women and demonstrated an extraordinary sensual dance, striking the floor with their feet in time to the music. The dance consisted of males and females, caressing each other, gyrating to the boisterous sounds, grinding their hips against each other and whirling in pairs around the room. Many participants became so involved in the physical play, they disappeared in side halls, only to reappear later, having experienced, Kat assumed, intense satisfaction.

Before she managed a breath, Liandock captured her hand and led her to join the melee. He pulled Kat toward him and placing his hands on her buttocks brought her hard against him. Pressed against her, he moved his hips to the rhythm of the music. Aware she danced in full public view, Kat's eyes darted around the room, and, caught Mouse as he eyed her with extreme curiosity. "Liandock stop, I can't control myself."

Despite his eyes glassy from lust, he stopped. "I need you." He glanced around. "But not here." He grabbed her hand. "We will attend your quarters."

They ran from the hall toward her waiting room. She fumbled with the key, but managed to open her door and, once they'd entered, slammed the thing shut behind her.

"I'm sticky and sweaty, and I'm sure I'm stinky."

He growled at her. "Your scent is like a woman who is… ready." He licked her shoulder and stripped her blouse from her. "Mmm. Salty. You are even seasoned and ready for devouring."

They tore at each other's clothes, throwing them on the floor in their haste. He swept the table clear, laid her on the surface, and without waiting they joined in the timeless dance of male and female, riding to the peak of pleasure.

He reached and lifted her from the table. "I believe you are now ready for a shower. I suspect you would prefer to return to your guide without the aroma of us on each other."

He headed for the personal. Kat followed, hoping for another session.

In the shower, she began to soap him all over to encourage him. The air filled with need and sex. *I could do this again and again.* She moved her hips against him.

"Enough woman. I am a strong man, but lack of sleep and much expenditure of energy, advises me I need to recoup for a later battle."

"Oh."

"Perhaps, my greedy Kat, you need a group to satisfy you."

Kat stared at him, horrified. "What?"

He began to laugh. "A joke, only a joke. The only group you and I need is each other."

Do all these men speak of groups and teams? She gave a dramatic sigh. "We should return to the celebration. I found the dance so incredible. Do you Rifellans often indulge in such uninhibited ways?"

"Not often, and most of the time mated couples do not take part. The dance is a form of practice for future bonding."

They finished showering, and dressed to return to the chamber.

Did I fall under the spell of Rifellan pheromones, or only Liandock?

CHAPTER TWENTY-SEVEN

The celebrations, the entertainment, and the cacophony of sounds continued on. Dancers whirled around the room, and paused every so often to grab food on the fly from the enormous buffet. The celebrants sat down to rest for longer periods, and people began to take their leave, two or three at a time.

Murwenna and the heir appeared for another round of the chamber prior to the evening meal of the second turn of the celebration. Their appearance breathed additional life into the festivities, although the mating dance did not reoccur.

Kat yawned. "I believe I need sleep."

Irina laughed at her. "Of course you do. The majority of Rifellans who will continue to celebrate until the morrow are the young. Bardu and I are bonded and require no need to continue to play young mating games. Olwyn and Arrogol left for their home moments ago. We will be joining them for much-needed rest." She smiled at her brother. "Liandock, Arrogol moved your belongings to his home, so you will be expected to join us when you are ready to refresh yourself."

"I will not be much behind you, sister mine." He stretched and yawned as well. "I will need to sleep late on the morrow, as I must leave for Haligon on the following turn. I wish to replenish my supplies, and the metal available from these mountains is finer than silver from Kaylin."

He's leaving so soon. Damn, I wanted more time.

Liandock glanced at Kat. "I created your pendant from Haligon silver."

"It's beautiful, and holds my stone firmly." *Good grief, Kat is that the best you can do?*

They all rose, and Mouse reminded Kat of their plans. "I will meet you in the dining hall for the midturn meal, and we will take the opportunity to visit Lord Murwenna to report to her. Irina, will you request Arrogol join us, because his Lord will expect a report from him as well?"

She nodded. "I will pass on your wishes."

Mouse faced Liandock. "Perhaps Metal-Master, we may all travel together to Haligon, because the village is our first stop on our journey to Glowen."

Oh goody, I get to be with him at least one more day.

Liandock nodded. "I agree, Sire Mouse. This would be an excellent opportunity to journey together." He winked at Kat.

Wait a minute. Does Mouse suspect I have a relationship with Liandock? Is he inviting him to join us because of me?

Liandock ran his hand through his hair. "Sire Mouse, my return to Kaylin will be via visiting Lord Eduardo. Give some thought to things you may wish me to convey to others at his keep?"

"I will think on this, and I will give you some information when I meet you early on the turn following the morrow."

Liandock took Kat's hand, and they lagged behind the others who left for Arrogol's home. Mouse departed for his own rooms.

The Metal-Smith pulled her into an alcove and kissed her. "Sleep well, my Kat. Sleep well."

They parted and, leaving the remnants of the celebration behind, Kat dragged her feet to her room. Once in, she fed

Brade and Wink, dropped her clothes on a chair and staggered to her bed. As she slipped into dreamland, something small butted at her and curled around her head. *Mmm Brade—she missed me too.*

❦ ❦ ❦

A hoarse croak in her ear forced Kat to open one eye. "Brade give me a break. I need to sleep some more. Go play with Wink." The kamalona nudged her ear and croaked louder.

"Oh hell, Brade, you're being a nuisance. I need more sleep."

Another croak, and Kat slid from her bed. "Rats, I didn't want to wake up, but now I can't go back to sleep. I'll order some journeyklim for both of us." She pulled the tassel in the corner twice.

She visited the personal and snatched a hasty shower. As she completed dressing in her casual clothes, a knock at the door heralded the arrival of her morning repast.

She thanked the apprentice, and, setting a small plate of journeyklim on the table for Brade, she took her plate to a comfy chair, curled up, and consumed her own food.

When finished, she placed her empty plate on the table, and discovered Brade had licked every bit of journeyklim from her own plate. She glared down at the little creature. "Happy now?"

The only reply a resounding burp.

Kat shook her head, moved the dirty dishes to a tray beside the door, and brought out her journal to record the happenings of the celebration. She spent considerable time recalling the mating dance and wrote about the details of her enjoyment. *Whew. If I can convey but half of the sensual nature of the dance, this will be a winner of a game.*

She paused in her writing to crumple a piece of parchment in a ball, and tossed it to Brade. The kamalona appeared anxious to attract Kat's attention, but the piece of parchment did the trick. She batted the toy about and chased the paper around the room. Exhausted, she leaped on a chair, and sank on the cushion, panting.

I guess I should meet with Mouse.

Kat unlatched the pyrock cage and urged Brade to join Wink for a nap. She peered down at the kamalona, curled around Wink, who cheeped and yawned. *I'd better leave you here, Brade. Murwenna wouldn't appreciate you being close to the heir.*

❦ ❦ ❦

Mouse sat at a table with a Rifellan guard. He glanced up and waved her over. "Kat, meet Tythan. He is the head of a guard unit."

Kat smiled in recognition. "Yes, I remember. We met you in Geronna. What are you still doing at the keep?"

"I took the opportunity to report to Melindar, who is Lord Murwenna's chief adviser, a little sooner than normal. This way I am able to enjoy the festivities of the celebration. As part of our duties, all the heads of guard units report twice per path. This gives Lord Murwenna a clear understanding of what is happening throughout Rifella."

"She appears to possess a most practical way of governing your land."

"She does, Lady Kat. Although I am sure most Lords and Thanes keep similar checks on those they govern." He gazed at the ceiling, squinting. "Perhaps Glowen is not so efficient. They tend to prefer only pleasure to order."

Kat joined him in his laughter. "From what little I learned of the Glowens, I received the same assessments of them."

Tythan rose and bowed his head to Kat. "I must leave now for Geronna, as I wish to be at home late on the morrow."

Kat widened her eyes. "How can you achieve this? Travel through the Hellesmouth would take longer than one turn?"

Tythan smiled again. "I avoid the Hellesmouth and the Crystal Dunes, and travel instead via the Torrenton Forrest." He faced Mouse, and performed the odd Rifellan handshake thing. "We met well, Sire Mouse. May you enjoy a successful journey."

As Kat eyed his departure, Fenneth walked through the door and headed for their table.

"Fenneth, I'm glad to meet you again."

"Kat, I am here to conduct you to Lord Murwenna so you may report on your initial journey through Rifella."

Mouse stood. "Our midturn meal is complete, so we are ready to meet with your Lord now."

All three left the hall, Mouse carrying the route maps for the trip to Glowen.

⁂

Fenneth gained access to Murwenna's quarters and escorted them to the Lord's presence. She was again seated on the magnificent chair in the room with the throne-like atmosphere.

"My Lord, the Lady Kat is here to report on the initial journey through Rifella."

"Excellent. Guards bring chairs for my visitors, and for Arrogol."

At the sound of his name, Kat swiveled her head as Arrogol entered from a room to the left of the throne.

"I'm glad you're here, Arrogol. I'm sure you can describe to Murwenna the details of our trip far better than I."

Murwenna smiled at Arrogol. "I am certain you can, Arrogol." She faced Kat. "However, I would prefer to listen to you, Kat, about your recent travels. Arrogol can fill in details. Please begin."

Kat began her tale. "The Tirennians saved us from an enormous pack of brantors, and we thoroughly enjoyed eating those who intended to choose us for their meal… The Great Hellesmouth Desert, one of the most frightening places I've visited, possessed a type of strange attractiveness, and the busta are wonderful in the way they work with travelers. When we journeyed through the Crystal Dunes, I found myself overwhelmed by their beauty. Rifella is a land of many contrasts, but Rifellans appear to be people of honor."

Arrogol added information about Kat's bravery in the dessert and advised Murwenna of how Kat rescued Hamrid outside of Brevista. "This gave Kat the idea to use the chits she won in the game to finance the establishment of a training center for the refugees from Baklai and northern Morden. The center will enable them to learn new skills to cope with life outside their own lands."

Kat squirmed a bit as Arrogol told about her meeting with Hamrid. *It really wasn't that big a deal.*

Murwenna asked additional questions, which both Kat and Arrogol responded to.

Throughout the report, Kat scrutinized Mouse's face, and his eyebrows raised often at certain parts of the tale.

Murwenna leaned back in her chair, a pleased expression on her face. "You did well, Kat. Eduardo is right. You do indeed possess some talents as an ambassador." She laughed in her deep voice. "You also possess certain talents which are seen to be less than tactful. However, I am pleased with what you accomplished in Rifella. What is the most significant thing you learned?"

Kat sat puzzled. "Well… I guess the most important thing I learned is…things are not always as they seem."

Murwenna sat forward, a slight frown on her face.

"What I mean is, the touch of the beautiful blue furry plant can cause painful problems on the skin. And the kamalona whose saliva is a violent poison, can be a sweet and fine companion."

Arrogol bowed to Murwenna. "I believe, if Kat spent much thought on this, she would discover she also learned much about working with others."

Kat glared at him.

Murwenna laughed and faced Mouse. "Sire, you brought a route map for the journey from Rifella to Glowen?"

He nodded.

"Fine, you may leave a copy with me. I intend to travel, with my heir and my retinue, via the Brandish Forest to bid both of you farewell at the Orkanna shipyards. I thank you again for delivering the glorious pelt of the cathnog from Lord Rhognor." She leaned back in her chair again. "My thanks for your visit. Now I must rest."

As they departed the throne room, Mouse handed Kat a copy of the route to Glowen. "We will meet at the stables, after the morning meal on the morrow. Pack all, because we will not attend the keep again, but will head for the village of Haligon, as our first stop on the way to Glowen.

Haligon. Liandock's heading to Haligon. I wonder how long we'll have together?

CHAPTER TWENTY-EIGHT

Kat consumed her morning meal in her rooms, while packing everything for her trip to the Orkanna shipyards, and the continuation of the voyage to Glowen. With Brade fed and coiled around her neck and Wink transferred to the traveling cage, she placed the last few items in her diplo bag. In the outer pocket of her backpack, she stowed the glorious blue gem embedded with bands of citrine, which flashed in the lights of her room, throwing reflections on the walls. Brade wiggled with excitement and followed the reflections with her head.

A knock revealed a young assistant who waited at the door for her primary baggage, and Kat attached Wink's cage to her backpack, along with her longbow and quiver. Hoisting the pack on her back, and donning the diplo bag across one shoulder, she set of for the stables. Exiting the inn, Kat raised her face to Pridden's star and enjoyed the warmth of its light on her skin. The air, filled with the scent of lemons and fresh cut grasses, brought a sense of new growth and well-being to her. *Life is filled with possibilities.*

Mouse stood speaking with the stable master, and raised his head to beckon Kat over. "Our horses are ready, and the baggage animal is loaded for the trip. The innkeeper packed us some supplies, and Metal-Master Liandock will accompany us to Haligon."

Kat swiveled around and welcomed the sight of the well-muscled Rifellan, leading his horse. He walked toward them, his highland swagger exaggerating the sway of his kilt, and the breeze worried at his blond locks.

Oh my. I do love watching him.

Mouse walked forward. "Liandock, welcome. We are delighted you are able to join us. Shall we be off?" He stretched his foot up to reach the stirrup, and swung into the saddle.

How does he do the leap up? He appears much too short to accomplish the move to his saddle. Kat smiled to herself as strong hands around her waist tossed her up on her horse. She grinned down at her helper. "Thank you, Liandock."

The man in question placed his foot in his stirrup and seemed to simply step in the saddle.

I expect Liandock to make getting on his saddle appear so easy. But Mouse?

Liandock and Kat rode side by side, enjoying their conversation, while Mouse took up the rear, with the baggage animal attached to his horse.

A short while before they reached Haligon, Mouse distributed the snacks the innkeeper packed for them.

By the time they reached Haligon, all were ready for a more substantial midturn meal, and they entrusted their animals to the stable master, Mouse making the arrangements with him. "Liandock, you and Kat head for the dining hall, and I will secure our rooms."

Liandock nodded at him and catching Kat by the arm, led her toward the refreshments. "Do not expect we will be able to share a room tonight. I do believe your friend Mouse is attempting to keep us apart."

"I think you're right. But why?"

Liandock shrugged.

Kat reached into her diplo bag. "I brought you something." She handed him the glorious robin's egg blue stone with the bands of citrine. "I found this at the Crystal Dunes, and the colors reminded me of you."

"This stone is magnificent." He stroked the rock and rotated it again and again. "I will study this and determine the best way to display this beautiful gem. However, I will not be able to show you my appreciation of my gift in the way I would wish to. Your Mouse will be on guard."

"I wonder why he's acting this way. He has not interfered in any potential liaisons before."

"You mentioned he left on a mysterious trip, so Arrogol was needed to accompany you through Rifella. Perhaps something occurred during his excursion."

As they joined Mouse at the table, he called over an apprentice to place their midturn meal orders. "I am aware you wish to visit the mines of Haligon, Liandock, and perhaps we may join you. I am sure you can convey the importance of what we will experience to Kat."

"I would be delighted to do so." Liandock rolled his shoulders, stretching from the ride.

"I obtained rooms for us, and if you wish to refresh yourselves first, we can meet outside the inn."

The mouth-watering aroma of seared meat, and spices, which defied identification, drifted through the hall and caressed Kat's nostrils, as the serving men approached with a tray full of their meals. "I will meet you, Mouse, but first I need to surround my food."

"I am aware I said this before, Kat, but I never encountered a female with such a sizable appetite."

Liandock frowned. "I am not aware Lady Kat's appetite is any greater than one of a Rifellan female warrior?"

Kat, mouth full, managed a grin at him.

❦ ❦ ❦

After the meal, Kat took her diplo bag, backpack, and Wink's travel cage, to her room and fed both her and Brade. She unlatched the cage and settled Brade in with Wink. "I'm sorry to leave you again, but I think the miners might freak when they catch sight of you sitting on my shoulder."

She made sure the small blade of her 'little stinger' was tucked comfortably in the sheath around her ankle, and concealed by her boot. *I'm going to meet Mouse and Liandock to admire silver, so I shouldn't need the dagger around my waist.*

She left her room, made her way to the outer door of the inn, and found Mouse and Liandock waiting for her. "I hope I didn't keep you both too long. Feeding a pyrock and a hungry kamalona always takes more time than I anticipate."

"You did not keep us waiting, Kat. Both Mouse and I arrived only moments ago."

"Fine. Since you've been here many times, Liandock, perhaps you will lead the way."

The walk to the mine was not lengthy, and they paused at the two or three shops outside the entrance. The stalls possessed an excellent display of blocks of silver, lengths of chain, and a number of exquisitely wrought medallions and brooches. Each stall used light globes to place the best illumination on their products, so the silver glittered and twinkled, reflecting back bright bands of light on the potential purchasers.

"Oh, I love that twisted wire pendant." Kat pointed at an unusual creation. "I would like to give the necklace as a gift to Irina. If I buy this, Liandock, would you take it to her for me?"

"I will indeed deliver this to Irina, who will be most fond of such a beautiful piece. But do you not wish something for yourself?"

"I don't use much jewelry. I'm wearing my gorgeous pendant and the matching anklet you made for me, and I packed the pink stone bracelet I purchased in Shendea."

Liandock cocked his head and gazed at her ears, rubbing his chin. "You should have a gift from here, and I have an idea. This will be easy to pack, and will be a magnificent addition to any important outfit you wear." He pointed to a long silver wire, with silver beading throughout the length, and requested the smith hand a length to him, along with some fine pliers. "Sit here, Kat." He pointed to a stool at the side of the booth. "Do not move, please."

He wrapped and twisted the wire about her face, and she shivered when he trailed strands around her ear, across her cheeks and up to her eyebrow. Once satisfied in the way in which the wires lay across her, he cut the ends off, and striking a flint, heated and created small beads at the end of each one.

The shop owner supplied her with a mirror and Kat gasped when shown the result. Three thin silver wires, weaved around four drops of liquid silver, emerged from inside her ear, trailed down to her lobe, looped around and up behind her ear and through her hair to emerge in three separate stands. One curved under her cheek, another trailed partway across to her nose, and the third arched to the outer tip of her eyebrow. Each strand ended in a silver bead.

"I love this." The silver adorning her ear reminded her of scenes from *Lord of the Rings. Wow, Rifellan warrior and Celtic princess all at once. How cool.* She whirled in a circle. "Thank you, Liandock. This is the most beautiful thing I've ever owned." She wanted to kiss him in thanks, but Mouse was right there.

Liandock smiled and handed a chit to the stall owner. "I need some additional silver. Thicker wire, and bars as well."

Mouse peered over his shoulder. "How much do you purchase each time you visit Rifella?"

As Liandock turned to Mouse to reply, Kat waved her fingers at them. "I'm going outside to discover how dazzling such a beautiful piece of jewelry sparkles in the light of your star." She left the two in conversation.

Kat borrowed the mirror from the shop owner, and walked a short way from the stalls, admiring the reflected flashes off the ear jewelry. Her stone cooled against her skin, and glancing around, she encountered the Morden from Brevista.

He stopped and stared at her and snarled. "You!" He screamed, drew his dagger, and flew at her.

She dropped the mirror and eyed him intently, ready to kick the knife from him. *He's going postal. The fool. He'll be easy to stop.*

Before Kat moved, however, Liandock burst from among the stalls and flung himself at the man. The Morden although unprepared, whirled around and sliced at Liandock's arm.

Mouse appeared, dagger drawn, and moved toward both men.

"Stop." Kat yelled at all three men.

Her companions ignored her, and Liandock took advantage of the Morden's slight hesitation and struck him with a powerful blow to the jaw, rocking him backwards. The man lost his balance and flew straight back, impaling himself on Mouse's dagger and suffered a mortal wound. He dropped to the ground, red pooling beneath him. Without even a scream, he died in front of them, choking on his own blood.

Silence.

I was only going to stop him. I didn't want a death. Why did they interfere?

"You damn fools. What did you think you were doing?" Kat swung her head from Mouse to Liandock, eyes glared furiously at both men.

They lacked a chance to reply.

"Was I conscious? Was I standing? Was I moving?"

They both nodded, stunned into silence.

"I sized up the situation and intended to defeat him with ease, when both of you interfered. And now what's happened? You, Liandock, are wounded, and Mouse, you've killed a man, who we cannot now question as to why, despite our previous encounter, he wished me harm."

Liandock found his voice. "You are a woman, and you needed defending."

Mouse appeared to shrink further in himself.

By this time, Kat was beyond furious. "In this case, I did not — I repeat — did not need defending. I have handled situation such as this in the past, and would have disabled him and taken his weapon without your help."

Mouse seemed unable to remain silent any longer. "Lady Kat, Lord Eduardo insisted I be your guide and defender. I followed my duty to him."

"I understand you owe a duty to Eduardo, but I thought by now you learned I am a capable woman."

Mouse dropped his head. "Yes, Kat, I have."

"If I ask for help, my words mean I need help. Do you understand?"

He nodded.

She rounded on Liandock. "You, come with me. I'll fix the bleeding. I doubt your wound is life-threatening."

Liandock began to object, but Kat glared at him.

He followed her to her rooms at the inn, but as soon as they were inside, he began to object.

"Typical man."

Liandock ceased his objections and stared at Kat, startled.

"I am not some helpless Kaylin woman, trussed up in skirts, unable to defend myself. I am, in my own way, a warrior, which I am sure by now, you have realized. I may not be as strong as you, but I've many more wiles than most men. I'm far more like a female Rifellan guard and have strength in my own way. I have power of my own. You wouldn't treat a Rifellan female guard this way?"

Liandock gaped at her.

"You appear to enjoy the time we spend together? If you continue to act like a macho idiot, I guarantee we will never spend time together again. Do you understand?"

"I understand, and I apologize."

Kat raised her eyebrows in surprise.

"I said I apologize, but only for misjudging you. You are correct. I would not judge a female Rifellan guard in a similar manner. I do not apologize, however, for coming to your aid."

"You must admit, Liandock, your intended action as part of a group did not work."

"You are incorrect. Mouse and I were part of the group. You were the challenge. You always choose to do things on your own. What you call teams do not act in such a way."

"Oh." She took a step back. "I must admit I didn't consider your actions in this light. Perhaps we both acted in haste. You forgot I often prefer to act alone, and I should have remembered and understood your preference for acting as a group." She laughed. "I guess your words are the best I'll receive." She grabbed his arm. "Let me fix your cut."

Kat bound his arm, and when she was done he leaned down and kissed her.

"Alright, Liandock, I guess we understand each other better now. But I think we should return to the mine entrance. We left poor Mouse to deal with a dead man. I suspect he may need help."

Men. Interesting. I never thought Mouse and Liandock considered me part of their team. Well, well.

CHAPTER TWENTY-NINE

Kat hurried back to the stalls at the mine entrance, followed by Liandock, and, at the end of the third stall, discovered Mouse speaking with the Miner-Master. She found no sign of the body of the Morden.

"Lady Kat, please meet Miner-Master, Ariang. He kindly aided me in removing the Morden prisoner who expired here."

Kat kept her face as bland as possible. *I wonder what tale Mouse told Ariang about the dead man.* She bowed her head, but only a fraction, unsure of how important a position he held. *I'm not going to ask what they did with him.*

Liandock moved forward. "Ariang, we meet again."

"Ah, Liandock." He smiled at the others. "Metal-Master Liandock is my best customer. We meet twice each path, when he returns for more supplies of our precious silver."

Kat eyeballed both Liandock and Ariang. *They resemble each other in a way, except Ariang is bulkier, and his hair is dark auburn.* The man filled her mental picture of what a silver miner would resemble, right down to his huge, barrel body, the smudges on his cheeks, and the dirt under his fingernails.

Ariang handed the three of them the equivalent of hard hats, which resembled the armor from Pakanna. "We will take a tour of the top two levels of our mine." He also gave them each a globe light encased in a cage, and started off down the primary tunnel. "Keep close to me, and step with care. Strewn over the floor is much rubble you might trip over, and we are not prepared to deal with injuries within the mine."

Ariang led them to a sizable square hole in the tunnel floor, from which ladders led to a flat area some twelve feet below. They descended and, once on the bottom, waited for Ariang to continue his tour. "From here, a tunnel stretches forward, until a right turn travels to another pit, leading down to a second and third level. However, if you move to your left, we can locate a further shaft which heads toward an abundant vein of silver."

He moved to their left and, after about twenty feet, arrived at another pit. Once again, they climbed down ladders to the third level of the mine and, when they reached the bottom, paused at the intersection of three passages. Four grimy miners presented themselves, when Ariang put dusty fingers in his mouth and gave a short sharp whistle.

He introduced the four men, but due to pressure on her ears from being so far underground, Kat did not catch their names. Ariang yelled at her group. "Ask them any questions you wish, although you may experience difficulty hearing because of the pressure and the noise of the miners digging." He pointed to some streaks of a dark metal running through the rock, and yelled again. "You can find veins such as this, and sometimes they will appear much lighter and are silver in color." He smiled. "We need experienced miners to discern what metal we want and what is to be discarded. We will be more than happy to answer any further questions when we return to the surface."

Oh joy, I don't like this dark, dusty and creepy place. I wouldn't wear silver if I needed to mine the stuff myself.

As they exited the mine, Kat raised a relieved face to the warmth and light of Pridden's star.

Mouse stood beside her. "I do not understand why some people find pleasure in exploring underground. I am not comfortable standing beneath tons of rock. I can imagine the weight sitting above me."

"Mouse, for once, we agree. The only reason I felt safe in Lord Rhognor's Stronghold was that the ceilings were so high." Kat shuddered.

"You both worry for no reason." Liandock stepped between the two of them. "Because the miners tunnel though rock, the walls and ceilings are solid and will not collapse on them. If you ever toured the Morden gold mines in the north, you would understand how safe the Haligon mines are."

Kat stared at him. "Are you suggesting the Morden mines are not safe?"

"I am, and they are not. Much of the area is black shale, and to tunnel through the shale, the miners must brace the walls and ceilings at every step. The shale also creates a fine black powder, which is filthy and is breathed in by the miners. Every day, they face death by collapses of the tunnels or develop problems breathing because of the shale dust. The Haligon miners are respected, and their safety is of concern to all. This is not the case in Morden."

Kat peered up at Liandock. "I'm told many stories of challenges in northern Morden. Does their Lord not care about the safety of his people?"

Liandock snorted. "Remember, they are ruled by a Thane, not a Lord. Galdin is his name." He turned to Mouse. "As a southern Morden, Mouse, you are more aware of his reputation than I."

Mouse is avoiding Liandock's eyes. Why?

"I have overheard many say Thane Galdin is less concerned about his people."

Kat stared at him. "Many people told me of situations that paint a picture of a despot. What is your opinion of him, Mouse?"

"I am not in a position to express an opinion. I do not spend time with the Thane." He glanced around. "The sky is darkening. Kat, you and I should consume our evening meal and retire early. We travel on the morrow to Farratown, with a brief stop in Rashnig. The trip is lengthy, and we must leave as soon after dawn as possible."

"Liandock, will you dine with us?" Kat hoped the answer would be yes.

"I cannot Kat, as I am to share the evening meal with the Ariang. I shall not stay long, as I too must leave early on the morrow. I am to travel via the Torrenton Forest to visit the Crystal Dunes. I will attempt to bid you a farewell on the morrow before I leave."

Damn. "I understand. In case we don't meet each other again, enjoy a safe trip." She swallowed to get rid of the lump in her throat.

He took her hand and kissed her palm. "You also."

❦ ❦ ❦

Kat ate in silence in the dining hall. *I already miss Liandock.* Mouse indicated their route the following day to Rashnig, where they planned a brief stop to water the horses, and obtain a meal for the midturn from the innkeeper. Thus, they would arrive in Farratown by early evening.

Kat, exhausted from the happenings of the day, glanced over at him, seated across the table from her. He appeared smaller and more grey than usual to her. *Poor Mouse. I don't think being my guide is easy for him.* "Forgive me for becoming so angry at you and Liandock. I worried about you both. And when I worry, I yell." She smiled at a memory. "My father used to do the same thing if an accident happened to me as a child. Rather than comfort me first, he would shout. So, I'd cry, and he would kiss my wound better. I adored him and, in many ways, still miss him."

Mouse responded with a weak smile.

Kat frowned at him. "This doesn't mean I'm going to hug you to make everything better. I'm only apologizing for yelling."

He rolled his eyes. "I understand, Kat. I suggest we both head for our beds. I will send an apprentice to call you for the morning meal. I suggest you pack everything before you sleep."

"Fine idea." She rose and headed for her rooms.

⚘⚘⚘

With Brade and Wink fed, and her bags packed and ready for the morning, Kat indulged in a brief shower in the personal, flopped on her bed, and slipped beneath the comforter.

She dreamed Liandock knocked at her door, and finally woke when she realized the knock genuine and not part of a dream. At the door, Liandock stood, yawning.

"You can come in, but no hanky-panky. I'm overtired and gotta leave early on the morrow."

He wrinkled his brow. "Hankie pankie?"

"An expression for love making."

"Interesting expression. But you are safe from me. I too am weary, and also must leave early because I am faced with a long journey on the morrow. I wished one last night enveloped in your warmth."

He wants to be with me. And I with him.

She closed the door, led him to the bed, climbed in and cuddled against him like a spoon. She murmured and fell asleep at once.

❦❦❦

The first streaks of light penetrated Kat's eyes and she moved against a warm body. *Hmmm. Liandock brought a pistol to bed.* She smirked to herself.

He moved against her and kissed her neck.

A knock.

"Oh no." Kat raised herself on her elbow. "Yes?"

The man remained outside the door. "I am your assistant, Lady Kat. Sire Mouse requested you be advised he waits for you to meet with him for the morning meal."

"Please tell him I will join him soon." She shrugged at Liandock and left the bed. "I can't find the time to be greedy. I must leave. Now."

He sighed. "I too. This is not the last time we will meet, Kat."

"I hope you are right."

"I am. I suspected when I first saw you in Kaylin, we would enjoy a deep connection."

"What made you believe this?"

"You are a strong woman, and yet have a sense of humor which you attempt to hide from others. I found this fascinating."

"I've never in my life been accused of having a sense of humor. When we traveled through Rifella, Arrogol constantly picked on me for wishing for more comfort. He insisted I was not as good as Rifellan women. I did not find his remarks amusing, so I doubt that I smiled much."

"Kat, you tend to conceal your humor as if it weakens you, when in truth, it is a strength. I see how you react with your guide Mouse. He may not always appreciate this in you, but I do believe he respects you. As to Arrogol, he and I are two very different males. He is a warrior, and warriors do not understand women's desires for comfort. Your friend Bardu is similar, but has softened his outlook by his bonding with my sibling. I suspect Olwyn will also soften Arrogol in time."

Kat eyed him, forehead creased. "You certainly regard women in a different light than most of the warriors I met in my journey."

"I am not a warrior but a lover of beauty, which is why I create with metals and gems. I find women enticing, and you, with all your strange ways, even more so."

"Oh. I had no idea." *Is Liandock a bigger part of this trip than I suspected? I hope he is.*

He leaned down and deposited a feather kiss on her forehead. "I must leave, and you must meet your Mouse."

With those words, he eased from the room, and Kat headed for the personal to grab a cool shower to wake her. As she dressed, she tugged on the tassel in the corner, and, when the assistant appeared, requested he make sure her bags, with her long bow and quiver attached, be delivered to the stable.

Dressed in leathers, she allowed Brade to settle around her neck and attached Wink's cage to her backpack, which she donned. Her dagger, sheathed at her waist, was concealed by a substantial leather belt and her little stinger, comfortably stowed in her boot, concluded the balance of her preparations.

Last, she picked up her diplo bag, which she slung over one shoulder.

She shivered. *I wonder when Liandock and I will meet again. He's so different.* She smiled, remembering.

CHAPTER THIRTY

Kat entered the dining hall and spotted Mouse seated and consuming his morning feed.

"I hope I did right. I ordered your journeyklim for you, and Karri-san as your beverage."

"Perfect, Mouse. I can't eat much this early, but I'm a bit chilly, so journeyklim will be a way to warm up. Thank you."

The young serving woman arrived with Kat's meal and place the food and a mug in front of her. "Do you wish anything else, my Lady?"

"This is enough, thank you."

She and Mouse ate in silence, and, as the food filled her, her body warmed. "How long will the journey to Rashnig take?"

"I estimate we will arrive well before the midturn. We will stop in Rashnig long enough to water our mounts and arrange for food for the journey." Mouse rose and turned to Kat. "Are you ready to leave?"

Kat nodded, grabbed her bags from the chair beside her, and followed Mouse as he exited the hall.

As Kat approached the stables, the wind was biting, and she shivered. *I wonder if I should grab a jacket from my luggage?* She shivered again. *Yup, I should.* She walked to the baggage horse, extracted a warm but light-weight jacket, which she wrapped around her shoulders. A croak startled her. "Oops, sorry Brade. Did I hit you?"

The kamalona croaked again, but snuggled under the warm wrap, leaving only a little blue nose exposed to the air.

Mouse brought a stool over to Kat's horse. She put her foot in the stirrup and pulled on the saddle horn to lift herself onto the now comfortable saddle, which Mouse purchased from Bardu.

"Thank you Mouse. It's cold today. I hope our journey will warm up later."

"It is early yet. and we will be traveling south, so you should be more comfortable later on." Mouse swung up to his saddle, and tied the reins of the baggage animal around a loop on the back end. They set off toward Rashnig, as the dawn sky turned from grey to pink and gold.

Kat followed, scanning the area, and brightened when she saw Liandock headed for Restin in the Torrenton Forest.

Almost as if he picked up on her thoughts, Liandock swung around in his saddle and glanced in Kat's direction. He waved and held his arm high, fist clenched in recognition of one warrior to another.

Kat laughed at him and returned the gesture. *With the sun glinting off his blonde hair, and the first bright rays casting shadows on the ground, he resembles a painting of heroes I remember from the covers of romance novels.* Kat shook herself. *I lose myself around him.*

⚘ ⚘ ⚘

Kat kept yawning all the way to Rashnig.

Without warning, Mouse reined in his horse and swung around in his saddle. "Rashnig is ahead of us."

She stifled another yawn. "I need to drink something to wake me up. I can't stop yawning."

"While our horses are being watered and fed, we can ask at the inn for a stimulating tea. After drinking it, we can indulge in a brisk walk to increase the blood flow in our bodies which will revive us. Our previous turn placed immense physical demand on us, and thus far, we received no opportunity to gain sufficient exercise. You will be refreshed after the tea and a walk."

"I can't wait. Let's hurry."

Mouse resumed riding, but Kat passed him and rode eagerly toward the town.

At the stable, as they both slid off their saddles. Mouse walked over to the stable hand and requested he water and feed their animals. With a signal of his head, he indicated Kat should follow him, and he made for the inn.

As they entered the hall, empty but for a scant number of customers, they sat at the nearest table, and a young apprentice approached. Mouse ordered for them both. "Two of your most liberal servings of Cantobean tea, please."

The apprentice nodded and sped off to bring their order.

He returned moments later, and set two mugs of tea, plus a filled pot, on the table.

Kat inhaled the scent. *Delicious. This reminds me of rich dark chocolate, and should wake me up.* She drank. *Oh glory. The drink reminds of my favorite candy in the whole world. Coffee Crisp. Yum.* She drained the mug, sat up straighter, stretched and poured another for herself from the pot. This time she sipped at the mug.

She smiled. "You people in Pridden have a tea for everything."

Mouse touched her hand. "Be careful though, Kat. You are not used to the stimulating effects of this type of tea. Do not drink any further cups, because you might not be able to sleep this night."

A disturbance at the door attracted her attention. Six men, Mordens from the south, by their appearance, strode over to the innkeeper and began a lengthy and noisy discussion.

Kat strained to understand their conversation.

Mouse leaned over. “They are seeking employment, Kat, and the innkeeper cannot help them. His inn is at maximum, and he cannot afford to hire more help.”

Kat rose and grabbed his hand. “Come with me. Perhaps we can help.”

She dragged Mouse over to the group and addressed the apparent leader. “I am Lady Kat. Did we understand you’re seeking employment?”

The man bowed his head to her. “Yes, my Lady. I am named Banhadron. Our families fell afoul of Thane Galdin’s group of assassins, and they confiscated our lands and stock. In attempting to right this wrong, some of our family members lost their lives, and we can no longer obtain work to feed those of our siblings and mates who remain in Morden. Our appeal to Thane Galdin received only silence.”

“Are you hungry?”

Banhadron blinked at the question. “Yes. Our food ran out two turns ago.”

Kat faced the innkeeper. “Feed these men, and my guide will supply you with a chit to cover the cost of their meals.” She turned to Mouse. “Can you give this man the necessary chit?”

“I can, but—”

“No buts, Mouse. This is the reason I gave all those chits to Arrogol and Olwyn. You’ll get your chit returned when we all meet up in Orkanna.” She stopped Banhadron. “My guide here will give you a note to take to Lord Murwenna’s keep, and to meet with Praetor Arrogol and his mate-to-be, Lady Olwyn. They will help you with this challenge you now face.”

Kat rummaged inside her diplo bag for a piece of parchment, which she handed to Mouse. “Will you write the note, because they will not be able to read my writing? Tell them these are the first of the people they will need to help."

Mouse led Banhadron to a table, and prepared the note for the Morden to carry to the keep. He stood and handed the piece of parchment to Banhadron, and reminded him to take the note to Praetor Arrogol.

The man thanked both of them profusely. He seemed so moved, Kat feared he might burst into tears. To allow him to maintain his dignity, she grabbed at Mouse to ease him from the inn. "Our apologies, Banhadron, but we must depart now, as we are on a limited schedule."

Banhadron sought her hand and bowed, "May the goddess be with you, my Lady."

Kat eased her hand from his and, pushing Mouse before her, rushed from the room as fast as possible.

As they left for the stable, Mouse frowned. "Your leaving of the man I perceived to be most rude."

"Not so, Mouse. He seemed to be on the verge of tears, and one thing I've learned about the men on your world, is they would never wish another male, or worse, a female, glimpse them cry."

Mouse stared at her. "Oh."

They arrived at the stable, mounted their horses, and set of for Farratown.

Odd that Mouse missed the expression on Banhadron's face.

CHAPTER THIRTY-ONE

Galdin paced his room. *Ssarff annoys me more each day. He takes too much for granted. Once I hold the woman in my hands, along with Eduardo, I will possess ultimate power, and Ssarff will suffer in accordance with his lack of respect.*

He frowned, drawing his brows close to his eyes. They loomed blacker than normal. His anger at the head of his Assassins' Guild caused him to narrow his eyes so he could only just see from them. He knew from practicing his facial expressions in a mirror, his eyes would glitter enclosed by the confines of his hood.

His face caused terror in the hearts of most men, and his guards, while maintaining stoic postures, experienced ice within their spines each time he faced them.

He paced.

A knock on the outer door of his audience room, attracted his attention. He strolled to his throne, and seated himself in a posture of one who waited for prey, and called out. "Come."

A guard opened the door a fraction, inserted his head in the gap and announced. "My Thane. Guild Leader Ssarff attends you."

"Send him in."

The leader of the Assassins' Guild sidled into the room, his movements emulating the snakes he worshipped. He dropped his head slightly.

Galdin ground his teeth at the hinted insult. *Ssarff fancies himself superior to me. The fool. He may think he controls the assassins, but since I control their purses, they will always choose me over him. When I am ready, he will rue the day he treated me with disrespect.* Galdin beckoned with two fingers for Ssarff to approach. "You are slow in responding."

Ssarff bowed lower this time. "My apologies, my Thane, but your messenger experienced difficulty finding me in the lower caverns of the Guild hall. We needed to deal with a recalcitrant apprentice."

"I can understand the importance of dealing with such an issue. I will overlook your tardiness this time."

Ssarff bowed his head again. "My thanks, your Liege."

"We are at last in a position to bring the woman to my keep." Galdin stood and paced about the hall. "We will seize her when she arrives at the Orkanna ship yards. We will enjoy a bonus delivered to us as well. Murwenna will also attend at Orkanna, along with the heir. We will capture and destroy the heir so another may inherit from Murwenna. Murwenna will be challenged by grief, and Rifella's leadership will fall in disarray. A candidate in Rifella exists who will be able to seize control, and Rifella will become our ally." Galdin smirked. "This will enable us to grasp control of Baklai as well." This time when he smiled, the expression unnerved the guards who remained in the room.

A flash of momentary fear crossed Ssarff's face when he beheld the venom in the smile.

Still grinning to himself, Galdin strolled back to his throne and sat. He waved at Ssarff, inviting him to sit at the chair three steps lower than his own. Ssarff complied.

Galdin rested his elbows on the arms of his throne and clasped his hands under this chin. "Once you control both our targets, you will board the ship we will indicate for the retrieval, and set sail for the Farralawn River. You will proceed up the river to the point where the waters enter Baklai territory. Once in Baklai, you will disembark and bring the captives across country to my Citadel."

Ssarff hissed out a breath. "You plan a lengthy journey for my assassins, my Thane."

"The route is indeed longer than I would wish, but I choose you to attend to the task, knowing full well I may count on your abilities and of those of your assassins. I assume you believe you are able to fulfill these obligations?"

"I do, Galdin. However, Rifella is a land filled with strong warriors. Can my group count on help from inside their borders?"

"Indeed, and this time, Ssarff you will receive aid from not one, but two persons in Rifella, and who will bring with them a large number of fighters. You will meet the two main allies in Brevista and travel with them to Orkanna. The first man is from Morden by birth. His name is Tiewellan and he is the adopted sibling of Janella, who is bond mate to Murwenna. Janella's family adopted him as a young man, but he continues to bear allegiance to his birth land of Morden. I approached him many paths ago and persuaded him to bide his time, and I would help him to gain a sense of power within his adopted land of Rifella." Galdin rubbed at his eyebrow. "My only warning about Tiewellan would be to scrutinize him with care. He is unpredictable and often acts out of haste without considering the repercussions. He will need to be guided with a strong, capable hand."

"I am more than able to handle this Tiewellan. Who is the second person who will aid us?"

"We are most fortunate here. Our second ally is Melindar, Lord Murwenna's womb mate. This woman is displeased with her position. Her birth occurred but a few moments after Murwenna's, and as such, she did not receive the Lordship she craves to this day. Some of the viewers of the births suspected the healer made a mistake, slipped, and birthed Murwenna when Melindar lay on her parent's body. Melindar always blamed the healer who claimed Melindar was birthed after Murwenna. The healer disappeared ten paths ago without a trace. There are some who suspect Melindar held responsibility for her disappearance, and perhaps for her death. The healer's whereabouts are still unknown, and if killed, her body remains undiscovered. Those who suspect Melindar, remain silent about their suspicions around Murwenna."

"What challenges might I encounter with Melindar?"

"She is only a woman, and although she is descended from Lords, she never indicated any ability as a Wielder. But do not underestimate her. Women are not ones from whom treachery is suspected, but my spies report, she is a powerful woman, and many people appear to vanish if Melindar is displeased with them. Spy on her with stealth and utmost care, and if you suspect duplicity, deal with her swiftly and without hesitation."

"This task speaks of more danger than you first conveyed."

"True. To ensure your adherence to my requirements of you and your assassins, I will triple the agreed-upon fee. I will advise my purser to advance you one half now. Another quarter will be passed to you once you hold the heir and the other woman in your clutches. The final amount will paid when you bring the captives to me here."

Ssarff rubbed his chin in a calculating manner. "I agree to these terms, Galdin. I find them adequate for the risk involved."

"One more item, Ssarff. At this time, the woman from the other world is being guided through Pridden by one of my men. My regret is the man is weak and a coward, and inadequate to the job. He did however, supply me with other valuable information, which is why I allow him to continue to attempt to bring the woman to me. However, should you find he becomes a block to you in achieving your task, do not hesitate to eliminate him, and bring the woman to me, without his interference."

"I believe we are clear, my Thane." Ssarff bowed his head and departed.

Galdin sneered at his retreating back. *With the Morden and the Rifellan aiding him, Ssarff should be able to complete what I demanded of him. When I possess what I need to control all Pridden, I will deal with him.*

CHAPTER THIRTY-TWO

Ssarff exited Galdin's keep and headed to the stables to obtain his horse to return to the Assassins' Guild.

As he approached the stable master, the man stopped him.

"Guild Master Ssarff, the day grows dark. If you wish, I would offer you a bed so you are not required to ride through the night or to camp near the Totawanga crevasses. Many others disappear forever when lost in the crevasse area."

"My thanks for the offer, however I am overdue to return to the Guild. I am well protected." *Plus I carry with me a number of syeths, who bend to my bidding.*

"As you wish, Guild Master." The stable master saddled Ssarff's mount and handed him the reins. The horse trembled as Ssarff mounted the animal.

As Ssarff rode from Galdin's keep, he shook his head. *Galdin is so pretentious. Citadel indeed. When all this is over, he must be brought down to the size he is, not the one he pretends to be.*

Ssarff rode toward the Guild hall, lost in thoughts on how to achieve his desired outcome. *This is the third attempt to capture the woman. I am aware I cannot count on Galdin. He assumes that all jump when he commands.*

Ssarff's horse floundered and tripped. *Syeth's kin. I became lost in thought, rode too fast, and paid no attention to my horse. He needs to rest.*

He slowed his animal to a walk and scanned the area for an appropriate place to set a temporary camp.

Finding a flat bare rock, with little brush surrounding the area, he cleared the space and headed to the trees to cut branches for a shelter. Once he prepared his camp, he walked to the closest crevasse and located a pool pouring into a shallow fissure. He led his mount to the pool to drink, and then to a copse of stunted trees on the other side of his camp. He fastened the reins to a tree, and hobbled the horse so it would not pull free and wander off.

He built a fire between his camp and the rift in the rock and created a hasty meal from the ingredients in his saddle bags. The result, bland in the mouth, but the bulk and warmth of the meal filled him. The horse ate too and cropped at the grasses in the immediate area.

He placed one more substantial log on his fire. From the other saddle bag, he removed a pouch, which wriggled. He hissed at the pouch, and movement ceased. He extracted two immobile syeths. One he placed to the left of his shelter, and one to the right. He hissed at the creatures again, and they raised themselves and, while keeping still, surveyed the area. Ssarff extracted a voluminous cloak from the roll at the back of his saddle and, wrapping himself in the many folds, lay on the ground beneath the refuge and slept.

The first rays of the star at the beginning dawn woke Ssarff to full alertness. He rose, removed all traces of his haven and his presence, freed the horse from his hobbles, vaulted on the saddle, and set off once more for the Guild.

❦ ❦ ❦

He relaxed in the saddle as he rode, considering his options in this new assignment. *I must send Ssestin to meet with the Morden and Melindar in Brevista for me. I intend to remain in the background.*

Ssarff slowed his journey again. He withdrew a messenger moth from the saddle bag, whispered instructions, and threw it in the air.

The moth beat its wings, gaining altitude, and set off in the direction of the Guild hall.

His horse, rested from the overnight stop, did not object when he ordered the animal to hasten toward the Guild.

When he reached the entrance, the guards saluted him and the gates screeched in protest as they rolled back to admit him. He slid off his saddle, passed the reins to the stable master, and headed for the guard unit's rooms. Passing one of the apprentices, he ordered him to bring Ssestin to the room and to fetch him some near-ale.

By the time Ssestin arrived, Ssarff, seated in comfort in his usual chair, drank from a steaming mug of near-ale.

"You requested I attend you, Guild Leader?"

"We are given an assignment, and one which will pay well for completion."

His second-in-command raised a brow in question.

"Ssestin, Thane Galdin requires we again attempt to capture the woman from the other world."

Ssestin stared hard at Ssarff. "I am hopeful Galdin will supply us with adequate help this time from his allies within Rifella."

"This is my hope also, Ssestin. From Galdin's analysis, both of the main allies have promised fighters to swell our ranks, and I hope Galdin is confident the numbers will be adequate for this campaign. However, he advises me the two are headstrong and most dangerous in their own right. This means, if necessary, we must prepare ourselves to either find our own help or be prepared to run from our losses and cease the attempt to bring the woman back to Galdin."

"Might this create future challenges with Galdin for us, Leader?"

"True, it might. However, we possess an additional challenge. He wishes us to also capture Murwenna's heir and bring the offspring with us when we return with the woman."

"May Ssayleese protect us." Ssestin tapped three times on his forehead. "I will follow you anywhere, my Leader. But I suspect this task is doomed if we rely only upon Galdin."

"We will not. We will plan as if we will receive no help from any other. I can perceive this may be the only way to achieve what Galdin wishes. The fee is also most lucrative." Ssarff stroked his chin. "We are not blessed with a long time to prepare, as you must meet with a Morden in Brevista. His name is Tiewellan, and he is an adopted sibling to Janella."

"Janella is Murwenna's bonded mate. How can we count on this Tiewellan's aid?"

"According to Galdin, we can. We are also meeting in Brevista with Melindar."

"Murwenna's sibling?"

"Indeed. Melindar, many suspect, lusts after the lordship of Rifella and wishes to eliminate the heir so she may achieve this."

"I am convinced you have considered this with care, Leader. We are facing a most dangerous task. How shall we prepare to rely upon only ourselves?"

"I wish to collect as many of our assassins as you deem necessary, and encourage them to carry with them as many adult syeths as they are able. Also make sure they prepare a potion of syeth venom, along with the Shendean antidote, and carry these as well."

Ssestin smiled. "I understand what you plan, Leader. You are most correct to utilize our own abilities to succeed in this task."

"With your guard unit of assassins, you will capture the woman and the heir in Orkanna. We are given to understand a ship awaits us to carry us via the Farralawn River across the border to Baklai. However, I intend we should continue on to Fangliven Ford and sail up to the end of the ford. At Fangliven, using the stages and pulley system, we will bring the woman and the heir to the land above the cliffs. Once at the top, we are close to our Guild if we need to escape, or we will be able to travel up Carrog Dunlan toward Galdin's keep."

"You may count on me, my Leader."

Ssarff handed Ssestin a small burlap-type bag. "In here are enough messenger moths for you to keep me informed of your progress."

Ssestin bowed. "I am more comfortable knowing you gave this assignment this much thought. I am at your bidding." He took the bag from Ssarff, bowed again, and departed the room.

Ssarff eyed the door as he left. *I hope this will be worth the payment promised by Galdin.*

CHAPTER THIRTY-THREE

With Mouse in the lead, Kat took time to view the forest to her right. The evergreens grew close together, and the wind rustling through the needles unsettled her. She imagined the trees whispered to each other, and the hairs on the back of her neck raised, and goosebumps formed on her arms. Brade croaked and snuggled deeper into her jacket. If the kamalona was unnerved enough to hide from view, it did not allay her disquiet. *I didn't experience this strange reaction to the Torrenton Forest when I passed through with Arrogol. Why now? Even the pendant is cool on my skin.*

Mouse paused their ride at a pool as they passed close to the Farralawn River, to allow their horses to drink. He passed the packets of food supplied by the innkeeper at Rashnig, and they sat on a log to eat. The horses, tied to a tree, took the opportunity to crop the short grass around them.

"This meal is delicious, Mouse. What is it?"

"I am not certain. I no longer ask what ingredients the Rashnig Inn supplies travelers. I learned to refrain from such questions."

"Uh, oh. Does this contain something weird?"

"Whatever the meal contains is nutritious and delicious. I once discovered the stew contained a creature I would not under normal circumstances consider devouring. So, I no longer ask." He pinched the bridge of his nose. "My suggestion, Kat, is to pretend the stew contains gornog meat, and enjoy the food."

Kat eyed the stew, suspiciously. She took another tentative mouthful, and fought to swallow. She finally swallowed and repeated to herself over and over. *Gornog meat is delicious. Gornog meat is delicious.* She managed to finish the meal, and cleansed the bowl in the sand, after which she stowed the container in the package supplied by the inn.

Mouse grinned at her. “You did well. We should leave now, as I always prefer to reach Farratown before dusk.”

Kat eyed him with misgiving. “Why? Do we need to worry about dangerous people?”

He laughed. “No. However, the roads approaching Farratown are peculiar and in the dark, one can become lost. Since I am not familiar with the area, I prefer my vision to be unimpaired.”

“Oh.” Kat jumped up and hurried to her horse. Standing on a nearby stump, she raised her foot to the stirrup, but could not reach high enough. “OK, Mouse, I do need help.”

He hurried over, cradled his hands, to give her a boost. When she gained the stirrup, he thrust her further to help her land in the saddle.

Wow, he’s so small, but he always surprises me with his strength. She settled in the saddle, swung her horse around, and set off in the direction they followed earlier.

Mouse trotted up from behind her, and overtook her.

⁂

They approached Farratown, and Kat understood why Mouse wished to arrive before dark. Pridden’s star began slipping below the horizon, and, since the road curved and twisted through tall grasses and stunted trees, they often blocked the view of the buildings. The route became almost invisible at dusk. *Do they want to hide their town from visitors?*

They arrived at the stable where they arranged to bed the horses for the night and the stable master directed them to the inn. "My Lady, Sire, we will deliver your baggage to your rooms."

Mouse passed on his various requests for the care of their mounts, but Kat wasted no time setting off for her sleeping accommodations.

"I'll meet you for the evening meal, Mouse? OK?"

He nodded at her, still in negotiation with the stable master.

Kat followed the assistant who carried her large duffle. She thanked him when they arrived at her quarters.

She hastened into her room and set up Wink's cage, and fed her. When Brade croaked for food as well, Kat soothed her. "Brade, I'll bring you some journeyklim from the dining hall, but I must leave you here. I'm not sure how willing the inhabitants of Farratown will be to accept you."

Brade grumbled and walked over to Wink's cage, her entire body language demanding admittance. Kat unlatched the door, and Brade stalked in the cage and nudged at Wink to move. They curled up together and slept.

Kat changed into her second set of leathers, and tugged on the tassel in the corner. She requested the apprentice arrange for the leathers she'd worn to be cleaned overnight, and she set out for the dining hall.

Kat followed the din from the hall to find its source without a challenge. She searched the room for Mouse who gestured to attract her attention. She almost lost sight of the little grey man among the blond Rifellan warriors, tall Shendean travelers clad in their colorful robes, Morden merchants from the south, and the fleshy, merry peddlers of Orenberry wines from Glowen.

She settled gratefully in a chair.

"We arrived at the most hectic time of the evening meal, but I took the liberty of ordering for you."

"My thanks, Mouse." She glanced around the room. "I can't believe how busy, and how noisy the place is."

"Farratown is where traders from most of Pridden come to do business. Kalins are the exception, since they find these types of gatherings too challenging to their moral senses. In return for the protection of Rifellans in their land, Baklai, as a rule, bring their horses for trading to the town of Barthon, which is our next stop."

A young server delivered their meals, and Karri-san tea for Kat.

"Is Barthon far?"

"Less than a turn away. We can find time to refresh ourselves before we continue through the Merrithan Forest to Brevista."

"Brevista is where we met Hamrid, and the foul Morden who attacked me in Haligon." She sniffed. "Why he attacked, I'll never understand. We paid him in full when we took Hamrid from him."

Mouse avoided Kat's eyes. "Yes, well. You will not need to arise before dawn on the morrow, and our journey to Barthon will be at a more leisurely pace."

"I appreciate a slower pace. This turn's trip is no vacation."

"Vay-kay-shun? What is a vay-kay-shun?"

Oh crap. "A vacation is time to rest and relax from your daily duties."

Mouse's face twisted up in puzzlement. "Why would anyone wish to rest and relax from their daily duties? We enjoy our duties."

"Come on, Mouse. You can't tell me Rifellan guards enjoy fighting?"

"Of course they do. Rifellans are fond of fighting. And weavers enjoy making cloth, and healers enjoy bringing people back to health. You appear to wish to make our lives complicated. They are not."

Kat sighed. "Forget I said anything. Our people are different." She shook her head in irritation. "I'm tired, and I want my bed."

"I shall not be far behind you."

Kat rose and, on her way to the exit, requested a small dish of journeyklim. Within minutes, journeyklim in hand, she left the hall.

Once in her rooms, Kat set the plate on the dresser, and opened Wink's cage to give Brade the opportunity to feed. The kamalona leaped to the dish and gobbled the contents. She licked her messy mouth, gazed up at Kat, and burped loudly.

"Brade! Your table manners need to be improved." She opened the door again to Wink's cage, and Brade entered and emitted a second burp.

After a warm shower, Kat snuggled in her bed.

⚘ ⚘ ⚘

The following turn, Kat, dressed in her newly cleaned leathers, and, packed and fed, met Mouse at the stables. "I didn't find a chance to inspect anything of Farratown except the inn. I hope we'll be able to spend some time in Barthon."

"You missed little, Kat. Farratown is a trading station and other than business being conducted on a regular basis, nothing about the town is unusual."

"I'm truly not fond of shopping for its own sake, since I would need to lug anything I buy, all over Pridden."

"I believe you may find Barthon more interesting, since most of the people in the town are either Rifellan or Baklai. Even though we will be close to Morden, the Mordens prefer to travel to Farratown to do their trading."

Kat handed the luggage to Mouse to load the pack animal, and the stable hand helped them saddle and, bridle their horses. Kat attached her backpack and diplo bag to the side, and stepping up on the stool the assistant brought her, slipped her foot in the stirrup and sprang into the saddle. She attached her bow and quiver of arrows within easy reach.

Mouse mounted his horse, attached the baggage animal to the back of his saddle, and led the way out of Farratown.

❦ ❦ ❦

Mouse, riding in the forward position, huddled in his grey cloak, immersed in uncomfortable thoughts. *Did I or did I not view an assassin lurking behind the stable as Kat and I departed? Perhaps the messenger moth from Galdin last night upset my equilibrium.*

He glanced behind him. Kat frowned and rubbed at her forehead.

Did she catch something as well?

He slowed his horse and, as Kat rode up beside him, called to her. "The visibility is excellent on this route, so you can ride in front."

She nodded and moved ahead of him.

Galdin's moth last night told me he considered sending me help to bring Kat to his keep. What does he mean by help? Are his assassins in the area at this moment? Mouse shivered and rubbed his forehead. *I hope not. At least, Barthon is filled with Rifellan warriors. Galdin's assassins are not likely to attempt anything in the town.* He peered behind him again. *I am sure we are being followed.*

Mouse had whispered to the messenger moth they would enter Brevista for the night of the following turn. He swiveled in his saddle and glanced backwards again. *I am experiencing discomfort. I am positive someone is behind us. Someone who intends us harm.*

Mouse rode up beside Kat. "We are but a short distance from Barthon. The horses need a little more exercise. Move a little faster, and I will stop you when I determine they are exercised enough."

Kat glanced at him, surprised. "Fine." She urged her mount into an easy canter.

Mouse listened intently. No sounds of horses behind them. *Perhaps I am imagining things.*

As the horses began to breathe in a labored fashion, the outlines of the town of Barthon emerged. He yelled to Kat to slow down, and walked his horse up beside her. "Our mounts are well exercised now, and the town is ahead. We will lodge at the inn in the middle of town."

❦ ❦ ❦

Something weird is going on. Mouse's been jumpy all the way from Farratown. Kat pulled at her ear. *Brade also senses something is wrong. She keeps hiding in folds of my jacket collar. And my stone is cool. I'm not usually aware of it at all.* She sighed. *Mouse is sure something's wrong.*

They rode to the stable, and Mouse arranged with the master to bed and water their horses. He mentioned they would be staying at the inn in the center of town.

The stable master snapped his fingers, and his young apprentice brought a cart, on which he loaded their luggage, and set off for the inn. Kat followed close behind.

Mouse remained with the stable master for a few moments. "I will come soon. I only wish to arrange for our horses to be ready on the morrow to travel to Brevista."

He's worried.

Mouse's forehead was all scrunched up, and he massaged his hands, as if nervous.

I wonder what he's asking the stable master. Kat walked toward the inn, keeping note of groups of Rifellans bargaining with the Baklai. She laughed at the sight of a six and a half feet Rifellans standing beside a five foot two Baklai, gazing down at him, immersed in serious bargaining.

"What are you laughing at?"

Kat startled, turned and found Mouse beside her. "The Rifellans are so tall, and the Baklai so short. From a distance you might suspect they are arguing with their sons."

Mouse stared at her, a horrified expression traveled across his face. "Do not say anything of such a nature out loud. The Baklai are most sensitive about their height, and despite their size, they hold their own with the Rifellans. An enraged Baklai is not a pleasant sight."

"Oh Mouse. I'm not a complete idiot. I wouldn't make comments which might hurt someone's feelings. Plus I'm familiar with angry Baklai folks."

"My apologies, I realize you do not possess the lack of awareness common to the Glowens."

Kat grinned at him. "I think I received a compliment." When she regarded Mouse's puzzled expression, she sighed. "Never mind. I'll drop my things in my room, take a walk around the town, and perhaps find one of those food stalls to grab an evening meal."

Mouse offered to accompany her. "The innkeeper in Faratown suggested a small vendor who is said to possess enormous talents as a cook."

"Fine, I'll meet you at the front door of the inn."

❦ ❦ ❦

After an uninspired and unpleasant tasting meal at the small stall, Kat walked back to the inn. "Mouse, I do believe the Farratown innkeeper can't discern fine cooking from bad. I found the meal at the stall to be one of the worst I ever encountered. I left most of the food on the plate, and wish I'd refrained from swallowing any of the stuff. At this moment, I can't face any food at all. My innards are queasy. I'm only going to arrange for some Karri-san to be sent to my room." She hesitated. "Although I do believe I need to rid myself of the contents of my stomach."

"I am not familiar with the word kweesie, but I understand the meaning. I am not well myself. In fact I will avoid eating on the morrow, and will meet you at the stables unfed."

"I agree, Mouse. If I'm hungry, I would prefer to consume pyrock treats. Oh I don't feel well."

Mouse waved a weak hand at Kat and proceeded down the corridor to his rooms.

I must hurry. I think I'm going to throw up.

CHAPTER THIRTY-FOUR

When Kat dragged her body from her bed, she regarded her unpacked luggage with gratitude. *Great, less to pack today. I thought I'd never stop gagging last night.* She wrapped her arms around her stomach and rocked back and forth to ease the pain. It did not reduce the agony from the Japanese drumming troupe practicing in her head.

She pulled the tassel in the corner, and when the young apprentice arrived to wheel her luggage to the stable, she stopped him. "After you take my bags to the stable, can you locate something from the kitchens which will settle my stomach? I do believe I ate some rotten food the previous turn."

"Of course, my Lady. I will bring you red-leaf tea. You will benefit from the soothing remedy."

She waited for the drink to arrive, ensuring her backpack, diplo bag, plus her bows, arrows and pyrock cage sat ready to be transported to the stable.

The tea arrived, and when she sniffed it, the aroma reminded her of ginger and mint. The first sip helped. Brade leaped on her shoulder as she picked up her equipment, and, carrying the mug with care, she sipped at the tea as she made her way to dining room.

At the entrance, she spied the innkeeper and requested a supply of red-leaf tea for two people, in mugs which she could carry with her. He brought two mugs and asked her to leave them at the inn in Brevista. They were wrapped in a type of thin, waxy parchment around the rim so they would not spill on her journey to the stable.

Arriving at the stable, suffering much less, she beheld a pale, weak Mouse standing dejectedly beside his horse.

"Your appearance is terrible."

"I feel worse than I look." He stood seeming more grey and shorter than usual.

She pushed a mug toward him. "Drink this. You'll be better in no time."

"Caleesh save me." He rolled his eyes upwards. "I do not believe I will be able to drink anything."

"Mouse. Don't complain. Drink the tea. You will improve. I promise."

He drank. He stood straighter, moved his head around and gave a faint grin. "You are correct, Kat. I am much improved. What is this tea called?"

"Red-leaf tea."

"I am not familiar with the name or the tea itself."

"I spoke to the innkeeper, and, from what I understand, the bush from which the tea is made grows only in a little unknown section of Baklai. All I'm aware is, for me, red-leaf tea is miraculous."

They drained their mugs, and handed them to the stable master, then accompanied by the baggage animal, set off, moving through the Merrithan Forest soon after their departure.

Good, we didn't need to drag the mugs with us.

Kat had forgotten how the underbrush flourished in a tangled way in the forest. The trees thrived in such close proximity, but they allowed little light from Pridden's star to reach the ground. In the upper levels, however, birds sang and flew from tree to tree. The forest, filled with rustlings of small creatures, did not conjure up memories of fear in Kat. But now… *Why is my stone so cool? What is bothering Mouse? The forest never seemed creepy before.*

Mouse, riding in front, kept glancing behind him, concern etched on his features. He appeared jumpy and started every time a branch crackled.

Brade seemed spooked as well. She buried herself within the enveloping folds of Kat's jacket and exposed only the smallest tip of her nose. Because the wrap glowed a brilliant blue, she blended in, and no one would guess at her presence.

Mouse twitched again when a branch snapped.

"What is going on with you, Mouse?"

He shot a glance at her. "What do you mean?"

"You're as jumpy as a cat in the presence of a gornog."

"Nothing is wrong."

"Oh yes, something is very wrong, and you're making me nervous as well. I'm asking again. What's going on?" *My stone is cool.*

Mouse snapped his answer. "Kat. Nothing is going on. Stop annoying me by asking all these silly questions."

Kat humphed. *He's gone all grey again, and he's shrinking into himself. He should tell me if something's not right.*

At last, the buildings of Brevista showed through the trees. *Ah, Brevista. Perhaps I can persuade Mouse to join me for a midturn tea, and I can grill him.* She groaned at the thought of the word grill. *I don't want to think about food.*

Mouse took over at the stables and arranged for the horses to be kept for two turns. He studied Kat. "I am advised Murwenna will meet us here, instead of Orkanna, but not until the evening of the morrow's turn."

"I assume Janella will be with her?"

"I believe so. Why?"

"I like her, and she's easy to talk to. You and I can converse on certain subjects, Mouse. But some things I prefer to speak about with a woman." She wrinkled her forehead at him. "Can we meet here for a light midturn meal?"

"I cannot. I need to prepare much for our journey to the Orkanna shipyards, and I must also enquire about a boat to Glowen. However, we should be able to enjoy the evening meal together."

He mentioned boat, and I almost gagged. Boats make me sick. "I suspect this will suit me better, too. I can enjoy something light in my room, and bring my notes up-to-date. I might be able to grab a quick nap. Last night I slept poorly because of the foul meal we ingested."

After arranging for her luggage to be delivered to her rooms, Kat followed the young man who carried her major bag. She entered with a key, closed the door, and settled herself. She fed both Brade and Wink and drew out her journals.

⁂

Mouse scratched and cocked his head, listening intently to the sounds in the corridor of the inn. *Something is not right. I am positive someone followed us to Barthon. On our way to Brevista, I believe our follower increased to two. Is this the arrival of Galdin's "help" which troubles me?*

He headed toward the dining hall, and encountered an apprentice outside the door. "Young man, can you arrange to request the leader of the Rifellan guard unit in Brevista to meet me here at the inn with one of his men, as soon as possible?"

"Is your request urgent, Sire?"

"Yes."

"I will go myself and bring Guard Leader Nooville to meet with you."

Mouse rubbed his hand over his eyes, and sat on a bench outside the door to the hall.

The young apprentice, true to his word, reappeared with two Rifellan guards in tow.

Mouse jumped up from his seat. “Guard Leader Nooville?”

The bulkier man nodded. “I am Nooville. Who are you, and what is your problem?”

“I am called Mouse, sire. I am escorting the Lady Kat through Rifella at the behest of Lord Murwenna. We encountered some challenges during our journey, and I am convinced Kat is in danger. I am unable to guard her through a complete turn, and we await Lord Murwenna and the heir to join us two turns hence.”

“How can we help?”

“I need someone to help me guard her. I would like to request you place one of your men outside her door until the morrow? We might need another for the morrow’s full turn as well.”

“We are aware of the visit of the Lady Kat and are most honored to help you guard her life. Here is one of my best men, Kurdin, and he will remain outside the Lady Kat’s door for the rest of this turn and this night.”

“My sincere thanks to you, Leader Nooville. I will lead you to her rooms.”

The two men followed Mouse to Kat’s door, and Nooville gave instructions to Kurdin about remaining awake at the door.

Kurdin nodded and saluted Nooville.

The Guard Leader spoke to Mouse again. “I would find further conversation with you to be most helpful, Sire Mouse. Perhaps we may partake of a near-ale in the hall?”

Mouse nodded. "My thanks, Leader. I would be most willing, and I will be more than glad to answer any questions."

With a last command to Kurdin, Nooville walked beside Mouse toward the inn's dining hall.

⁂

A young apprentice appeared at the door to the kitchen behind the dining room, and requested a tray with stew and Karri-san tea for the Lady Kat. The man appeared to be from Shendea, as he wore a pale green robe.

One of the kitchen helpers stopped him. "Are you new here? And why are you picking up a tray for Lady Kat? We are told she orders herself, and we deliver her meals to her directly."

The apprentice shuffled his feet. "I am aware, sir, but she stopped me in the corridor and made the request of me. I am told she is an important visitor, and I located no one else, so I thought I should fetch her food on my own, because she would receive the meal quicker if I did so."

The helper twisted his mouth. "You are correct, she is an important person. Are you new to Brevista?

"I am, sir. I am on my way to Glowen to assume a position there. However, I am required to serve in every inn on the way, to cover the cost of my travels."

"Fine, I shall prepare a tray for you to take to her." He stared at the apprentice from under bushy eyebrows. "But do not perform such an act again. Breaking protocol is frowned upon."

The young apprentice lowered his head, and shuffled his feet again. "I understand. I attempted to help."

The kitchen staff member patted the young man on the back, and turned to prepare a tray, on which he deposited a bowl of stew and a sizable mug of Karri-san tea. He handed it to the apprentice and sent him on his way.

When the apprentice moved from the sight of others, he deposited the tray on a counter in the corridor, and pulled a small sack from his pocket. He sprinkled some of the contents, a green powder, over the food and stirred the mixture well, to blend the ingredients. He added a further sprinkling of the powder in the mug. Smiling to himself, he walked the rest of the way to Kat's quarters and presented himself to the guard. "Sir, I bring Lady Kat's meal which she requested."

The guard glanced up at him. "Fine." He rose and knocked on the door.

When Kat replied from inside the room. "Come," the young apprentice entered and walked over to the desk.

"Your meal, my Lady."

She glanced up at him, surprised. "Excellent, they anticipated my wishes. Put the tray on the desk, please."

He moved to do so. "I also brought additional towels because the innkeeper suspected you might need more."

She moved to the desk. "Ah, how kind. Deposit them in the personal."

He entered the personal and, making sure Kat did not catch him, put two towels on the bench beside the shower, two syeths slithered from the towels and hid. He exited, keeping the door open a crack.

"Please advise us when you wish the tray removed, Lady Kat."

She glanced up, and nodded.

The apprentice left the room, and headed down the corridor in the opposite direction from which he'd originally come. Once around the corner and out of sight of the guard, he shed the green Shendean robe, revealing black clothing.

He wiped his face with the robe, removing the bronze color he had previously applied. He knew only his own stark white features were now visible. A second man, also clad in black, approached him from farther down the corridor and signaled the apprentice to join him.

The two whispered to each other. The man originally disguised as a Shendean apprentice extracted a listening device from his clothing. "Ssestin, I brought a set for you as well."

"Excellent, Ssorin. You succeeded in dosing her meal with the sleeping potion?"

"Yes. I found this easy to do. They suspected nothing in the kitchens. And I left a pair of syeths in the personal."

"We need to determine when the potion takes effect."

They both inserted the listening devices in their ears and placed the other end against the wall.

"Can you determine what she is saying, Ssestin?"

"She is talking to someone… or something."

From inside the room they heard the woman. "I don't like the flavor either. I must still be affected by the meal from last evening. Eat some pyrock treats instead."

"Ah, she speaks with her pyrock." Ssorin chuckled.

She continued. "I must drink the Karri-san. I'm so thirsty."

They continue to listen. Silence. They glanced at each other. Ssorin shrugged. "Is she asleep?"

Then a scratching sound which seemed to be a pen writing on parchment.

The woman yawned quite loudly. "I'm so tired. I need a nap." Then nothing.

The two exchanged glances. "I believe, Ssorin, she is now asleep." A snore from inside the room, confirmed Ssestin's opinion.

"Wait." Ssestin stopped Ssorin with a hand on his arm. They stood motionless until they heard the guard outside the woman's door utter a choking cry. They peered around the corner, and saw the Rifellan lying on the floor, twitching violently.

"Ssestin, with haste. Now."

Both ran for the door, and Ssestin inserted a pick to open the lock. He collected the syeth and concealed the snake in his robes.

Once in the room, Ssorin ran over to Kat. "The second syeth is dead. How? What is the piece of blue matter on the floor? The item appears to be a part of a tail."

"I do not understand, Ssorin, but we must gather the woman and leave with haste."

They placed Kat on the rug in the middle of the room and rolled her up in the carpeting.

"Fling her over your shoulder, Ssorin."

They left the room, Kat rolled in the rug and draped over Ssorin's shoulder.

Ssestin turned and fiddled with the key at Kat's door and sealed the lock. The keyhole disappeared, and the lock solidified. "Hurry, Ssorin, we must leave for Orkanna now to meet with our companions"

The two left by the rear doors of the inn and hurried to the stables outside of town. Moving quietly and carefully through back alleys, they avoided encountering any Rifellans, but met up with three more assassins. They secured Kat, flung her over a saddle, and tied her down. The assassins wrapped sacking around the horses' hooves to muffle the sound of their movements, and set off toward Orkanna.

⁂

Brade crept out from behind Wink's cage, most of her tail missing. After she killed the first syeth, the second bit her tail, and, in defense, she shed the appendage from inches above the bite. The removed section lay still and lifeless, which in normal circumstances would continue wiggling and writhing.

Brade peered at Wink. The pyrock sat frozen, eyes dilated in fear. Brade croaked with as much volume as possible and batted at the cage. Wink roused and began fluttering around, squeaking and peeping.

Brade batted at the cage again.

Wink shrieked a high-pitched sound and popped out of existence.

Brade sat back against the cage to wait for her return.

All fell silent.

CHAPTER THIRTY-FIVE

Mouse, roused from a deep sleep by Wink flapping, squeaking and batting his face with her leathery wings, sat up startled.

"Wink. What?" *No note attached? Something is wrong.* He leaped from his bed, threw on his clothes and cloak, and rushed toward Kat's room. Wink followed him, still peeping frantically.

The Rifellan guard, Kurdin, lay on the floor. Mouse pounded frantically on Kat's door. No response. *What's wrong?* He leaned over Kurdin and checked for a pulse. He found only a thready beat. *The man is dying. What is killing him and how?* Mouse attempted to open Kat's door, but it was locked. He threw himself against the door, and rebounded painfully when it refused to move. He gasped in dismay when he realized the lock was sealed.

Wink disappeared with an audible pop, and Mouse assumed she re-entered Kat's room. *I cannot duplicate Wink's accomplishment. I must go for help*

The dying Rifellan groaned and grabbed at the hemline of Mouse's robes. His lips moved.

Mouse bent and put his ear to the man's mouth.

"Sire, I heard them—they plan to capture Lord Murwenna… " He coughed up blood. "They will kill the heir." He coughed again and, racked by a violent spasm, uttered his final death rattle.

Mouse rose, wheeled around and raced for the innkeeper's offices, but as he approached, the man himself appeared.

"Sir, please send one of your apprentices to contact Leader Nooville. His guard lies dead outside Lady Kat's room, which I cannot enter."

"Yes Sire." He grabbed a passing apprentice. "Find Leader Nooville at once and bring him and his guards to Lady Kat's quarters. Inform him one of his guards is dead."

With huge round eyes, the apprentice nodded and ran off to complete his orders.

The innkeeper grabbed a heavy bronze key from a board filled with keys of a mixed variety of shapes and sizes. "Sire Mouse, I will follow you and we will use the master key to enter the room."

"But…" Before he could tell the innkeeper there was no lock, the man was running down the corridor.

Mouse set off after him, and the sounds of many booted feet echoed in the corridors.

They reached the door, and Nooville and his guards appeared behind them.

The innkeeper gulped. "The lock. The lock is gone, disappeared. How is this possible?"

Nooville moved up to the door. "Stand aside. We must break the door down." He motioned to his largest guard.

The guard lifted a leg, with thighs as immense as the trees in the Torrenton Forest, and kicked the door with a colossal racket which reverberated throughout the inn. The huge wooden barrier fell off the splintered hinges, allowing them entry.

Mouse pushed past the guard. Brade's tail lay on the floor, next to a dead syeth. "I believe a syeth felled your man, Nooville."

Nooville's usual calm face, reddened and twisted with rage. "Mordens? Morden assassins dared to enter Rifella and kill one of us? They will not escape my wrath." He gathered his men and issued instructions for the pursuit of the assassins. He conferred with Mouse. "We cannot guess whether they headed for the Right Farralawn River to escape via Baklai, or to Orkanna to escape via boat."

"Leader Nooville, the river route will be too slow. They will leave from Orkanna and sail to the Fangliven Ford. Many paths ago, Galdin arranged for a series of platforms to be built at the site. Each is equipped with a series of pulleys and cages, to bring people and goods to the top of the cliffs. We must reach them before they gain passage on a boat."

"I believe you are correct, Sire Mouse. We will head for Orkanna."

"I will exit the Merrithan Forest, and I anticipate I will meet with Murwenna and her guards and will advise her of the challenge facing us. Then I will proceed to Orkanna."

Nooville nodded. "We will intercept these foul assassins and rescue your Lady Kat." He and his guards left the room at a run.

Mouse swiveled his head, searching for Brade. He spotted her hiding behind Wink's cage, which the little pyrock once again occupied. The kamalona approached, her once beautiful tail reduced to a stump. She croaked to attract Mouse's attention.

He moved toward her. "Brade you did well."

She ran up his arm, but she slid down back to the desk.

"You cannot place your tail around my neck, so we will need a compromise." *I am speaking to an animal. Kat is affecting me more than I realize.* He gently lifted Brade's small person, opened his cloak and deposited her in an inner pocket. She uttered a minute croak and she settled inside his robe.

He dropped the bag of pyrock treats from the desk in Wink's cage, without touching her. He attached the cage to his belt, also concealed by his robe, and wasted no time striding to the stables.

I must intercept Murwenna's party.

To his surprise, his mount, saddled and bridled, waited for him beside the water trough.

The stable master handed him the reins. "Leader Nooville advised us you would need your animal the moment you arrived here, Sire Mouse."

"My thanks. You performed an excellent service this turn." Mouse swung up to his saddle, whirled his mount around and set off as fast as possible, given the tangle of bushes and trees facing him in the forest.

⚘ ⚘ ⚘

Mouse and his horse cleared the Merrithan Forest when four Rifellan guards appeared. He hailed them.

"Are you Lord Murwenna's guards?"

The tallest moved his horse forward. "Who are you to ask such a question?"

Mouse explained his assignment to guide Lady Kat, and advised the guards about her abduction by a party of Morden's assassins. "Leader Nooville and his guards set off in pursuit toward Orkanna. But…" Mouse spread his hands. "You must warn Lord Murwenna. Another group of assassins are waiting for her there, to capture and kill her and her heir."

The guard's eyes widened, and he turned his horse and galloped to the royal party a few hundred yards behind him.

Mouse followed, knowing Murwenna would need to question him.

When she received answers to her questions, she sat still for a few moments. She began issuing orders. "Janella, you and Fenneth will take the heir back to Geronna. Remove any finery you may be wearing and take Grendel with you." She pointed at one of her guards. "Grendel, remove any insignia which suggests you are part of my honor guards. You will assume the role of a mate of Janella. The three of you are a simple family traveling to Pakanna."

Janella's face reflected fear. "Murwenna, you must come with us."

"No. I must go to Orkanna. Eduardo would never forgive me if I did not help rescue the Lady Kat. Plus, we must pretend we know nothing of the intended attack on us. The only way is to continue on to Orkanna as if nothing has occurred." She held her hand up to stop any further comments from Janella. "You guard the heir. I am expendable. He is not. I rely on you to protect him."

Silent now, Janella and Fenneth removed their fine cloaks and replaced them with plain brown wraps from their luggage. They re-swaddled the heir in cotton and bound him across Janella's chest.

Grendel ripped off all his insignia, and removed his tufted helmet. He descended from his horse, and rubbed the lighter places on his armor with dirt to age it and make it appear well-worn. Then, he rubbed more dust on their three horses, bridles, and saddles.

They now resembled an ordinary family traveling to a new home.

Murwenna, still mounted on her horse, issued orders for the rest of her guards to ride with her to Orkanna.

Mouse approached her. “Lord, might I request some parchment and a pen? I possess Lady Kat’s pyrock, and I shall attempt to discover where she is being held prisoner.”

Murwenna snapped her fingers. “Guards, bring the items Sire Mouse requires.”

Mouse wrote only three words in Kat’s runes on the parchment. *Where are you?* He removed the cage, unlatched the door, and handed the note to Wink, which she held in her mouth. “Find Kat and deliver this to her.”

The little creature flapped her leathery wings and popped out of existence.

Murwenna examined the entire process. “Excellent idea, Sire Mouse. Will you accompany us to Orkanna?”

“I would be most grateful, Murwenna.” *No wonder she is Lord of Rifella. She and Kat are so much alike. They are both impressive females.*

CHAPTER THIRTY-SIX

Kat dreamed she stood beside the sea, with waves washing at the shore, and a bell ringing in the background. *Bell? And I'm freezing cold.* She stretched her neck, but her poor head ached abominably, and the sudden movement nauseated her.

She opened her eyes, one at a time, the light around her dim and red. *Am I in hell?* She sat up, and a hissing sound filled the room. Horrified, she inspected her surroundings. Syeths lay coiled on the floor all around the cot she sat on. *I am in hell. How many of them are there?* She turned her head in little movements, hoping not to disturb these nasty creatures, and counted thirteen syeths now writhing on the ground. When she stilled all movement, the snakes settled back in a pattern around the room. *They're standing guard. The room's not cold, my stone is cold as ice.* She moved her arm. The syeths hissed and slithered toward her.

Yuck, they're like motion detectors. A bell tolled. She cocked her head to listen for more sounds. *Water lapping too. I must be near a sea.*

The click of a lock opening, and the syeths hissed and squirmed toward the entrance. A tall black-haired man, with a complexion devoid of all color, entered. He hissed at the syeths and they moved as one to the back corner of the room. The man, so thin he appeared anorexic was dressed entirely in black. *He must be a Morden assassin.* Before Kat could question him, Melindar and Tiewellan strode in behind him.

Kat jumped off the bed. "I'm so glad you're here. I need help."

Tiewellan uttered a nasty laugh, an expression of loathing on his face. "Help you? I do not think so. You deserve this. We are being well rewarded to help capture you and bring you to Morden."

"Janella's family took you into their home to be part of their family. I find you reprehensible, Tiewellan. But a traitor?"

"I am no traitor. I am a Morden. Janella and her parents considered themselves so superior. I owe them nothing." He spat at Kat's feet.

Melindar stepped forward and sneered at Kat. "The Mordens want you, and as far as I am concerned, they are welcome to you."

"So Tiewellan's a traitor, but Melindar, you're her sibling. How can you do this to her?"

"I birthed first and should be the Lord." Her face twisted in rage. "The stupid healer cheated me out of my birthright. The fool listed Murwenna as firstborn. When she realized her mistake, she refused to correct it. My male parent agreed with her. He insisted Caleesh deemed this error to occur. Therefore, we should accept things as they are."

"What you're doing is beyond treason. Murwenna is your family. How can you?"

"Easily. He broke the rule of succession. He claimed Murwenna would become a better Lord than I would be. I laughed when he died."

Kat narrowed her eyes. *The snakes are in the corner. Can I escape? I must keep her distracted.* "Surely you didn't kill him?"

"No I did not. He died during a battle." She shook her head. "The old fool. He insisted on leading his men against the Morden assassins. He departed this world leaving Murwenna in place as the Lord, and left me helpless to interfere."

Can I overcome all three of them? "You're not going to kill your own sister?"

"No I cannot find a way to kill her without revealing myself. I can remove her progeny from this world. I will arrange for the heir to be destroyed."

Kat slowly tensed to run. *If I rush them, can I make it?* She glanced briefly at the syeths which remained immobile, hypnotized by the assassin. "If you do this, you will destroy Murwenna as well."

"Most likely." Melindar's smile lit her face with pure evil. "I will be at her side to comfort her, and as she becomes submerged in melancholy, I will be beside her to relieve her of the reins of the Lordship." She eyed Kat, suspicion on her face. "Do not attempt to escape. I am aware you are hoping to distract us."

Melindar turned to Tiewellan. "Move the bed against the wall farthest from the door and bind her hands and her feet."

He dragged the bed to the wall, threw Kat back on it, and bound her.

She did her best to keep her hands expanded while he wrapped the rope around her. *Ha, he's made a mistake. He's tied my hands in front of me.*

Melindar turned to the assassin standing behind the two of them. "Where is the food?"

He turned to leave and Melindar stopped him. "Make sure those things remain where they are."

"My syeths will not move until I give them permission." He left the room, and moments later, returned with a tray with food on a plate and a mug of water. "Here."

Melindar took the tray from him, and turned back to Kat. "You are a meddling fool, but we are committed to feed you.

We promised to keep you alive and well. We will leave this tray on the cot beside you. Do not attempt to leave this bed." She laughed. "The syeths will kill you."

"If I'm killed, you'll be punished."

"No, we will not. Those who are stupid enough to attempt to fool a syeth pay with their lives."

They turned and walked from the room, sparing time to nod at the assassin.

He hissed at the syeths before he left the room and locked the door behind him. The syeths resumed their earlier pattern.

Kat sat for a time, studying the snakes and the possible path to the door. *I don't see a key to the door, which is too far from me anyway. I would never reach the entrance in time.*

She remembered her dagger on her desk at the inn. She furrowed her forehead, moved her foot slightly, and then smiled to herself, despite the sudden hissing of the syeths. *They didn't find* my *little blade in my boot. Oh joy. Something positive at least.* She lowered her bound hands to her feet, a bit at a time, twisting until she slipped two fingers inside her left boot, and withdrew the small blade, shifting with extreme care so she didn't disturb the syeths. With tiny moves, she maneuvered the sharp blade across the bonds on her wrists. By the time the ends frayed away from her hands, she dripped with swe*at.*

First step to freedom.

She shifted the small dagger and made short work of the rope around her ankles.

Second step to freedom. But now, how to escape.

She gulped down the food from the tray as she thought about possible escape scenarios.

She shivered at the sight of the syeths, and leaned back against the wall, first laying the cut rope over her hands and feet, as if it was still in place. *If they come in unexpectedly, they must not realize I'm free.*

I must keep my eyes open around syeths. She trembled with fear. *How the hell can I get out of here?*

She considered and rejected a number of ideas. *I wish I knew how to contact Mouse.*

CHAPTER THIRTY-SEVEN

Kat attempted to meditate. *I've got to calm myself, and clear my mind. I can do that if I meditate. But I must also watch the syeths.*

A muffled squeak in her ear and a fluttering sound startled her and sent a rush of adrenaline through her. *Crap a syeth is about to bite me.* But something soft and furry nudged at her neck. "Wink, you came," she whispered, doing her best not to disturb the mass of slithering monstrosities on the floor. The pyrock carried a note in her mouth, which Kat took from her. Wink settled next to her and nosed at the remains of a sandwich on the plate.

A syeth hissed.

Both Wink and Kat froze. The syeth in the middle of the room gazed around, and at last coiled back on the floor.

Kat opened the note. *Brilliant Mouse, he wrote in runes. How am I going to tell him where I am?*

She scanned the room for anything to use as ink. Nothing.

A tiny snort from the plate attracted her. Wink lapped at the juice from the sandwich.

Yes. Kat removed the small dagger from her boot and picked up a frayed end of the rope which previously bound her hands. Making as little noise as possible, she sculpted the rope to a point and, stiffened the fibers by rubbing them with left-over sandwich. She now had a pen.

A couple of syeths rose and hissed. Kat, shivered. *They sound like steam engines. Dangerous ones.*

She searched the room again for something to replace ink. *I must be able to use something. There's not enough juice on the plate. Of course, I'm such an idiot.* She picked up the small dagger once more, and drew the blade across her finger. *Careful Kat, don't cut too deep*. She placed the parchment on her lap, and held her finger over the plate. The blood dripped on the plate, and she dipped the end of the rope in the few drops available. She wrote on the parchment with a painstaking attempt to make the note legible… *in bare room near sea and bell, child to be killed by Tiewellan and Melindar, working with assassins and syeths.* She blew small breaths on the note to dry the blood.

While the note sat on her lap, drying, she pulled a strand of fiber from the rope, and cut a short length.

She tested the blood. *Dry enough.* She rolled the parchment and tied it to Wink's leg with the strand of fiber.

She whispered to Wink to find Mouse. Wink stood and flapped her wings twice and winked from existence with a loud pop.

All the syeths in the room rose and began hissing.

Kat froze. Sweat popped from her forehead.

The creatures kept scanning the room, for the sight of something moving. Nothing moved. No other sounds occurred so they relaxed once more.

I pray Mouse finds a way to free me.

CHAPTER THIRTY-EIGHT

Mouse, Murwenna, and her guards traveled to Orkanna as fast as their mounts managed. Mouse, convinced that Murwenna now assumed her role as a Rifellan warrior Lord, was confident they would find Kat before the assassins spirited her on board a boat for the Fangliven Ford. *Murwenna appears assured the heir is well protected and she is now concentrating on the rescue of Kat.* He breathed a partial sigh of relief.

Once at the inn near the docks of Orkanna, Mouse set up his room as a command center. *How did they manage to overcome Kat? She is so capable normally.* He sat at a desk, surrounded by maps of the area, and drank from a mug of near-ale, when a pop alerted him to the arrival of Wink. He read the note. *Syeths! They poisoned her before. My only hope is Galdin insisted she be kept alive.*

He scrubbed at his face. *Tiewellan and Melindar? Murwenna will be devastated to learn of her sister's treasonous actions.* He stood and tugged at the tassel in the corner. He invited Wink to enter her cage, which he again attached to his belt, and gathered his maps, so when the assistant appeared, he would be ready to request the man show him to Murwenna's quarters.

The guard at Murwenna's door recognized Mouse, and knocked and advised her of his approach.

The Lord, clad in full Rifellan armor, stood at a desk laden with a similar stack of maps. "Mouse is word from Kat here as yet?"

"Yes, and the news is not pleasant." He read the contents of the note to her.

Murwenna's mouth dropped open, and her face reddened with rage. "My own sibling plots against me? I find this almost impossible to believe, but I must admit I suspected some dissatisfaction from her in the past number of turns. My poor Janella will be shattered to learn of Tiewellan's betrayal." She sank into a chair beside the desk, scanned the maps on the surface, and addressed her guards. "Gwinrick, you and six of your men, go to the shipyards and the guard units in Orkanna, and solicit aid from them to accompany you and Sire Mouse to help in the search for the Lady Kat."

Gwinrick saluted and summoning six men with gestures, left the room on the run.

Murwenna stood and faced Mouse. "Do you, Sire, possess any knowledge of the meaning or location of the bare room to which Kat refers in her note?"

"I cannot locate the place where Kat is being held with the few words she supplied. I do believe an idea presented itself how I might locate her."

"Excellent. We will allow Gwinrick enough time to return with reinforcements. Do you anticipate we will need horses?"

"I do not believe so. The room appears to be near the waterfront, most likely situated in an abandoned warehouse."

"I suspect you are correct. However, she mentions syeths. We must be prepared for those foul creatures." She turned to one of the guards still in the room. "Do you possess supplies of the killing gas in Orkanna?"

"Yes my Lord."

"Send two guards to gather an adequate supply. We will meet here in ten parts."

As the two guards left the room, Murwenna spoke to eight of the remaining guards, leading them to the maps on the desk. "Each of you will work with a group of the additional men and women brought back by Gwinrick, and begin your search in these areas." She pointed out to each of the five men and three women, a section for which they would be responsible. "Do you understand your assignments?"

The eight nodded, almost in unison.

"Leave ten men at the inn and at my door, in case Melindar and Tiewellan come here to attempt to kill me or the heir, whom they believe is still with me."

Murwenna turned to Mouse. "What is your idea, Sire?"

"I will rely on Kat's pyrock." He picked up the cage. "Wink, can you fly straight to where Kat is captive, without performing an instant transportation?"

Wink squeaked, as if in agreement.

Murwenna, Mouse, and all the guards left the room and gathered in the courtyard of the inn. At that moment, Gwinrick appeared, accompanied by a crowd of guards and burly shipyard workers.

"Gwinrick, you and your group will accompany Sire Mouse, as he may be the closest to discovering where the Lady Kat is being held. The rest of you are familiar with the sections of Orkanna you will search." Murwenna designated four men as runners to advise the groups where they would be needed when they found Kat.

Gwinrick and his group gathered around Mouse. They agreed they would follow him to where he thought Kat might be.

Mouse unlatched the pyrock cage and again asked her to fly to where Kat was concealed. Wink rose in the air at about twice the height of the men, and began her flight to locate Kat.

Wink flew faster than the men could travel, but she needed to rest often to replenish her strength.

She must use considerable energy doing a non-instantaneous flight. Mouse threw a pyrock treat to her each time she rested. Wink swooped down and caught the treat mid-throw. Refreshed, she ate it and continued on her flight. *Kat will never forgive me if I exhaust her pyrock.*

Wink arrived at a derelict warehouse and hovered above the door.

She's here. Mouse signaled to his group of men to halt. He motioned to the runner to advise the other groups of Kat's location, and for them to join him and his group. *I will be willing to wager many assassins are in the area.*

When they arrived, one of the dock workers picked the lock to allow them entry. Mouse signaled to part of his group to enter the warehouse in silence.

Wink headed for the rear, where she flew to a perch near the ceiling, and waited. Mouse and his men crept forward, and peered around the corner of a corridor. A few steps away, an assassin sat cradling a syeth in his hands.

Mouse pulled Gwinrick aside and murmured to him. "I suspect the door is to the room where Kat is being held. Kill the syeth first, and then the assassin. We are fortunate they have not detected us already. Prepare your man with the gas to release the fumes under the door. I assume the gas is heavy and will not rise above the floor. Correct?"

Gwinrick nodded. "The gas will kill syeths because they are small, but will only make Kat's breathing slightly difficult. She will not die or suffer any permanent damage."

"On my mark, Gwinrick. Go."

The guards surged forward one of whom raised a sword and split the syeth in two. The assassin sprang to his feet, but before he took two steps, was struck down by another guard. Gwinrick pulled at the man holding the gas, and directed him to insert a tube under the door, to release the vapor in the room. Almost at once, syeths slithered swiftly from under the door, many dying as they did so. Some managed to crawl into the corridor, to sink their fangs into the guards, who writhed in agony and died within minutes.

Those guards still on their feet slashed at the remaining snakes and ended their lives. As though summoned by their hideous creatures, assassins poured through the corridors from elsewhere inside the warehouse. But those in the building were aided by the protection of the men from outside the warehouse, their numbers swelled by the additional units, who now joined in the fight.

Inside the building, the cries of men and assassins, wounded or dying, echoed off the walls in a spine-chilling din. Men slipped and slid in the corridors, awash with blood, and littered with corpses.

A door at the far end of the hall opened and Tiewellan and Melindar ran through an outer door to escape. Mouse noticed them fleeing, but his primary goal was finding and freeing Kat.

Two brawny dockworkers smashed open the door to Kat's prison, and the battle surged into the room.

❦ ❦ ❦

Inside the room, Kat gaped at a fog streaming from the other side of the door. The syeths hissed and slid over each other to escape. Some slipped beneath the door, but others died before they reached freedom. Within minutes, all the syeths lay dead, or disappeared beneath the door. Kat jumped down to the floor, but before she moved further, the door crashed inwards, and Rifellans and assassins flooded in, accompanied by blood and the clamor of weapons and the cries of men.

Kat grabbed at a short sword on the floor with which to defend herself. She ran toward the door and stopped short at the appearance of an assassin holding a dagger. He rushed toward her, and the sword she held plunged through his body. Blood sprayed over her, but she couldn't remove the sword on which the assassin impaled himself. The metallic odor of blood assaulted her nostrils, and she gagged at the sight of her hands covered in the sticky red fluid. *I need another weapon.* She snatched the dagger from the dead man's hand. The blade, slick with gore, slipped in her hands, so she wiped it on the assassin's robes. She shuddered in horror.

She began to rise, when she witnessed Mouse aim a spear at her. *Is he's trying to kill me?* Shocked she ducked. Behind her, she heard a liquid gurgle, and glanced backward to see Mouse's spear protruding from the chest of one of the enemies.

Poor Mouse, I keep misjudging him.

CHAPTER THIRTY-NINE

Ssestin lurked in a darkened doorway, three buildings away from the scene of the battle, as the Rifellans routed the assassins they had captured. Most were already wounded. *Who is to blame for this astounding defeat?*

His second-in-command, Kasseeus, tapped him on the shoulder. "Leader Ssestin, what should we do? Only twelve of us remain free and unharmed. We cannot possibly engage with the Rifellans. There are too many, and they are too strong."

"You are correct. I cannot understand why the woman Melindar and that annoying creature Tiewellan did not bring us reinforcements, as they promised Galdin." He rubbed his forehead in agitation. "I wonder how sure Galdin was of their support with additional troops."

"Their lack of that support cost us this battle. I doubt Ssarff would have accepted this venture had he known we would not receive more fighters from the Lord's sibling and her Morden partner."

"I wonder, Ssestin, if Guild Leader Ssarff was aware of this challenge."

"No matter now. We must return to the Assassins' Guild and advise him of what has taken place." Ssestin shook his head in frustration. "We will wait until the darkest part of the night and board the boat that sails on the morrow, apparently for Baklai. We will take over the crew, as we originally intended, and continue instead to the Fangliven Ford."

They faded in the dark corners of the building, and waited.

Ssestin sighed. *Three times Galdin has failed to give Ssarff the promised support. The Guild cannot afford to lose so many of our members.*

CHAPTER FORTY

Murwenna and the guards who accompanied her, arrived in time to witness the final dispatching of assassins. Three apprentice healers moved among the injured Rifellans, repairing those who would be able to walk, and arranging for litters for those with serious wounds. The dying, they assisted by supplying pain relief.

The dockworkers agreed to stay and help cleanse the area of the gruesome after effects of the battle.

Murwenna and her golden circle of guards, along with Mouse; Gwinrick, who suffered only a minor wound to his arm; and Kat returned to the inn. Murwenna sent her own pyrock to fetch Janella, Fenneth, the heir, and Grendel to join her at Orkanna, the way now safe.

Mouse, held up Wink's cage, to which she returned, rolled in a tight ball of fur, and slept before he completed latching the door. He handed the cage to Kat, who reached a trembling finger through the bars and stroked the furry little body.

Thank you Wink. Good grief, I'm still shaking.

They entered the building and began to wend their way to Murwenna's quarters when without warning, Gwinrick stopped, placed his finger to his lips and held up his other hand to prevent the group from proceeding. He moved to Murwenna. "Lord, I believe I can identify Melindar's voice ahead of us."

Kat, right behind Murwenna, was the only one who caught his whisper and the Lord's reply. "You are aware of what to do."

Gwinrick faced the other guards and gestured to them, indicating they should creep without any noise to Murwenna's quarters and capture the enemies ahead of them.

The well-trained team advanced in complete silence, rounded the corner before the entrance to the Lord's rooms, and, without alerting either Melindar or Tiewellan, seized and bound them both and dragged them into Murwenna's rooms. The Lord strode past them to her meeting room, and seated herself. "Bring the traitors to me."

Kat became a silent viewer of an extraordinary drama. *How will Murwenna handle this?*

The guards dragged the bound figures into the room, and stood them before Murwenna. Melindar, ashen, but silent, held her body erect and defiant.

Tiewellan, sweating, bent before the Lord, without meeting her eyes. "My Lord, forgive me. Your sibling seduced me with honeyed words and threats of violence if I did not help her. I could not escape her clutches. This was all her idea, and she forced me to aid her."

Melindar curled her lip at him. "Coward."

Melindar is right on that point. Kat could finally breath normally again.

Murwenna, nostrils flared and her elbows braced on the arms of her chair, placed her chin on her interlocked hands and stared at the two. The silence in the room stretched on. When she spoke a hint of puzzlement sounded in her tone. "Melindar. Why?"

Melindar's reply dripped ice. "I am firstborn, and our male parent understood this, but never corrected the error. He said Caleesh determined you would be a better Lord than I. But I am the firstborn. By Rifella's rule of succession, I should be Lord. Our male parent broke with tradition."

Murwenna gazed at her sibling. No warmth existed in her face. "Based on our current situation, I would agree with our parent's assessment. By harboring such ill will for so long, you proved he chose the correct path for us." Murwenna shook her head. "Your decision to kill me was flawed. None with such a plan would be considered a responsible Lord."

"I did not meet with the Mordens to kill you, my sibling. I planned to eliminate your heir. I estimated his loss would make of you an ineffectual leader, and the people of Rifella would demand you step down. I would be Lord at last."

Murwenna's face held an expression of disgust. "You entertain so little regard for life you would kill a babe? Unbelievable." She placed both hands on her cheeks and stared at Melindar, with a horrified expression on her face. "What arrangement did you agree to with the Morden assassins?"

"They would help us to gain access to your heir, and we would help to capture Kat." She smirked at Kat. "But we discovered more than one faction became anxious to gain custody of the woman, and none of them worked in concert to bring the desired outcome to fruition."

Two factions want me? Why? Kat shook her own head in astonishment.

Murwenna shook her head. "Melindar, I find your explanation beyond belief. I almost doubt we are siblings. I will tell you, we received warning, and my heir never faced danger. He is not in Orkanna." Murwenna sighed. "Tiewellan your sibling, when she joins us, will be appalled to learn what a traitor you became. Your adoptive parents will be likewise shocked, and will rue the day they embraced you and welcomed you to their family."

Melindar sneered. "You will not kill us. You cannot afford for your Rifellans to perceive you as a murderer."

Murwenna sighed again. “You are correct, I am no murderer. I do possess, however, a number of ways to deal with the two of you. Janella will arrive well before the evening meal. I will wait to discuss your sentence with her.” She addressed the room. “Gwinrick, place these two traitors under arrest. Feed them, bind their hands and feet, and chain them to the wall in cells of the below-ground prison of this inn. I will call you to convey them to my quarters again after Janella and I discuss their fate.”

“I will do so with pleasure, my Lord.”

The audience left the hall, and Kat touched Mouse on the hand. “My thanks, Mouse, for once again saving me from the assassins. I am convinced they are one of the factions looking to capture me, but I can’t think who would be the second.”

“We will, in time, discover their identity. But for now, let me advise you I arranged rooms for you at this inn, and did send for all your baggage from Brevista.”

“Thank you. I hope I’ve got time to grab a bite to eat. I feel a bit shaky, so I must be hungry.”

“I am positive this can be arranged. Let me show you to the room assigned to you.”

They reached the entrance, and Mouse handed her the key. She unlocked the door, and pushed it open.

“Wait, Kat. Something else. When you received drugged tea in Brevista, they also released two syeths in your room. Brade attempted to save you, and killed one of the syeths. However, the second attacked her.”

“Oh no.” Kat felt a sharp pain in her heart. “Is she dead?”

“No, she’s not.” He reached in the inner pocket of his robes and withdrew the curled up kamalona and handed her to Kat. “The syeth bit her in the tail, but she ejected the poisoned section, so the venom would not reach the rest of her body. The tail will grow back, but I believe she is a little worse for wear."

"Oh Brade, you're alive. I'm so glad. You poor little thing. Don't you worry, your tail will grow back, and you'll be as beautiful as ever."

Mouse rolled his eyes.

"Oh come on, I'm positive she understands me. She is looking pale, and I'm sure she's sensitive about losing part of her tail. I think when I talk to her she improves." *I'll feel better at least.*

Mouse shrugged. "If you believe your words, Kat, I suspect she does too."

"Whatever. Mouse, I must feed both these creatures and indulge in a shower. I feel so itchy from being surrounded by syeths. I will meet you in the dining hall afterwards. Although they claimed the need to keep me alive, Melindar and her pal Tiewellan did not feed me well. I am hungry."

"Hungry? At least I am convinced you are well, Kat."

Kat frowned at him as he left her room. *Mouse? Sarcastic? Hmph.*

CHAPTER FORTY-ONE

Wink ate four pyrock treats. *You expended an awful lot of energy didn't you?* Wink cheeped up at Kat, who deposited her within her cage, where she walked around three times, curled in tight ball and fell asleep.

Kat caressed Brade's brilliant blue head, decorated with the emerald spots. "You appear to be much better, don't you?"

Brade croaked at her and butted at Kat's hand.

Kat lifted her up in her hand and brought her to face height so she managed to butt her chin against Kat's. "Your color's brighter, and your tail's growing surprisingly fast. Before you know it, you'll be back to normal."

Kat placed Brade in Wink's cage, where she settled for the night. Dueling snores drifted from the cage.

The hot shower eased her aches and pains, and removed the scent of blood and death, in the jets of water. She slathered on a lavender body cream and then dressed in clean leathers.

Before she left her room, she pulled the tassel in the corner and handed the apprentice her dusty, well-worn Rifellan outfit. "Would you please request someone at your inn to clean and restore my leathers?"

He nodded and, as he bore her clothes away with him. she called a thank you to him.

From her room Kat walked to the dining hall, and at the entrance stood and breathed in the aromas of roasting meats, the under-scent of near-ale, and something sweet which reminded her of the glorious fragrance of ripe strawberries. The usual noise of the dining hall seemed subdued. Many friends lay dead and needed remembering. Those who emerged unscathed sat sober in their thankfulness to be alive and well. *They were after me. It's my fault all these people had to fight, and so many met their deaths. I didn't mean for this to happen.*

She scanned the room as Mouse raised a hand to attract her.

"I arranged for Karri-san for you, but decided I would let you order for yourself."

A wait person placed a pot of Karri-san and an enormous mug in front of Kat. "My Lady, we are serving an exceptional meal of sea-swimmer fillets this evening. Our cook managed to locate a number of remarkable seasonings, and, having sampled some myself, I recommend the dish."

"Sounds excellent. I will order some. Are you also serving a dessert that possesses a sweet aroma?"

"Ah, your nose is well educated, my Lady. We received a distinctive food from Glowen in the form of redline berries. They are not often available, so I urge you to order them. You will be enthralled by the flavor."

Kat nodded. "Fine, include the redline berry dessert."

She turned to Mouse. "It's my fault all this happened, isn't it?" She hung her head.

"Kat, you heard Melindar. Someone does appear to be after you. That is hardly your fault."

"But, Mouse. I must have done something to annoy someone. I don't know what it is, or who I angered."

"We cannot solve anything now, and I truly cannot see anything you have done that could possibly create such anger.

Speak to Fenneth, if that will help. Or even perhaps to Murwenna."

Kat's meal arrived, and when she took the first mouthful, she moaned aloud at the flavor of the sea-swimmer dish. A delicate fish, with seasonings that hinted of lemon and a piquant suggestion of Peri Peri sauce, prompted Kat to ask for the name of the hot spice.

"We call this Fire Mouth. Our cook trades for the spice with the Baklai. The seasoning is very rare, and we are not able to enjoy its tang often."

When Kat finished the fish, the wait person, smiling with satisfaction, placed the bowl of redline berries in front of her with a dramatic flourish. The fragrance of strawberries in sunshine reminded her of the time when she picked her own at a farm. The picking took on a rhythm of its own, two for the box, one for me, two for the box, one for me… When she paid for her purchase, the farmer took a glance at her red mouth and stained fingers and charged her an extra dollar per box. The experience was worth every penny.

Redline berries did resemble strawberries, except they reminded her more of strawberries smothered in rich heavy cream and with a sensuous dark chocolate under taste. Kat groaned again with pleasure.

She glanced at Mouse, who ordered the same dessert.

He smiled as he ate.

We're both using food to mask what happened today.

Kat drank some Karri-san. She and Mouse sat in silence. Kat was still concerned about her responsibility for the fighting.

Their wait person approached the table. "My Lady. Lord Murwenna requests the attendance of you both in her rooms."

Mouse thanked the man, and they left the hall to meet with Murwenna.

The Lord sat in her chair, with Janella to her immediate right. Down each side, Fenneth and Gwinrick, sat at one table, with Kat and Mouse on the opposite side. The rest of the room was filled with Murwenna's honor guards and many of the leaders of dockworkers and townspeople.

Once all attendees located seats, the doors opposite Murwenna opened, and guards led in the chained and bound Melindar and Tiewellan.

Janella's mouth twitched at the appearance of Tiewellan.

The Rifellan guards forced them to kneel.

Murwenna addressed the pair. "We thought long and hard over the sentencing of both of you. The law is never easy to adhere to when one is required to pass judgement not only on a citizen, but also a member of one's family. To require death by hanging or beheading is far too onerous a responsibility to place upon the head of your Lord, when the responsibility lies not at her door, but at yours, since you are the traitors."

Murwenna shifted in her seat. "Stand and listen while I deliver your sentence.

The guards lifted them to their feet, and Murwenna continued.

"Melindar, my sibling, and Tiewellan, sibling to my mate, Janella, you are sentenced as follows. You will be delivered to center of the Great Hellesmouth Desert, where you will each be given water for one day. You will not, however, receive the benefit of horses nor of bonded busta. The busta, in their own wisdom, refused to accompany you. They regard the crimes you committed to be distasteful."

Both Melindar and Tiewellan blanched at the news.

Murwenna continued. "Should you survive crossing the Hellesmouth, and we will know if you do, you will be banished to the island off the coast of Rifella close to the Mora Waters. On the island, without access to boats or anything with which to build a boat, you will live for the rest of your days. Should you not succeed in exiting the Hellesmouth, the challenge of your sentence is solved." Murwenna stood, and the rest of the room followed suit. "May Caleesh be with you."

The guards led the sentenced traitors away to prepare for their trip to the Hellesmouth. Murwenna remained standing, and the rest of the room waited.

"My people, many of you suffered this day with losses of your friends and relatives. We cannot thank you enough for the sacrifices you made. On the morrow, therefore, after the midturn meal, we will hold a celebration of the lives of those to whom we say farewell.

"Each Rifellan who gave his or her life will then be transported to the place they called home, and will be bonded with Caleesh via the warrior's fire. Those who perished who do not claim Rifellan birth will be helped by our healers to be celebrated in their own traditions.

"The warriors of the Rifellan guards will pay homage to their fallen comrades at the outdoor arena on the edge of Orkanna. Any others who wish to, are invited to attend as well. May Caleesh settle your hearts and help you in this night's sleep."

Murwenna turned and, with Janella, exited through the rear door.

Kat stood beside Mouse. *Wow. This woman is a Lord in every meaning of the word. What will she say when I tell her I believe I am responsible for all these deaths?*

CHAPTER FORTY-TWO

Mouse beckoned to Kat. “The celebration on the morrow of the lives of those who fell in battle will be lengthy. I would prefer if we depart Rifella the turn after that, so I would suggest we partake of our morning meal in your rooms. I will bring the information we will need for our journey to Glowen, which I will explain to you.”

“Agreed. I need to sleep soundly. I’ll request the assistant advises you when he brings our meals.” She yawned. “That way, I won’t worry you might catch me still in my bed.”

“A sensible suggestion. I shall not arrive at your door before I am called.”

Kat yawned again and, nodding at Mouse, set off for her rooms.

❦❦❦

Kat stood at the edge of the Torrenton Forest. Poor visibility and shadows lurked among the trees making things difficult to locate. She spotted him as he emerged from behind a group of tall bushes. The man in black. Icy sweat trickled down her spine. *He’s coming for me.* But he didn’t move. He stood still among the foliage, waves of black rage roiling through the trees toward her. But the inky churning mass stopped at the forest’s edge. *Something’s protecting me*. She moved away from the perimeter of the trees. His rage pummeled at the barrier, each blow venting blasts of thunder.

Kat sat up in bed, gasping. A nightmare. Again. *This time different. Someone or something stood between me and the black specter*.

She slipped from her bed and stepped over to the dresser to drink from a mug of water. The cool liquid washed the fear from her. *A weird nightmare, but I can go back to sleep. I am safe. My pendant is warm.*

She returned to her bed and snuggled in the cozy covers. And slept.

❦ ❦ ❦

Plaintive squeaks and hoarse croaks penetrated Kat's consciousness, and she sat up, only one eye open, and surveyed her dresser. "You two are noisy enough. Keep your shirts on. I'll feed you, but first I need to visit the personal." She bounded from her bed and once showered she fed Brade and Wink, and then dressed in one of Brith's softest shirts, and the split skirt.

She tugged the tassel to order the morning meal for Mouse and herself. When the assistant appeared, she requested an extra plate of journeyklim, and asked him to request that Mouse join her when the food was delivered.

She undid the latch on Wink's cage, and Brade bounded out, croaking. "Your journeyklim is coming. Be patient." Wink was rolled again in a furry ball, sleeping.

Kat cleared the table and brought a second chair to it.

A knock on the door aroused Brade's interest. She croaked again.

Kat called to the assistant. "Come."

Mouse entered, carrying a tray with food and mugs of liquid for them both, plus a case containing maps. "I relieved the assistant of his duty. I decided I would be foolish to have him to come to your quarters as well, when I was on my way to visit with you this morrow."

"You're most efficient, Mouse." Kat motioned to the cleared the table. "Sit, please." She brought Brade over to the table. She placed the kamalona across from Mouse and set the third plate of journeyklim in front of her. "Poor Brade, she's not as adept at leaping from place to place without her full tail to balance her."

Brade stuck her mouth in the plate and began to eat, rather noisily.

"The animal devours journeyklim?"

"Yes, she's fond of this as her morning meal, and I can't obtain any of those prickle-fur berries that Arrogol mentioned, for her. She will eat pyrock treats, but I don't want to carry bags of them on my travels. So the journeyklim is the perfect solution."

"Interesting. I do discern her tail is re-growing most quickly."

Brade cleared all the food from her plate, and burped.

Mouse raised surprised eyebrows.

Kat grinned. "I'm aware. She possesses no manners at all."

"Er…she is an animal, Kat. I do not believe they practice people's manners."

Kat sighed at him. *I was trying to be humorous.* "I'll put her in Wink's cage and they can both sleep." As she picked the kamalona up around her middle, Brade burped again, louder this time. Kat rolled her eyes at Brade, carried her to the pyrock cage, and deposited the kamalona inside. Soon two gentle snores issued from within.

Kat moved the dishes from their meal to the tray, which she laid on the bed.

Mouse pulled a number of maps from his bag and spread them over the table. "As you can perceive, these are the Orkanna shipyards and the town of Orkanna itself. The harbor they sit on is vast but well protected from the storms which sometimes manifest at sea. Rifella boasts the finest harbor in all Pridden. The harbor at Baklai is deep, but is part of a lengthy inlet, and the Baklai are considering building a series of protective sea walls to allow them to possess a safe harbor, the equal of the one Rifellans enjoy."

"I notice on your map, Glowen also has a well-designed harbor. I expect the curve in the land acts as a sea wall for them."

"Correct. We will leave Orkanna either on the morrow or the turn after, depending upon the weather and the sea. The boats to and from Glowen are rigged to allow the passage of horses on board, so we will not be required to leave our mounts behind."

"How long will we be on board a boat?"

"We depend on the weather for any boat journey, but if the waters are comfortable, we should be at sea for only two turns.

Eew. I hate being on boats. I'm an accomplished sailor, but I tend to travel by rail. The rail of the boat, I mean. "I should warn you, Mouse. I become seasick."

"You mean you become ill on the water?"

Kat, glum, nodded.

"How odd. Few people are ill on the water. However, we will run with the wind, which makes for a stress-free journey. The prevailing winds and currents flow from Shendea, southward, and continue past Baklai. This is much more pleasant than sailing against the wind. I am certain you will be fine."

"Perhaps."

A knock disturbed them. "Come."

The young assistant stuck his head around the door. "We are requested to inform you, the celebration of life will begin soon."

"Thank you." Mouse packed away his maps, and rose. "If you are ready, Kat, we can head to the dining hall for the beginning ceremonies. If I may, I will leave my maps in your rooms and will collect them later."

"Fine. I'm ready."

❦ ❦ ❦

The dining hall assistants, because of the crowds of people, moved tables to the sides, and spread chairs throughout the area for seating. Fenneth, motioned Kat to two seats beside her. Kat sat and called Mouse over to the other chair.

Lord Murwenna, seated in an enormous chair resembling a throne, with Janella seated beside her, held the position of power at the front of the room. When Murwenna stood, the room hushed. "My people, this day we came through a violent attack on our way of life from an unexpected source. I experienced such pride in the way you conducted yourselves and I cannot express my thanks enough to you all. Janella, my bonded mate, will read the names of those Rifellans who perished the previous turn." Murwenna stepped aside.

Janella stood and began to read from a parchment she held.

Kat listened with concentration. She hoped to catch names she might recognize, and she was surprised at how limited the list of names was.

Janella sat, and Murwenna moved forward again. "Now our healer, Fenneth will read the names of those from other lands who fought with us." She moved back.

Fenneth rose and read the names from the parchment in her hands.

Once more, Kat experienced surprise listening to so few names being read out. *From the sights and sounds of the blood and the noise of men dying, I thought many more perished last night.*

Murwenna moved forward again. “When dusk falls, Leader Grendel of my honor guards, will hold a memorable ceremony to celebrate the passing of Rifellan guards who defended us and paid with their lives. All who wish to take part, please attend at the arena on the outer edge of Orkanna.”

She raised her arms. “And now, to celebrate the lives of those we loved and honor today, we will raise our voices in our anthem of Rifella.” She motioned to a group of musicians in the corner, and they lifted their instruments and began to play.

Kat recognized the song Arrogol and Bannigus sang near the Merrithan Forest. When the two of them sang the patriotic version near the forest, Kat’s blood had stirred. Now, the hymn-like song of praise pulled at her heart and she blinked rapidly to avoid tears. *Because of me.* She swallowed.

As the music ended, all in the hall sat still and silent in their seats. Kat suspected they were not yet ready to return to normal living.

Murwenna spoke once more. “I, and all you in this hall spent this evening thanking those who helped us, with one exception.” She gazed around the hall. “Lady Kat, would you please stand beside me.”

Kat rose and headed over to Murwenna. *Uh Oh, What now?*

“This woman, Lady Kat—” Murwenna placed her hand on Kat’s shoulder, “—conveyed enormous service to the land of Rifella. Sent to us by Lord Eduardo of Kaylin, Kat exceeded our expectations.”

Kat stared at Murwenna. “But—”

“You unearthed two well-hidden traitors. You freed a Baklai man who sold himself into slavery without understanding the ramifications. You helped to supply funds to begin a training center for refugees from both Morden and Baklai. These are significant accomplishments, in particular coming from a woman who often trips over our customs. Thus, you have created a greater bond with both the Baklai and the southern Mordens. We thank you, Lady Kat."

The hall burst into applause.

How do I respond to this? "I am not the one who helped you. You are the ones who helped me and taught me so much. My biggest lesson as I lived among you is that when people work together, they are so much stronger than individuals. I will put this concept in my dealings with all people from this day on, and I hope this will allow me to trip over your customs less often. I am so sorry I was the cause of this battle and so grateful you helped to save me. For what you all gave me, I thank you."

The entire hall laughed and clapped at the same time.

Kat turned to Mouse and opened her mouth to thank him in public, but stopped when he shook his head. *Weird.* She turned back to Murwenna. "May I speak with you in private, Lord Murwenna?"

A puzzled frown crossed the Lord's face. "Follow me."

In a small room attached to the primary hall, they sat at a round table. "Murwenna, I find your world compelling, but I miss my home more and more. Eduardo promised me that he and others who possess power, and who agree to help me, will attempt to restore me to my own home. As a Lord, you are a Wielder of power. Will you agree to supply aid when the time is right?"

Murwenna blinked. "I am not sure how much power I wield, Kat, but I will help in any way I can."

"Thank you."

Kat returned to Mouse. “I want to attend the homage to the guards. May we stop and eat a brief early meal?”

He nodded. The efficient assistants, during the meeting with Murwenna, had set up the hall for a meal, so he and Kat chose a table and sat.

❦❦❦

The meal complete, Kat excused herself from Mouse to change into her Rifellan leathers. “You should accompany me and retrieve your maps.”

He followed her to her rooms, and, after collecting his bag of maps, departed for his own rooms. “I will meet you at the arena, Kat.”

I guess he’ll put on a fresh grey robe. Kat chuckled to herself—and stopped. *I shouldn’t make fun of Mouse. He doesn’t deserve it.*

CHAPTER FORTY-THREE

Kat washed her face of any makeup, and donned her clean leathers from the previous turn. *If this homage to the guards this is anything like the one in Kaylin, makeup won't last long.*

Once dressed, and, making sure both Brade and Wink still slept, she left for the arena.

All the guards in Orkanna gathered in a circle around the bodies of their ten fallen comrades. In a ring outside of the circle stood torches, which flickered in the light breeze of the evening. Each body rested on red fabric, laid over a piled stack of wood.

Mouse moved beside her. "Do you need an explanation of what is to occur?"

"No. I attended a similar ceremony in Kaylin for Bardu's second in command, Kadnu. I'm aware of what will happen."

Mouse nodded and lowered his head toward the fallen.

The utter silence, broken only by the sound of the bell attached to the buoy at the entrance to the harbor, weighed on the crowd. Grendel stepped forward with a parchment in his hand. "These are our comrades whom we honor today." He read from the list of names. After the tenth name, the entire gathering of guards called out, "Caleesh accept us."

The guards began the patriotic anthem. They stamped their feet and their spears. The rhythm quickened. The song, exuding the power of the deep bass voices of the men and glorious sopranos of the women vibrated in the pit of Kat's stomach. All the audience joined in, even Kat who, without remembering the words, hummed the tune. The pounding of feet and the vibrations of the voices intensified, soaring through the night as the guards set their torches to the wooden stacks. The rhythms expanded in volume, as the flames from the pyres increased. Smoke rose from the arena—not black, but billowing up as a pure white sacrifice. The stacks of wood, engulfed in flame, lit the entire area with red, surrounded by pale white smoke. Soon the flames began to reduce, and the voices decreased in volume. The song reached its end, and the pounding of feet and spears stopped dead.

Faces ran with tears, but everything stayed silent. The crowd dispersed and the guards moved away, their expressions filled with joy.

The lump in my chest broke apart. I am lighter.

Mouse walked next to her. "We will depart on the morrow after the midturn meal. Meet with me for the morning meal, and I will give you final instructions."

"I'll join you on the morrow."

❦ ❦ ❦

Kat woke refreshed. The sleep she enjoyed ran deep and soundless. She climbed from her bed, showered, and dressed. Before she left to enjoy a morning meal with Mouse, she packed everything. She fed Wink and promised Brade she would bring her some journeyklim. Brade's tail was longer, but not long enough yet to fit around Kat's neck.

She set out for the dining hall and waved at Mouse sitting at a table in the corner. "So, when do we board this boat?"

"After the midturn meal."

"Wonderful, because I need to attend to some minor items. I am packed, so where should I ask the assistants to send my baggage?"

"Ask them to convey your bags to a boat called "*The Warrior*".

"A most masculine name. I thought boats always bore the names of females?"

"What made you think so? Boats bear the names of whatever their builders choose to call them." He peered at her, an amused smile on his face. "In Rifella, Kat, warrior describes both males and females."

"You're right." Kat closed her eyes, feeling heat in her cheeks. "I apologize. I wasn't thinking clearly."

Mouse said nothing.

They ate in silence, and as she finished, Kat asked the serving person to bring her an additional plate of journeyklim.

"For Brade?" Mouse grinned.

She accepted the plate from the assistant, glared at Mouse, and set off for her rooms. *He's enjoying my gaffe.* Once inside, she wrote a note with painstaking effort, copying the words from both Wynneth and Mouse and advising Fenneth of her nightmare. "Can we meet?"

She inserted the parchment in a tube and attached it to Wink's foreleg. "Go find Fenneth."

Wink took off with her usual popping noise. Within minutes, a return note read, "I will come to you".

Kat pulled out her journal and added all the latest happenings. She completed her notes, when a knock sounded at the door. "Come."

Fenneth entered, and Kat rose and hugged her. "Fenneth, I hope you can help."

"I will do my best."

They sat at the desk, and Kat described the nightmare. Fenneth's face reflected puzzlement. "What an odd dream. You dreamt about this being before, yes?"

"Yes."

"What is odd about this one is he became stopped by a barrier. This seems to herald a better outcome than before. I believe we may assume someone is watching over you."

"I suspect the same thing." She clutched at her warm emerald stone.

A loud croak from Brade interrupted them. Fenneth peered at the kamalona, and seemed startled at the stunted tail. "What ever happened to your little creature?"

"She saved me, by attacking a syeth. The poor thing sacrificed her tail in my defense."

"Small and beautiful and yet so brave."

Brade leaped from the desk to the table and walked over to Fenneth. She stood before the healer, gazing up at her, and croaked.

"What does she want?"

"Not sure." Kat reached over and picked up Brade, who struggled and slipped from her hands and again walked over to Fenneth and croaked up at her.

"Fenneth, she can't leap on your shoulder without the full use of her tail. But I believe she wants you to adopt her. Pick her up and bring her close to you."

"Are you sure I am safe with her?"

"I'm certain you are. She's acting with you like she did with me when we first met.

Fenneth gingerly pickup up the kamalona and brought her to face level. Brade reached out as far as possible, and butted at Fenneth's chin. She croaked again and settled in Fenneth's hand. "I think she likes me."

"Brade, do you want to stay with Fenneth?" Kat stretched her hand toward the creature, but Brade turned her head away and gazed toward Fenneth. Kat laughed. "She doesn't want to leave Rifella, so she's picked you as her friend. Congratulations, Fenneth, you are the proud friend of a kamalona named Brade."

"I do apologize, Kat. I did not intend to take your Brade from you."

"Relax, Fenneth. I can't travel all over Pridden accompanied by various creatures. Brade understands the time is here for her to leave me."

"I shall treasure her. And Kat, based on your dream, I believe you are in capable hands."

Fenneth hugged Kat, picked Brade up with care, and returned to Murwenna.

Brade is intelligent. She knew it was time to leave me. Kat sighed and smiled. *I wonder why she chose Fenneth? Well, time to head for the boat. Ugh.*

Kat tugged at the tassel and, when the assistant arrived, requested he deliver her baggage to *"The Warrior"*.

She eased her arms through the straps of her backpack and settled it in place. Only her diplo bag, her bow, her quiver of arrows and Wink's cage still sat on the table.

Was Liandock responsible for Brade? She did help save my life.

Kat removed a scrap of parchment and her pen from her diplo bag. She gazed at the ceiling in thought as she chewed on her thumb. Nodding to herself, she reached a decision, and penned a message to Liandock. *I hope I remember the words Mouse taught me.* "You possess power, I know. Will you be one of the helpers who return me to my world?"

I hope my writing is clear. I can produce most of the words. She brought Wink from her cage and fed her a treat. After inserting the rolled up message in a tube, she attached it to Wink's foreleg. "Take this to Liandock, please, Wink."

She tossed the creature in the air, and the pyrock flapped her wings and disappeared with a snap.

Kat attached the cage to the side of her backpack, placed her diplo bag across one shoulder, and slung the bow and quiver across her chest, warmth radiating through her body from the emerald held in place by the twisted silver necklace.

She took one last glance around the room, opened the door, and left. She glanced back.

I wonder what Liandock's reply will be? She breathed in and sighed. *What do I want it to be?*

DRAMATIS PERSONAE

NAME	DESCRIPTION	FROM
Aenid	A hunter from Tirenna	Rifella
Anwen	Apprentice Healer & Guide for Mouse & Kat	Shendea
Ariang	Master Miner at Haligon	Rifella
Argelwyd	Original Lord of Pridden	Morden
Arrogol	Praetor of Murwenna's guards Bond mate of Olwyn	Rifella
Bardu	Praetor of Eduardo's guards Bond mate of Irina	Rifella
Ballinor	Leader of Guards in Roothlan	Rifella
Banhadron	Refugee from Morden	Morden
Bannon	Caretaker of Pontis	Kaylin
Benden	Stable master at Geronna	Rifella
Brigden	Leader of Morden travelers in Shendea	Morden
Brith	Seamstress for Eduardo's keep	Kaylin
Bodeth	Assistant to Tythan, with the guard unit in Geronna	Rifella
Bronwyth	Head of functions for Eduardo	Shendea
Bannigus	Horse-master in Rifella	Baklai
Caleesh	Goddess for Pridden (except for Morden)	Pridden
Carlo	Designer/coder for Nick	Our world
Carrog	Busta bonded to Brynn	Rifella

NAME	DESCRIPTION	FROM
Casseg	Busta bonded to Kat	Rifella
Clune	Financial clerk for Eduardo	Kaylin
Colwin	Apprentice serving Kat	Shendea
Cranna	Busta bonded to Arrogol	Rifella
Dafid	Door guard for Eduardo	Kaylin
Deleth	Healer to Lord Rhognor Womb mate of Wynneth	Shendea
Derwynn	Head of Thieves Guild	Shendea
Drainin	Counselor to Eduardo	Morden
Eduardo	Lord of Kaylin Related to Mouse	Morden
Fardith	Assistant to Halfin	Shendea
Farnon	Headmaster for Dizerth	Shendea
Fenneth	Healer to Murwenna	Shendea
Flank	Burgmaster of Magwin	Shendea
Galdin	Thane of Morden	Morden
Godrith	Tapestry Master in Shendea	Shendea
Grendel	One of Murwenna's honor guards	Rifella
Gwinrick	Leader of Murwenna's guards	Rifella
Halfin	Lady of Shendea Rhognor's bond mate	Shendea
Hamrid	A servant to a Morden, rescued by Kat	Baklai
Haydar	Horse-Master for Eduardo Mayda's father	Baklai
Hesginn	Grey Magician head of Magicians Guild and advisor to Lord Rhognor and Brother to Walden	Shendea

NAME	DESCRIPTION	FROM
Illian	Apprentice builder Penrow's daughter	Kaylin
Irina	Member of Keep guards Bardu's bondmate & sister to Liandock	Rifella
Istra	Serving woman at Vendi's Inn	Shendea
Janella	Murwenna's Bond Mate	Rifella
Kadnu	Bardu's second in command	Rifella
Kaleen	Met Kat at Ponti Inn	Rifella
Karen	Friend to Kat & Nick's Wife	Our world
Keedin	Rifellan warrior stationed at Roothlan in Shendea	Rifella
Kat Karim	Katherine Karim - Mother a Scot, Father Arabic	Our world
Kaydith	Serving woman for Kat	Shendea
Kasseeus	Assassins' Guild member Second in command to Ssestin	Morden
Kraklin	Grey Magician	Shendea
Kurdin	Rifellan guard in Brevista	Rifella
Laylin	Serving woman for Kat	Kaylin
Liandock	Master Metal-Smith of Kaylin Brother to Irina	Kaylin
Lanerch	Lord of Kaylin prior to Eduardo, and adoptive father to Eduardo	Kaylin
Makinti	Praetor for Thane Cathked Bardu's friend	Rifella
Mayrin	Wife of Horse-Master Haydar Mayda's mother	Baklai

NAME	DESCRIPTION	FROM
Mayda	Serving woman & apprentice to Wynneth, Daughter to Haydar	Baklai
Mazon	Family who welcome guests	Shendea
Melindar	Chief Advisor to Murwenna Sister toMurwenna	Rifella
Merrindock	Prefect of Pakanna	Rifella
Morshag	Legendary horse thief of Now a Baklai curse word	Baklai
Mouse	Serves Galdin Related to Eduardo Guide for Kat in Pridden	Morden
Murwenna	Lord of Rifella	Rifella
Neerin	Assistant to Walden	Shendea
Nick	Kat's supervisor Husband to Karen	Our world
Nooville	Guard leader in Brevista	Rifella
Penrow	Master Builder of Kaylin Illian's father	Kaylin
Pentramore	Prefect of Tirenna	Rifella
Pilar	A Tirennian hunter	Rifella
Ponsin	Leader of Glazenwyth	Shendea
Rantor	Store Owner in Blain	Rifella
Rhognor	Lord of Shendea Bond mate to Halfin Titular Head of all Guilds	Shendea
Saglit	Ssarff's second-in command	Morden
Salssin	Agent of Assassin's Guild	Morden
Sherwyn	Head of Housekeeping for Eduardo's keep	Kaylin
Souris	Waiter at hotel in Tortola	Our world

NAME	DESCRIPTION	FROM
Ssarff	Leader of Assassin's Guild	Morden
Ssayleese	Snake Goddess in Morden Spirit only	Morden
Ssestin	New assistant to Ssarff	Morden
Ssorin	Assassin in Brevista	Morden
Tannis	Brings Gornog Meat to Rifella	Kaylin
Thontook	Master Weaver of Kaylin	Kaylin
Tiewellan	Economic advisor to Murwenna and adopted brother to Janella	Rifella/ Morden
Tythan	Head of the Rifellan guards in Geronna	Rifella
Walden	White Magician Brother to Hesginn	Shendea
Wealin	Taylor in Murwenna's keep.	Rifella
Wolfdrang	2nd in command to Arrogol	Rifella
Wynneth	Healer to Lord Eduardo Womb mate to Deleth	Shendea

FLORA AND FAUNA OF PRIDDEN

NAME	DESCRIPTION	FROM
Blicks	Small rabbit like creature delicious in a stew	Rifella
Bonbrie	Delicious fruit similar to peach	Shendea
Boradai	Furred creature size of a kitten who can read minds.	Shendea
Brade	Kamalona which bonds with Kat	Rifella
Brantor	Small, short-legged, carnivores who hunt in packs, with massive claws, two small horns and black teeth	Rifella
Brynosh	Tall plants which are used for tapestries and by Rifellans for their leather armour.	Shendea
Busta	Intelligent creatures who bond with Rifellans to fight the Crosa (see specific busta in Personae)	Rifella
Cantobean	A chocolate-like bean for a stimulating tea	Rifella
Cathnog	Large ferocious cat-like creature with four huge canines resembling a sabre-toothed tiger.	Shendea
Drag	Largest snake in Morden, similar To a python in that it crushes it's prey	Morden
Eethnaire	A root vegetable which produces a delicious and nutritious stew	Rifella

NAME	DESCRIPTION	FROM
Fire Mouth	A hot spice that is similar to Peri-Peri sauce	Baklai
Gondal	Two foot long lizards with black tongues, and which are excellent for eating.	Baklai
Gornog	Pig-like animal, size of a jaguar, grey & black, covered in stiff bristles, two set of tufted ears, six clawed feet, 12-inch tusks in a mouth with warts. Meat is tender, sweet and delicious, although causes gas in those who consume it.	Kaylin
Gwindle	A health tea for mind & body focus	Shendea
Haggapoe	Large carrion bird which is attracted to shiny objects.	Rifella
Hissar	Rodent-like creature 1.5 feet, with the temper of a Tasmanian devil and three rows of barbed teeth, and the strength of a creature 10 times its size.	Baklai
Horse	Almost the same as in our world, except much larger in size.	Baklai
Hydodd	Large elk-like animal with huge horns, cantankerous and a match for the ferocity of the Cathnogs.	Shendea
Kamelona	small scaled creature which which resembles a chameleon. Spits toxic saliva causing swift death for its prey.	Rifella

NAME	DESCRIPTION	FROM
Kithra	Dog-sized rodent with black eyes, needle sharp teeth and brown hair.- travel and attack in packs.	Kaylin
Klim	Plant which produces nut-like Seeds and is cooked into journeyklim- A porridge like meal.	Shendea
Panwon	Thick glue-like substance made from the horns, claws & hooves of brantors.	Rifella
Ponti	Resembles a horse, but with very large head for its body size, large splayed feet, short legs, wide girth very sure footed in mountainous regions. Pontis grow to about ten or eleven hands high.	Shendea
Prickle-fur	Blue plant with red berries and Soft barbs on the leaves, is toxic to human skin and leaves a red itching rash when touched.	Rifella
Pyrock	Tiny, furry animal, with long tail and leathery wings can transport instantly, and locate any person anywhere on Pridden. Answers only to one person during lifetime. When rolled in a ball, fits in one hand.	Kaylin
Red-Leaf Tea	A tea which helps quell nausea and settles the stomach	Baklai
Red-line Berries	Sweet berries which taste similar to strawberries	Glowen

NAME	DESCRIPTION	FROM
Red Rash	A dangerous virus, which emerges every 7 years, and can cause pain & death	Pridden
Sea Swimmers	Fish from the Bay at the Mora usually either roasted over coals or presented in a stew called cassolet	Shendea/ Rifella
Shade	A huge black panther-like animal with brilliant emerald eyes that becomes Kat's protector in Shendea	Shendea
Syeth	Small but deadly poisonous snake, venom causes almost instant death but is used by Shendean Healers to produce potion to combat Red Rash	Morden
Wullawerth	Sheep-like animal with masses of fine soft hair, excellent for clothing. Prized for eating.	Kaylin

ABOUT THE AUTHOR

J. M. Tibbott has been writing since childhood. The Arrival was her first published novel. As a writer of magazine and newspaper articles, being an editor for an online newsletter, and a writing instructor, J.M. belongs to a community of local writers, all of whom are dedicated to the upgrading their own skills.

While the initial intention was to publish a myth/fantasy novel, as J.M delved further into the creation of a new world in which The Arrival takes place, it became obvious that the complete story required multiple books. Thus Book 2, The Healers is published, and Book 3, The Warriors is now complete.

J. M. is currently hard at work on the fourth book in the series

SNEAK PEAK

We hope you enjoyed this third book in the Pridden Saga, and just to entice you, we've included a peek into the next novel in the series, The Pleasure Seekers

THE PLEASURE SEEKERS

CHAPTER ONE

I'm too young to die. Kat raised her head and caught sight of Mouse. *Bloody hell, he's eating.* She clutched the rail and heaved. Her stomach hurt. and her head pounded. She groaned as her insides spasmed again, and she retched.

Another flash of lightening lit the sky. *Thankfully the rail is wood. Although if it were metal, it could elecrocute me and I'd die sooner.*

The ship climbed a gargantuan wave and pounded down the other side, leaving her stomach somewhere in mid-air. She moaned. *The weather was supposed to be fine*.

"Kat." A hand touched her arm. "Drink some of this red-leaf tea." Mouse held a cup out to her.

She attempted to shake her head, but the pain was too great, and she leaned over the rail and dry-retched again.

"This helped you before. Remember? Drink some." He thrust a cup into her hand.

"Go away. Let me die in peace."

"Drink, Kat."

Just to shut him up she sipped at the tea. She blinked. *It stayed down*. She took another sip. When the boat gave another lurch, she hung over the rail once more, sure the small amount of liquid would reappear.

A huge form, greater in length than the boat, crowded alongside the vessel. *What's that?* The creature lifted its head out of the water and opened a gargantuan mouth, ringed with three rows of enormous, yellowed teeth. Water and small fish gushed from the jaws. It raised its body so close to the deck of the boat, Kat thought it would reach out and pluck her from the vessel.

She shrieked and pushed back from the rail. Losing her balance she staggered into Mouse, who caught her before she fell. The cup dropped from her hand, and tea splashed over the deck.

"Kat, what is wrong?" He steadied her, ran to the rail and glanced over. "What did you see?"

She began to reply, but hurriedly covered her mouth, as the small amount of tea she swallowed threatened to re-emerge. She coughed. "Whale."

Another flash of lightening, this time accompanied by a belch of thunder.

Mouse frowned at her. "Wale?"

She nodded, afraid to speak, and possibly retch again.

Mouse led her to a chair bolted to the deck. "Can you sit? I will bring you more tea. It will help."

He settled Kat in the chair, wrapped a warm blanket around her, and handed her a fresh cup of tea. As the blanket warmed her, shet felt less shivery, and, while her stomach felt delicate, at last, it stopped spasming.

He sat in a chair beside her. "Are you able to talk?"

She nodded. "A little."

"What did you see in the water?"

"I'm not sure what it was, but it stretched the full length of this vessel, and had loads of teeth. A shark or a whale?"

"I am not familiar with either of those creatures. There are stories of massive sea animals appearing in the waters around Glowen, but none have been seen in many paths. There are no tales to suggest they ever attacked anyone, so we can assume they are benign."

"I don't care. The worst they can do is kill me, and I still feel that would be a blessing."

"Drink more tea, Kat. We have entered the harbor, and the storm is also passing. We will be landing shortly, and you will feel much better." He patted her hand.

Kat barely noticed his gesture, but closed her eyes so she could no longer see the rise and fall of the ship's rail.

Those teeth. A shark?

A Message from J. M. Tibbott

Although I acknowledged the main people who have helped me through the process of this book on the pages near the front, I would like now to acknowledge you, as a reader for your contribution.

Like all writers, I adore creating a world with different creatures and people, and I really do all of this for you.

I was fortunate enough to grow up with parents who were themselves readers, and who took me weekly to the library. As a youngster I was only allowed to borrow two books at a time, and as we lived a fair distance from the library (a mile walk plus a 35 minute bus ride) we only visited my favorite building every Saturday. Two books could not possibly keep me occupied for an entire week, so I regularly invaded my parents' library, which is why my reading level was way beyond my tender years.

It was the joy I received from books, that prompted me to write my own novel, so that I could foster the same delight among my readers.

So thank you for reading.

J. M. Tibbott

If you have not yet read The First Two Books, The Arrival, and The Healers:

Please go to Amazon.com

Sun Dragon Press Inc. recommends two previous Pridden Saga Novels by J. M. Tibbott: -- at Amazon.com

The Arrival: The Pridden Saga: Book 1

What happens when a solitary but brilliant video game designer is thrust into an unfamiliar world? Offered a chance to return home if she will help save the inhabitants from the winds of war, Kat must decide what risks she will take and what restrictions she is willing to accept. Beset by bizarre and ferocious creatures, narrow minded social mores, seductively erotic men, and with no idea who is friend or foe, she must wend her way through a minefield of challenges. Can she do it?

The Healers: The Pridden Saga: Book 2

Kat, in her continuing quest to return home, wends her way among the spiritual healers of Shendea, but encounters heart-stopping challenges from a ferocious cathnog and unknown and violent strangers. Still tasked with the demand by Eduardo of Kaylin to help Pridden avoid a devastating war, but without clear instructions, she is escorted by her mysterious guide, Mouse. Despite her tendency to blunder through odd customs, she is astonished by a Thieves' Guild who do not steal, a Magicians' Guild who demonstrate no magic, and learns to sidestep the wiles of the alluring Rifellans. How will she keep her word to help Lord Rhognor, and still return safely to her own world?

www.ingramcontent.com/pod-product-compliance
Lightning Source LLC
Chambersburg PA
CBHW072046190726
48294CB00005B/1424
9781738974269